W9-BXE-984

SHE MATTERS

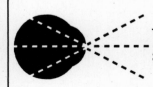

This Large Print Book carries the
Seal of Approval of N.A.V.H.

SHE MATTERS

A LIFE IN FRIENDSHIPS

SUSANNA SONNENBERG

THORNDIKE PRESS
A part of Gale, Cengage Learning

GALE
CENGAGE Learning

Detroit • New York • San Francisco • New Haven, Conn • Waterville, Maine • London

GALE
CENGAGE Learning®

LIBRARY OF CONGRESS CATALOGING-IN-PUBLICATION DATA

Sonnenberg, Susanna, 1965-
    She matters : a life in friendships / by Susanna Sonnenberg. — Large print edition.
        pages cm — (Thorndike press large print core)
    "Unabridged"—Title page verso.
    Originally published: New York : Scribner, 2013.
    ISBN-13: 978-1-4104-5592-5 (hardcover : large print)
    ISBN-10: 1-4104-5592-0 (hardcover : large print) 1. Sonnenberg, Susanna, 1965– 2. Sonnenberg, Susanna, 1965– —Friends and associates. 3. Female friendship. 4. Large type books. I. Title.
CT275.S5918A3 2013b
362.29092—dc23   2012042936

Published in 2013 by arrangement with Scribner, a division of Simon & Schuster, Inc.

Printed in the United States of America
1 2 3 4 5 6 7 17 16 15 14 13

for Saidee Brown
and
for Carole Van Wieck

CONTENTS

SHE MATTERS

Patricia will be late. As I think this, with a tolerant fondness, she texts that she'll be late. It doesn't bother me. I've known her eighteen years, and she confirms herself, the deeply known friend, which reminds me of love in its greatest warmths, its common comfort. I haven't seen her in months. After her father died a few years ago, she left Missoula with her family, took a job two hours away. Our e-mail is sporadic and bright, not more than that. We have our work, our teenagers, family health concerns, et cetera. None of these intersects anymore. She comes to town once in a while, stays with her mother, and sometimes, last minute, we squeeze in a lunch. Otherwise, our correspondence has lapsed into late-delivered major news.

My father has died in New York where I grew up, and I've been dazed for months, home in Missoula, yet not home. I hunger all the time and nothing answers me. Absence the new habit, I am shedding people, no longer sure how to show interest, how to let friends care; but I need care, and Patricia's has always been keen, persuasive. With her sweet intention she might make me visible again. Was she coming to town soon, I e-mailed. She was, and guess what! "We're moving back!" A flicker of gladness. We made a date, but her weekend changed. We had to postpone. That used to make me crazy.

Patricia pulls into the metered spot as I am passing it on the sidewalk, and she waves hugely before shutting off the car, as if she can't wait to get out. The windshield frames her gathering-ups, the strap of her bag onto her shoulder, familiar motion. In a second, we'll reunite, and she'll shower me with enthusiastic greeting. I remember there's a song we do. I can't sing.

After I arrived in Montana, twenty-seven years old, Patricia became my guiding, buoyant older sister. She jollied me along, made things regular when I found them a regional confusion. When we met — her encouraging pursuit met my ready affections — we each had one dog and one cat, one husband (well, boyfriend for me). Both of us were earning a little money as freelance writers. Our birthdays were close together. She delighted in these coincidences as if they were delicious and rare overlaps. Later, when we were interested in having babies, we wondered how it would affect our writing. We asked, Where will we find the *time,* not believing we had to worry. At one point I had a therapist I liked and recommended, and Patricia started to see her, too. Sometimes, our coats in our arms, we passed in the waiting room, which always amused us because we had steady plans with each other every few days. "Hey, sweetie," she'd cry, her greeting big no matter the room. "I didn't know you were coming on Mondays now!" When she took a leave from her job at a magazine, she put me up for the interim position. Every morning, sitting in her chair, I logged her password into her office e-mail account for the day's business. We had a long period of doubleness.

Patricia embraces me, the musical surge of *hello how are you,* her raised voice exclaiming, "Just getting away from *the kids!*" Her mother's with them, she says. I try to match her and relate, which feels nice, nudges me closer, even though to me such family reliance is peculiar.

"I *know,*" I say. "Some time to ourselves."

But I embody strain.

11

"How *are* you?" she repeats.

"I'm so sick of it here," I say. "I don't want to look at this town anymore."

"Don't say that. I'm about to move back."

"That's true, I'm glad."

Inside the bar we debate tables. It's afternoon. I'd texted, "Shall we drink?" She wrote back, "Hell yeah," which made me smile. She always had the balm, gave me a glad heart. Music overhead, a call to a crowd that doesn't mind it, we are drowned out. Close to my ear she says, "Where we can talk." I nod. "God, it's good to *see* you."

"It's good to see you." I take her in, really. She looks older; I must look older.

We pick a corner table with a right-angled banquette. The waitress comes and Patricia treats her warmly and agrees to the suggested wine. The waitress goes away for the wine and my whiskey. At first Patricia's absence, as brutal as her unsold house unoccupied a few blocks from mine, beat at me. I'd sent a card to her new address. "Don't forget to write," I wrote, meaning it both ways. Don't forget you're a writer. Don't forget me. Gradually, such disorder righted itself. This was life, people moved. It wasn't, after all, disaster. You coped with it, and, when I considered it, coping felt like

12

a right step, maturity. We'd grown nimble with changes. Women handle the shifts, keep friendships afloat, in spite of all that other shit and demand, the being needed.

We start our protocol, the updates of our children first. It's been eight or ten years since her children have had an impact on me, although I remember how the corral of new motherhood contained our friendship, limited us. When our kids were babies, toddlers, then starting school, we'd shared kitchens and rooms and cluttered activities. We knew the arsenic hour, as Patricia loved to call it — not yet dinnertime, the house filled with doom and shrieks — and nothing worked, no entertainment, no fruit, no limits. We'd phone each other. I know, I know, we said back and forth, the din at our backs.

We take turns — Does Daniel have a Facebook account, does Tasha? Has he friended you? Do you recognize her friends? — and I listen not for the information (I'll forget most of it by evening, the family's constant details enough, my tattered mind empty each night) but for what's at work in her heart and surfacing. We have different styles. Patricia starts with the reports, I start with mood. I pierce, hunt for the biggest truth, restless until I've divined it. People —

new acquaintances, old friends — tell me I'm intense, sometimes too much. "Are you never simple?" a friend once asked, just wanting a hello. Patricia, light at the outset, asks questions twice, first for the information, propping that up like a painting against the wall. Then she steps back, asks again, mulls feeling. The eddy of her repetitions used to annoy me. *I just answered that,* I'd think. *Aren't you paying attention to me?* But deep knowledge has replaced irritation, wiped away the personal grievance: she is herself. She is like this. And I know myself — reflexively anxious that I won't be properly heard. In the security of true knowing, these traits can be set aside. She pours out details of her return, and I spark and lift. Sun creaks back over a mutual world.

Next month she'll be here for good. I hear her tell me the real-estate logistics, lament the hassle of switching schools, and I offer encouragement, but I'm thinking: me, I get Patricia back. Later I note I hadn't offered help. In crude mourning I don't feel competent at anything.

We darken our talk, that tough underlayer I wait for, private hopes, the kids' real scares and questionable behavior, uncertain parenting, sex in our lives, silent humiliations, hatreds. Then we come to our fathers.

Our grieving spreads over the table. She says things I've heard her say about her dad and the event, her frequent echoes, but now I've been repeating myself, too, unable to progress from the day of my father's death, the hospital's dull effects, how he *was* here but *is* not, and I get it: you go over and over it, you look for sense, try to place yourself, insist. Her father had been dead a few weeks when she collected all she owned, undid her kids' bedrooms, and moved away. I never saw what grief made of her, what she did with it. I couldn't follow. My father was alive.

"What was I thinking, that year?" she says. "Moving then. I must have been out of my mind. I barely remember any of it."

"Yes, this year." Its wash is blinding. What will I recall? How will I return to myself?

"It'll be great to be back. Helena's fine, we've loved the house, but I don't have friends there like this. Only you talk like this." Her voice has settled, shed its vibrant rise and rise. She is just speaking.

"I have to ask you something," I say. "When Jack was born, the first few weeks, you didn't see him."

"I didn't?"

"No, you didn't come."

"Was it summer?"

15

I'm briefly annoyed. "It was November." Both my sons were born in November, Daniel first, Jack four years later. Patricia and I were very close by then.

"I wonder why I didn't. God, I'm sorry." She looks a little stressed. I don't want that for her.

"It's okay," I say. "I just wondered."

This isn't true. I've stored hurt for ten years and let it seep into the friendship. That's what I should tell her. Come clean, Susanna, unmask and voice regret. Apologize. A decade on, together in a bar that hadn't existed then, I can't fathom why it's important to bring this up, why I need her to know she hurt me. Except that grief disdains normal procedure, and my behavior keeps surprising me, as if it has snapped off from its source, broken away. I've been accounting for disappointments. Patricia isn't actually one of them. It was Patricia who packed the full Thanksgiving dinner in paper bags and left them covered on our porch the night Christopher and I brought our first newborn home. Until then, she and I had been happy to be friends, glad at the sound of the other's interested voice, but that night, when I'd been a mother for fifty-eight hours, as I dressed my baby in diaper, Onesie, fleece bunting, Patricia planned,

16

baked, drove over, and changed our friendship. She marked what mattered between friends, what mattered in a couple, in a town. She showed me how simple: you witness and love, and you feel loved. She wasn't asking for anything.

Four years later, at the birth of my second son, she hadn't come to the hospital or to the house. Other people dropped by, brought wrapped presents and bouquets. I waited for my deep-down friend. She didn't even call. I'd been counting on her to remind me how I fit in this life, how connected I was to solid people. Patricia's eager, easy devotion in the past few years had helped to grant me mothering skills. I didn't have a reliable mother like she did, the experienced model and steady backup. Her mother worked polling tables on election days, where she chatted with a stream of lifelong neighbors. My mother, whom Patricia met once in a state of fascinated disbelief, was publicly fabulous and grand with a gesture but, for me, a notorious crisis. She didn't follow through, and when together, we did her, not me. In times of critical transformation I couldn't have her around. Before knowing me, Patricia wasn't aware such creatures existed.

Finally, a couple of weeks later — the time

a new baby remakes everything, scrambles all intentions — Patricia appeared. I was mad, fed up. She sat at one end of the couch, I at the other, Jack shielded in my arms until I set him between us. She leaned over him, wowed and wondered, as others had, but there was something stiff, she was distracted. I might have asked, figured her out, led her to open up. I was good at that. But I didn't inquire, a punishment. I didn't let anger go, habit from the dangerous family I'd left behind, from being leery of women. I was good at that, too, the guarded disappointment.

The moment divided the first years of our friendship from those after. We'd known each other almost a decade when I had Jack, but as I pulled myself in against hurt, I let a single oversight decide our future.

Patricia strains to remember why, ten years ago, she hadn't come. As she reconstructs daily history out loud, I feel dumb. For so long I'd wanted apology and explanation, but now that I've asked for them, I find neither matters at all.

We move on, talk about her mother, how she's managing, about the rearranging in a family when one person dies. We didn't use to know. We'd been adding people, choosing people. Patricia puts down her wine.

18

She says, "There is nothing that anyone can get past a forty-five-year-old woman." We laugh hard, the first honest sound I make that afternoon, or in many days, each of us feeling the ravages of experience, our debt to enduring. We are not to be fucked with. We rule. Even as we age and help our children push past us, as we worry about the estimate for the roof, forget things we meant to do, regard our widening bodies, we rule. We've returned again and again to our original selves for another look; we have refined our purpose. Changes we thought we'd been resisting have anyway been wrought, and they have made us unbreakable. On an early-spring afternoon, in a dark bar off a sleepy Missoula sidewalk, we sing the unbreakable. We spread out the landscape and, as we've always done, coax narrative out of unruly change.

Patricia found me. I was working in a restaurant, and I'd stopped at her table to fill the water glasses. "Susanna, right?" She reminded me we'd been introduced. "Aren't you from New York?" In Missoula a blurry month, after finding the apartment, the two jobs, I was aching for more society than my boyfriend. She invited us to a party, *lots* of writers, you'll *love* them, the MFA students, and *faculty,* just come! We came, my boy-friend and I, stuck near to the door at first, and Patricia, her face flushed with glee and gin, hugged an arm around my waist as she stitched together one person she liked with another. She gestured with her plastic cup and kept me by her side.

We were on. I dialed her number. I loved a new beginning, launched myself at candidates, hoping for the perfect companion. Until Missoula and its adventure of revised identity, my main company had been men. Usually, they'd been lovers first, then became my close friends. I knew how to make men last, trusted their allegiance and their reliable limitations. Women didn't last. Unable to help my hope and longing at the start, I opened myself, gave away everything, immersed in a woman as if I wished to disappear. Things blew up, or we lost focus on each other. I never saw it was a pattern, the fruitless lesson. Each friendship ended, like a fabulous limited run.

Patricia took me to Blue Mountain, a hike that gave us a view of the Missoula valley. Little rocks spit out from under my new sturdy boots as we worked our way higher, and then we stopped, out of breath, the vista at an angle to the river below so that stands of trees aligned to erase the new develop-

20

ments and tracts of box stores, revealing soft hills, the gaping sky. She told how she'd met her husband, Mark, laughing at how young she'd been. I told how I'd met my boyfriend Christopher six months earlier, and now here I was. Here I was, living where he wanted to, in Montana. We compared favorite Alice Munro stories, which had affected us when, our desperate admiration. Let's read each other, we said, flattered by the other's interest.

"You guys should come to dinner. Sunday?" The friendship would hurry and deepen. On that night she opened the door, releasing a fragrant spell, smells of roast chicken, sauces. Mark clapped our shoulders and pulled us in. He poured us all scotch, turned the blues music up. At his friendly questions, Christopher and I explained ourselves, and the two of them remarked, their opinions noisy and enjoyed. Ice melted in the glasses and made room for itself. I stood before their wall of books and recognized editions. Patricia and I had started our collections at the same cultural moment. That bright red Cheever, the accumulated Norton anthologies of college, the sporty Vintage trade paperbacks of first apartments. Far from my home city and reliable friends, I could trust the books and

21

the lovely woman who had hung on to them, and who wrote fiction, wanted to feed us, laughed big at embarrassments and literary gossip. "Tell me more," she said. "What were the *Paris Review* parties like? You've met so-and-so? What's he *like*?" She couldn't believe I'd volunteered to evacuate such a world.

Patricia lived where she'd been born. Her parents had been born here. She'd grown, gone away, come back, and inhabited a town peopled by doctors and florists and mechanics who'd walked the halls of the high school when she did; lawyers, professors, bakers, engineers whose brothers had been arrested after parties; arborists, farmers, journalists, real-estate agents, and landscapers whose sisters had divorced her cousins. She shrugged at the casual exposure, felt happily known.

In our early days, Patricia loved to do "big city" things with me, as if we were our own dolls. She'd suggest places for cheap lunches, seeing if I liked them, enjoying the fresh take a newcomer could get away with. Service always took awhile, me at first in an urban huff, but I copied her manners and learned the local way. She often walked the neighborhood mile from her house to her parents', which was on the National Historic

Register. In summers the whole family went to a cabin. You picked huckleberries until dark, she said. You floated the rivers, tubing, casting. I'd never heard of huckleberries, or morel mushrooms, didn't know these river terms. She tended tomato plants in the sunniest spot of her yard. In spring she gave me garish orange poppies dug up from her garden, shaking earth from the roots as she handed them over. "Just put them in anywhere," she said to dubious me. "They'll do great."

A year and a half later I was waiting for her at a rear table, impatient, a bitter day in late winter. The restaurant was dark and almost empty. Patricia was late. From the table I watched the white space where the windows looked onto the street. A silhouette broke through the whiteness, her shape grew distinct. She was undoing scarf and layers as she hurried in.

"Hi!" she said. She was too cheerful to resent, bending to kiss me, breathless from the cold. "The sun's out! How *are* you, sweetie?"

"Okay."

She dropped her gloves and hat by her feet, sat, laced the strap of her handbag over her chair. I waited. Again, but as if for the first time, she said, "How are you?"

"Not good," I said. "I have to — I'm having an abortion."

Her face then. I saw the change. The ashen shadow, the tense retreat. Christopher was my closest friend, but he was, by definition, too close for this. I needed a woman, someone who understood the body's rebellions in a way he could not, its sneaky devastations. She was concerned for me, mustered support, but her distress loomed. I ignored this. I had to speak my own trouble, my double disaster of accidental pregnancy and intentional abortion. I'd already had the preliminary appointment, was forced to stay pregnant one more week, stew with unsayable anger and fear, with the ruin and confusion in my marriage. Patricia had been married much longer. She'd show me the point to all this.

"Don't do it," she said. This startled us both. I actually pressed against the back of my chair. "I mean, but are you sure this is the right choice?" I wondered if I'd misjudged, mistaken our mutual literary admirations and social pleasure for allegiance.

"We've decided, we have to," I said. We did have to, a decision-less decision made in days of compressed, obsessive hours. Our relationship wasn't steady enough, it would

24

have to find more definition. I was resigned, not yet brokenhearted.

"It's just —" She started to cry, her turn. Trying for so long, wanting badly to get pregnant, nearing forty. I felt the affront of my decision, then longed for magic — let me transfer the pregnancy, *you* make the baby. Please relieve me of this mission.

I think what happened at that table was that she hated me. She saw me squandering the precious. I saw she couldn't help me, that in our rawest moments, no matter our goodwill, we weren't better than casual friends. We made a gap then — her longing, my burden, the blankness in between. We forgot our food, strangled through the hour, parted. I called her the evening after the abortion, and she was kind. To honor my mood, my act, she was kind, but I knew she didn't want to talk any more about it, so I didn't.

A year later, at her baby shower, I hated her. It had been a complicated year, as Christopher and I had recovered from the abortion, reconsidered parenthood, decided to try. I'd swallowed my anger — *Now* you're ready? — and I got pregnant. I felt urgent and possessive in the first weeks, guarding gestation without joy. But a few days before the shower I miscarried, and I was so sour and gone, hated all fertile worlds, especially Patricia's, filled with her mother and father, her friendly sister, her longtime friends. I dropped my present in the pile, sulked in a chair across the room as she opened them all.

In another year, Patricia threw my baby shower, bottles of sparkling cider to mimic champagne open along her kitchen counter. It was a sweet afternoon, women I admired and liked welcomed into the house, directed to the enormous, happy me by Patricia with her determined, boundless generosity, which only faltered between us when we'd been arrested by pain's inexplicable hand.

Patricia, Liza, Judith, Susanna. We gathered each Monday morning, ten o'clock. I couldn't wait, up since five or six, dragging through the repetitions with my sunny baby, my energy devoted to the mental catalog of his clean clothes, his diapers in diminishing stacks by the changing table. Hoist him, change him, nurse him, sponge him, hoist him, nurse him. He couldn't do anything without me. At ten I'd be with Patricia, Liza, and Judith, all of us collapsed and loud, and someone would bring coffee cake. Women to notice, nod. Someone would have had a worse night than mine. Someone would tell a tale on her husband, or scald him, and then I could say the same, or be glad for not having to. I'd become part of a quartet, which was a responsibility, a privilege, that didn't feel natural. Patricia had invited me to join the playgroup when Daniel was still in arms, meet her two dear friends. Clubs seemed tedious to me, book clubs, knitting groups, artificial associations that demanded you relinquish independence, specialness. When I wanted a friend, I wanted her across a table. Confide, reveal, dish, commiserate, then go. For strife, I coped on my own or with one dedicated other, didn't want a chorus. Also, I was suspicious that the playgroup women — this prominent Liza and Judith — ate away at my friend's allegiance *to me.* "That's not really my thing," I said. Patricia, with her faith in communal reliance, scoffed. "You'll love them," she said. She possessed an abiding belief in the happy outcome.

Several weeks in, I did love them — Judith's harried warmth, her voice laced with resigned Jewish humor, Liza's intense face inquiring as she checked my expression up and down; our delicious and dense loose laughter. The three of them had daughters, girls older than Daniel and already walking. The daughters could squat, open cabinets, pick up one black bean at a time, one goldfish. Their nakedness appalled my eye, no penis. The playgroup lasted through our next pregnancies, then past those babyhoods. Once two writers and early friends, Patricia and I became a crowd. In the space of five years, we'd become a quartet of mothers, each with two children — twelve of us massed into a living room in winter. In warm weather we met on the grass in the park, handing the bottle of sunblock around, working the many limp arms with cream as we talked. We talked. We talked in cars and in parks, we talked at birthday parties, at weddings, relegated to the periphery as we bounced our restless children in weary arms. I found us interesting in the very things that otherwise made us infinitely dull. Tasha's meltdown in the parking lot? Tell! Tell of the perplexing hives on Frieda's back, your worry over Maddie's teeth, the bully at day care, the dingy smell of stubborn pee. Describe the appointment with the specialist, the rudeness of the pediatric nurse — What does *she* know — the dreary bathroom mess at day's end, the pink vomit after a wasted dose of antibiotics, the defeated glance at the kitchen floor; the preposterous neglect of the laundry room, pets, sex life. Tell what you said when you called poison control, and then what they said. You did the right thing. I would have called, too. How tired are you? When did you last pee?

We reminded one another to drink water, to keep appointments, we reminded the others of our degrees and achievements — Liza the scientist, Judith the educator — the desired careers that had taken root, then been put on hiatus or abandoned as we obeyed the mystifying compulsion to bear children and tend them. With equal heat we could talk about the anthrax scare or the manufacture of strollers; we talked of news stories — that *mother* who drowned *all* her children in the tub ("How horrible," "How could she?" "Oh, I could see it . . ."); or of certain, future dangers: People would break our children's hearts, unimaginable cruelty in our gigantic new business of love. Prom, we said. Driving, we said, laughing so hard, as if they'd ever be larger, as if they'd ever zip their jackets or use a Kleenex. We talked and talked, and when our babies in a roaring foreground were cranky or truculent or unfit for common errands, we scattered fragments of that talk, hands on their backs, our attention filtered, diluted, exasperated, but no one missed a Monday morning.

I'd never had such friends, women to

count on, who counted on me. It sounds simple, a natural equation, but I hadn't succeeded at it before. A code emerged. One woman would gather another's child in any situation. Emergency, hurry, helping. We swept each other's floors, after Cheerios, frozen blueberries, then put the broom away. None of them could have done a single thing I'd have protested, and they granted me the same absolute permission. What a thing, balance with women. I didn't wonder who liked whom better, who got more; camaraderie reassured me. Collective strength prevailed. I liked baking the apple cake on the fourth Mondays, everyone at my house, liked talking about ingredients and allergies and recipes. I liked the sight of our breasts, three or four of us nursing at the same time, the room quiet, except for our voices, delicate and pitched to reverberate through our chests, another calming trick to mothering that I could see at work around me. We hoisted car seats, strapping in extras for the afternoon while someone went to her shrink, while my husband and I went to our shrink. Christopher and I had become workers, united in dry tasks, neither noticing what the other did, just needing the other to do it. I saved romance for Patricia, Liza, and Judith, thinking up cards

30

for them, or corn chowder, coaxing out their triumph or woe, sharing the hardest, storing my best till Monday.

Our husbands were undone from us, phantoms of some former interest. I had nothing to say to men. Men! I could barely fathom their use, now that we'd made children. The men didn't speak our minutiae, or pass hours gathered with toddlers and strangers' babies, overhearing bad parenting in waiting rooms and supermarket aisles. They did not gentle the kids' stiffened legs as we did, lifting them from the carts. What else could be important? *Today,* I could say to my three friends, on the weariest, hopeless days, *I fed my family. That is enough,* they said back. *That is so much.*

Just because we were friends, Patricia let me attend the birth of her second child. When I'd asked, she hadn't hesitated. "I'd love it," she said, as if I'd come to her with a great idea. "Let me check with Mark." Daniel was a year and a half old, and I'd been trying to make sense of the reordered self. I'd already done so much of that in Patricia's encouraging company, becoming a mother. She trusted me, which made me feel trustworthy. Mark called me when her labor started. I drove fast, slammed into a parking spot. I needed to be back in the delivery room, to revisit this gamble and inside-out undoing, where my boy had changed me. How could that be an ordinary room? The hospital door slid open for me, time machine, on my way to my crucial friend.

Patricia didn't greet me. Next to her Mark looked up, said hi. I went to the elevated head of the bed and pressed my forehead to hers. "You're doing it," I said. We knew the body's dire work.

She moved deeper into labor, and Mark whispered at her ear, face turned against hers and hers altered by the fury of intent. I couldn't hear, but I watched his words form. Her arm in Mark's grasp, his hand inside her thigh, her head tilted to him, her chin squarely into her sternum. The couple's gravest truth, never meant for exposure. It backed me away, this haunting privacy beyond friendship. The baby's head crowned, and he was properly born, and there was a sweep of activity, paparazzi movement around them.

Patricia was gone into the baby, and as I quieted my absurd emotion, the little-girl feeling of *What about me,* I knew I should leave. He's beautiful, I said, kissed her. I made my way to the car and sat cupped in the seat. The ecstatic adrenaline of a birth was buzzing through my body, and I cried. I cried for all I'd lost when I gave birth, the unbidden changes, and for all I'd gained with the enormous, replenishing love for my son. And I cried, amazed by the friend who would share her private efforts with me, without worry. Uninhibited with her intimacies, Patricia assured me of a way to be the right woman and right friend. She didn't demand more or prepare for less. She gave me a closeness I hadn't known how to have without its being awful. How could I thank her?

When Patricia's father died, I understood that it was major, or rather, I had a mere sense. By then, our kids were in middle school, uninterested in one another, which seemed incredible to us, the linked mothers. We no longer met on Mondays, sometimes went weeks without calling, but at the service I found Judith and Liza right away, and we moved as one to sit in the last pew, we still-whole daughters, each with two parents. *How is she, have you talked to her,* we said in low asides. *I did last night, I left minestrone, I took some groceries over.* This was our benediction in the face of our friend's pain. Our radiant, optimistic Patricia had crossed over, fatherless. She'd lost big. The eulogies began, and we stopped our talk, watched her closely. I realized we were going to lose, too. She guided us.

Once, after Patricia gave a reading — I wasn't thirty yet, she wasn't forty — I asked for a copy of the piece, and read it many times, marveling at tricks I wished to try. She used to come to my readings, sit in front, cheer afterward her unabashed cheer. In the next years, motherhood's inescapable assignments and the struggles of our marriages made us forget writing, how we had first studied each other, enjoyed each other and connected. Now our husbands earned most of our incomes, our independence thinned by their money, trumped. Something had happened to us. And Mark and Christopher, they also were writers, and we said to each other how proud we were, how jealous. We wanted what they had, their selfish time, their closed doors and concentration, their bodies ignored by the babies. We knew something of writer unions that other friends didn't get, the artist husband, the artist wife vying for praise, for success, wanting to outdo each other, pretending not to want that. A room of one's own, we often said, if only. After the first babies, Patricia and I stopped talk of our writing, that sacrifice a greater sorrow than the dozen others parenthood demanded. We washed out each other's sippie cups, dropped off library books. At the Monday gatherings we could look at each other over the heads in need of a shampoo and bemoan our loss without a word. At least the kids are worth it! We love them so! And then we could say, but only to each other, we could whisper, *Maybe they aren't worth it. What about me, where have I gone?*

Patricia's back. I see her at the high school, her enormous smile visible at a distance. We stop and hug in the hallway, read each other's faces.

"How *are* you?" she says in her way. I feel such good relief. She's frazzled by the move, not quite at home yet.

"Can you *believe* this," we say, "they're *sophomores!*" We compare the kids' schedules, which we're holding in our hands, and see they have two classes together. We're thrilled, imagining their rediscovery, and then we laugh at ourselves, our enthusiasm, because we know we must resist urging them to be friends. Such alchemy is private and unplanned.

"How are you?" she asks again, and I tell

her about the book I'm writing — my friendships with women.

She glows. "I've almost finished my novel."

Together, our voices warm and matched, we are saying, "When can I read it?"

■ ■ ■ ■

YOUNG.

■ ■ ■ ■

WOMEN ARE LIKE THIS

Here's my home of women, blood's beginnings: I share a bunk bed with my sister. We live on the fourth floor of an apartment building on the Upper East Side. Even though it's east of Park Avenue, what my mother calls the unfashionable side, the monthly rent is an "astronomical" $400. My mother tells us we deserve this, having stayed in the residential hotel after we left our father. His parents pay the child support, and she has money for the rent, and for coats and chokers at Bonwit Teller, and for restaurants along Third Avenue, where she knows the owners and the maître d's, men's names her special song. She drove a taxi, briefly, and had a small part in someone's movie, but she doesn't work. She doesn't go anywhere. The grandparents also pay for private school, the pediatrician and dentist, the Cape Cod camp in the summer. We see them when our father takes us down

Lexington Avenue to the mansion where he grew up. He comes to collect us, and he and our mother tease each other in the front hall. Then he kisses her, her pale arms up around his neck, and takes us. I'm not sure why they're separated, then divorced, but I am sure he's not one of us. He doesn't belong in our apartment.

My mother had been nineteen for a month when she gave birth to me at the London Clinic. Then my father, just twenty-nine, brought his new baby and his young wife from England to New York. We lived in a hotel on Fifth Avenue, with my father's valet and a nanny for me, while we waited for the town house to be ready. Later I asked to hear the chronicle repeated, me as the five-month-old on a ship as it crossed the wintry Atlantic. My mother threw up on the voyage, she told me, but I was perfect, such an easy, happy baby. I made friends everywhere. At twenty-one, she had my sister, and the next summer she left the marriage. In these stories, we make a triumvirate. My mother is cowed and overwhelmed; I am peaceful, sociable; and my infant sister, a siren of discord, is inconsolable. My father, before I'm allowed to remember him, is already invisible. Not until I grew up could I consider that when she arrived in New

York in 1966, my mother was a teenage girl, that she missed her best friend, that she was scared of her husband, who was often mean, and that she made herself sick aching for home.

A beautiful twenty-four-year-old and her two daughters, five and three, we move into the big apartment. The front door is propped open, men carry furniture in, and she directs them. We're settled. My sister and I get one room and in the first weeks sleep on the floor, heaps of blankets, which is fun, our Snoopies propped against the baseboard in the daytime. Then we get the bunk bed with a ladder, like a tree house indoors. We drape sheets and make caves. We catalog everything — toys, tights, markers; cardboard boxes deep with Barbies, their hair an unfixable mess and their plastic chewable shoes lost on the bottom; a clock with digital numbers in glowing segments; bracelets we fight over; diaries with gold locks. The keys dangle from black strings. We are six and four. I have a transistor radio, and on the top bunk I listen with the volume so low it almost isn't sound. I must hold still to hear, and shallow my breath, but it's worth it. I don't want to share. My sister likes pigtails, and I part her hair before school, snapping the colored elastics into knots that will hold all day. I am seven and she is five. I take her hand to go to the subway station, getting us to school, galloping the steps if we feel the train's approach. When we're late, I hail a taxi on Park and have the driver drop us half a block from the school. I've heard our mother say to drivers, "The far-right corner, please."

Our mother sleeps in the other bedroom, curtains pulled, her somber vault scented by tea rose oil and lingering soaps from yesterday's bath. She keeps vases of flowers until the water needs changing. The mirror on the bathroom door makes two of her, reflects her dark head on a pillow. She's twenty-five, twenty-six, twenty-seven. This room (and we *know* the soft spot where her doorknob gives, her carpet's tread under our naked feet) contains her swirl — the pillboxes, evening bags, pharmacy bottles, envelopes, our three passports, her sandals with tiny buckles on the ankle straps, the mess of *Newsweek* magazines and *Cosmopolitan,* sections of the *Times,* phone numbers on torn paper, and dollar bills, silk scarves. We take the scarves and make games, until she says from sleep to put them back. She has a "bad back"; she tells us it was from landing on her tailbone, a long time ago, and I hear the word *bad* as it would be for dogs or old milk, definitive. She sends us down to the pharmacy to pick up her medicines. My sister says, "Can we buy gum?" and I'm the one who gets to hold the money. Late in afternoon — some afternoons, the good ones — her door is wide, and sun pours into the hall, and our apartment fills with lifted voices, sparkling, the three of us one sweet sound. She skips across the living room. I watch my sister, I watch my mother. She watches both of us, and herself.

Our living room looks the way my mother wants it. She's chosen the lamps, the art, where it hangs (until she moves it in all-night frenzies). There's a Campbell's Soup can Andy Warhol signed at a party, which she keeps on the mantel, and a Cornell box she stole from somewhere. She explains Joseph Cornell, "The most important . . ." She decides on amaryllis in February, paperwhites in April, or jonquils. Hyacinth drenches the apartment in scent. She sings to Leonard Cohen and makes me sad: "Suzanne takes you down to her place by the river . . ." She sings to "Angie:" "You can't say we never tried," but I don't like the figure veiled on that record cover in smoky yellows, can't tell if it's a man or a woman;

43

and is that her on the front of the Bob Dylan record, a morning she was without us in some New York street? I know it's not, but I've seen her next to men that way, all leaned in and clutching, and she grips us like that, her daughters, when we're walking.

When I'm in high school, and she's divorced a second time, we will tighten further into a womanly purity, a common party, evening plans for going out together. We'll drink champagne from the same fluted glass as we get ready, passing it in exchange for the lipstick, the blush brush. She'll assess me, add a belt, reach it around and blouse out the silk shirt I'm wearing, which she has lent to me. "That's better." She tells us men notice us, but she's the one they talk to. We will trade our successes in the taxi, laugh at men's fumblings and at the bartenders, at the ignorance we are so good at spotting.

But before we are ourselves women with her, when we are still *hers,* our mother's friends are constant women. They ring the doorbell, embrace us, stalk past in their heeled boots — the gossip on the couch, the vulgar confidences, the vodka cold from the freezer (yet never frozen, a trick I assume only she knows). Men are the focus and the business, and the women, here in our apartment, conduct it. Olga is bitchy, and Corinne is tearful, and Melinda is regal — "It's her Latvian cheekbones, girls" — and Samantha lives with us for a bit, cross-legged on my mother's bed as she names her questions and mistakes, before she dyes her clothes orange in our bathtub and moves to India.

The women phone, and if our mother's asleep I take careful messages. She wakes and rings back, talks for *ever* as we pass with intended clumsiness outside her door-way, hoping for attention. "Come over," we hear her say. "Girls! Tidy up! Olga's com-ing!" She loves happy emergencies. Her friends bring her potted flowers, pull glasses from the kitchen cupboard, they flop and bare themselves, and my mother, only beginning to grow up — *I will be twenty-eight again this year, ho ho* — listens, plays, waits for praise and pleasures and op-portunity. She resists no one. The girlfriends inhale, take the spell and pick up their drinks; they have dark laughs, cries and barks, so much of *something. Knowing* something. We are sent to our room.

My mother always had a main best friend, a passionate, sudden sister who'd last a year, maybe. Bev lasted longest because she lived in our building. She was divorced, or about to be. They traded flirty banter in the elevator, their heads inclined above ours. Bev's Irish setters pressed against our legs, and my sister and I handled their silky jowls, wiped saliva on our pants. My mother used to say, "If you can't find me, come upstairs." I'd press the PH elevator button — a homework problem, a costume idea — ride up and knock. They stopped their low sounds and shrewd cackles. My mother's voice called, "Who is it? Come in!" She sat in the middle of Bev's couch, a wine bottle open on the table. They faced each other, a knee up each and a stemmed glass in hand. As the intruder, I sensed the precious mood, its boil they tended. "I'll be down in ten minutes," my mother said. Bev knew things that I didn't know, my mother's needs and calculations, certain whereabouts. This was okay with me. I was hoping some grown-up would take over. Thirty years later, after she'd gotten sober, Bev wrote to me, "I was not as aware as I should have been. I'm sorry."

Fiendish activity, her closet thrown open, spent theater tickets and unsheathed letters on the bed, my mother menaced the rooms and dug things from drawers and shoved them into her bag, before snapping up her keys. "Don't stay up," she called from the front door. "Telly off at nine!" We promised, and we disobeyed. We didn't want her to go, but then she was gone, wonderful, and we raced to the kitchen, stood on tiptoes, reached the back of the freezer for frozen yogurt bars. We rooted around in her closet, where the floor roiled with deflated boots and high heels tossed apart from their mates. The limp hems at various lengths, scented by tea rose, suggested her, reminded us happily but did not confuse us, did not complicate our business. In person she could frighten us, as her lips went white and rigid, her spit filled with accusations. She was the greatest storm, although I made myself brave, unshakable, tried to show that to my sister. Cocaine-fierce days were followed by sluggish comas on the bed, doll-size Demerol bottles mostly empty on the dresser. I didn't think it strange, just her, us — empty glasses back to the kitchen, syringe wrappers a litter to be cleared from the bathroom floor. When the phone rang, I ran to answer in the kitchen, erect with maturity, and used a quiet voice to preserve her sleep, our valued calm.

We could wake her for Pet. That wasn't her real name, but they called each other that, courting twinness, handing the name back and forth in conversation. They'd been fifteen together in England, sixteen, flaunting themselves. Pet shared the vital past, a land prior to me that baffled my comprehension. When they spoke my mother's voice grew precise with British consonants, and higher. On Pet's visits — deliriously rare — I'd hear their gushing tones, creep to my mother's door, and look. They sat face-to-face on the bed, cocaine drawn out in busy strands over a mirror balanced on my mother's legs. They babbled the names of schools, train stations, a boutique — our *hats*! — or a boy at a dance they'd both rebuffed but secretly desired, and they blurted long strings of events, so foreign they upset me, a wrong universe. "Come in, darling," my mother said, seeing me. She wanted me to feel the bestness of this friend, her importance. Pet held back her long, long hair as she bent over my mother's lap to sniff that energetic sniff.

I don't know my mother anymore. I don't know my sister. I splintered away, constructed a remote life. I did not want to be reachable. As soon as I left my mother for boarding school, she took in a new daughter. She'd moved to New Mexico by then with my sister. She'd bought a house, adobe, three-bedroom, one for each of us, she said. The new girl was a little older than I, her parents dead, and my mother began to tell people she'd adopted her, which she hadn't. She introduced Danni as her eldest, which I overheard the first time with the feeling of being batted off a cliff. When I protested my mother called me selfish, and said "Danni has *no one* but us." Danni got the room meant for me, and Danni and my sister grew inseparable, and in the next years Danni, my sister, and my mother shared the champagne, went out together, traded men's attentions. The three of them lived, it seemed to me, like a huddle of enormous mice, all warmth and squeaking enthusiasms. With no power to explain, no effect of my hurt, I started to uninvolve myself. I'd act polite at the news of Danni — her teaching certificate, her job interview — but fumed privately. She married and had daughters, whom my mother called her grandchildren, but, then, I'm the one who decided to break daughterhood, who kept my children away.

The last time I overheard my mother's voice, I was on the phone to my grandmother. My mother was with her, wedging herself into the conversation, although no one was talking to her. My grandmother, whose concentration at ninety-six was fading, kept trying to stop her, sweetly and with exasperation, so that she could hear my answers to her questions. Finally, giving up, she said, "Is there anything you want to say to Mummy?" "Tell her I love her," I said. It just flew out, uncatchable and a complete truth. I hadn't seen my mother in years — since the summer of 1998, and now it was late 2006 — refused to myself that I missed anything of her. "She says she loves you," my grandmother said. "I know she does!" my invisible mother sang, echoey, deeper in the room. "Tell her I love her, too." I know you do, I thought. My mother's perpetual *now,* tempting me with possibility. Weren't we silly, she might say? What was the matter with us? Let's be close again. My doomed and complicated longing surged, and I had to hang up.

The two of us had no *now.* Our furious fires had burned everything to the ground. As I'd grown, each time I brought my mother in, called for her, or let her advise my course, I was ruptured. She came up to college the first October weekend, for instance, and hit it off with my roommate. The girl, Amy, was athletic and suburban, a type I'd never encountered, but we'd steadied each other the first disoriented weeks, stood side by side in the uncertain gaggle for registration. I liked this potential, the reliable connection, not too intimate, born of random assignment. Just right. Amy and I didn't talk of her marketing major or my focus on Renaissance literature, but at night, while she toweled her hair, I flipped through the spiral bound face-book and we mock-imagined dating prospects. It was fun.

Then my mother showed up. She held my face to hers — "Oh, Sue, my bunny" — her searing gaze that always turned to sweet tears for both of us. Finally she looked at Amy, and wanted to know her secrets. She was so good at that, able to convince anyone that they were meant for each other. The girl gave away real truths about her mother and father and desires she'd never spoken of to me in our enforced rapport. Yes, Amy admitted, she was having sex with her new boyfriend, or was very close — "You are?" I said — and my mother went into high gear, how we were going to Planned Parenthood — *they* were — this very afternoon, getting her on birth control. The pill? A diaphragm? A little flustered, my roommate flashed me the your-mom's-great look I'd seen cross the faces of my friends. "She's cool," they said. "I wish my mom was like her," they said.

It seemed a good plan, whatever my mother organized, until later, when my roommate's parents appeared, and my mother, enjoying her dorm-room dominion, reassured them that she had seen to their daughter's contraceptives. My roommate moved out the next week. Twenty-five years later, she wrote to me in vicious recall of that ruinous afternoon. She told me that what she remembered of our acquaintance was that she hated me. My mother, before the weekend was out, had forgotten the episode, had no sense of its effects.

One weekend, one scotched friendship. That's not why you lose your mother, not why you and your sister stop speaking, but it's partly why, the exhaustions of hope at last overwhelming, the dramas of close women so incendiary. You are accustomed to telling yourself to try again, and you try again, again. Finally, you can't, and you stop.

When I was twenty-three or twenty-four, I went with a few friends — men — to a party and was pushed with great crowd energy from the door into the swell of the party, a central room pressed to the walls with people, mostly known to me, men and their girlfriends. No one was married yet. I was living with roommates then, two women I hardly thought about. Men were my focus, for flirting, sex, information, example, and for friendship. I could observe them, advise and hector them, be mentored and trust their harmless ways. I'd never been taught to know their dangers. Noise rose from the garbled talk on the couches, bounced off the walls. Guests had their arms and elbows lifted to pass, glasses held under their chins, and I was suddenly face-to-face with an older woman.

"I know you!" she shouted. "Your mother ruined my life!"

"Join the club," I said, thinking she was funny, but she was disgusted.

"It's Mina," she said. "Remember? Your awful mother ruined my life."

I remembered Mina, though this gloomy, worn woman bore no trace of that celebrity. I'd never seen her away from Barbados, where we used to go a lot. My grandmother had had an estate, a grand and annexed villa built into the coral cliffs above the sea, and Mina was part of my mother's set, the collection of young English and Americans who drew together each holiday. Once when I was a child, Mina had made an entrance at a Christmas party dressed as a present, sheathed in gold lamé and sashed with red velvet tied in a bow at her hip. My mother adored the nerve. "Look at Mina, everyone! Darling, you're *sensational*!" and they hurled into obvious conspiracy, whispers pierced by malevolent surges of volume.

Staring at me, Mina waited, a grim challenge. She'd called my mother "awful," and meant it, and I had an instant of schoolyard alert. I could tell she wanted me to hear, and I did want more, those specific, missing clues to the dominant woman of my life, my mother who pulled and pushed, evaporated and materialized, careened, undid things, brambled my intentions; but, also, I didn't want that. I wanted to stop looking for her. Another report of her petulant explosions, her indifferent betrayal, her absolute disappearance? She was a prism against the window, rainbow shards copious but intangible. Who could sort that out? The object — cut glass, the play of beveled edges — wasn't mysterious; it was the sorcery of light and sway that beguiled. My mother's friendship with this briefly favored woman had ended, and we never heard Mina's name again. Shamed, I had the instinct to apologize, to say to her, "I was not as aware as I should have been," but that wasn't my line. I excused myself and struggled through the crowd, away. Whatever she had to tell me, that burnt story of her brief fashion, how convinced she was they'd mattered to each other, how she'd been absorbed, then drained, cast off, her secrets used against her — I didn't need the news. It was in my blood. Women, my young mother had shown me, are the festival. Women are like this: fierce, supreme, capable. And devious and cunning. We lie, we win. And we're this: alluring, witchy. Women make throaty appeals, rant purely, persuade. We are right, but don't trust us. Prize loyalty, but don't count on me.

REAL FRIENDS

I remember, if I concentrate, the clutter of children, can't see the teacher more than a smudge. She wrote our names on the blackboard, and *Marjorie* in chalk, like fabric in the fingers, is the texture of first grade.

Marjorie was not my friend, but so central, bossy, taller than the rest of us, I never forgot her. She wore white tights and a tartan jumper with large white buttons at the waist to fasten the green straps that crisscrossed her yellow shirt between her shoulder blades (I sat behind her). Her name is still woven into plaid, into my idea of plaid. She was the first girl I saw wear a headband, and she had white patent-leather Mary Janes. The hairband, shiny red plastic, made grooves in the strands at her hairline. I don't remember anyone else in first grade. She commanded all my attention.

I had a certain standing in the classroom, allowed to be off by myself. Sometimes I'd cry. Marjorie would walk over.

"What's wrong?" she said, looming over me, pigtails rooted behind her ears. She hardly ever talked to me.

"I miss my best friend. She died." There was a pause. I'd suffered, had met the depths of life's mysteries.

"How did she die?"

At home my mother handled the story. "Your very first friend died," she'd tell me, and get sad, which made me sad. I loved to hear it: the first attachment beyond family, a tragic ending, my early heart broken but petted and mended by my mother. Sophisticated pain was part of me, and so, too, the passions of friendship. "Her poor mother!" my mother would say. "Just imagine how awful." I could not imagine, had no image of the woman, but could almost picture the girl, this golden wraith, this perfect beauty. Scarlet fever or a weakened heart, something sneaky, stole my beloved friend away. One day she was there, fine. I could remember us, just about, three-year-olds with chubby wrists and white tights, half a lifetime ago. The next day she was dead: the empty stroller. According to my mother, I was inconsolable at her disappearance. "Don't you remember? You thought she didn't want to be friends with you anymore. You cried

57

and cried. You kept asking where she was." She stroked the top of my head. "We used to push you in your strollers, side by side." I searched for any sense of proximity, any warmth. Blond curls? Did we dig in the garden with kitchen things? Did she cry when she dropped Ritz crackers in the dirt? She wasn't mean, ever, of course not. She was the sweetest girl anyone had ever met, not like Marjorie, who scared me, whose voice grated, whose very name bullies my memory. My dead friend gave me her dolls, to keep. She wanted me to have them. She brought candy canes. We read Little Golden Books on the couch and sucked the peppermint. I followed her, waiting my turn as she pushed the clacking bubble toy over the flagstones. In the park we chose the swings, and our mothers stood behind us, didn't they, their doubled voices sweeping far and near. All this I imagined, so I could miss her, feel kin. I pictured her stroller on the sidewalk, the waist strap to hold her in, her Mary Janes kicking up. See her dark curls; she clutched a doll under one arm; her big eyes were hazel, like mine. I tried to cope under this net of confusion — suggested drama, disappearing picture, willed memory.

"What's wrong, sweetie?" said the teacher,

who left what she was doing with the others to come over, crouch next to me, palms down on her stockinged knees. Marjorie walked away.

"My friend." I sensed longing in the word, but I couldn't quite touch it, arrive there. I needed more. "My friend died."

"Yes, that's very sad, isn't it? When someone we love dies."

Feeling better, I went back to the scissor table to work shapes out of construction paper. I kept pet mice, and one of them had died, too. So I knew. I really knew.

Marjorie wrote in big letters, so I started to write mine bigger. Her navy blue kneesocks. A gold pin in her skirt. My mother took me to Gimbel's to buy a tartan kilt with a gold safety pin. The fringe tickled my bare knees. On Mondays Marjorie looked different. Everyone else looked the same. Marjorie said, "You go there and you go here." "Yes, Marjorie." "What about me, Marjorie, pick me?" She didn't pick me. After lunch, we came back into our classroom, a slow rope of kids. Marjorie always went to her cubby, took out a white hairbrush and with a flick of fingers freed her pigtails, then brushed her hair.

I read *The Autobiography of Frederick Douglass,* a chapter book I picked because his stern face and white beard haunted me from a classroom poster over my seat. I made a timeline of his life, and the teacher taped it up under the high window. Come see, Marjorie, I wanted to say. I wanted that badly. She had a tutu in her cubby one day, and I asked to have ballet lessons.

On Thursdays I got to leave school early for ballet. My mother at the classroom door, I hurried, got my coat, and we held hands in the hall, which retained the odor of lunch. She sniffed me, the air, asked, "What did you have?" Every Thursday we had baked beans. I'd push them into an island on the plastic plate, saving them for last. I ate the lunch and the fruit cocktail and then allowed myself the syrupy beans.

One Thursday we had a fire drill at lunch, so loud and drastic it hurt my chest, and all of us stood right up and made a line by one door. The long-limbed second-graders were in giggling lines by other doors. In front of me, Marjorie's pigtails brushed her shoulders. "Shhh," said the teacher. We filed down the stairs, hands on the shiny black banister, and our teacher led us out the front steps, walked us to a leafy tree down the block, where we stopped and waited. We weren't supposed to talk until we were back inside. Marjorie talked. Not to me, but I stood close. The drill over, we were to go back in, resume what we'd left behind, but we returned to the lunchroom, and I saw just the shock of bare table and that my beans, my favorite comfort, were gone. I decided, *From now on, eat your favorite thing first, in case it gets taken away.*

The ballet teacher wore a long-sleeved leotard, pale tights, and a little flap of skirt tied on the side. We wore ballet slippers with graying strips of elastic to hold them on and black leotards that showed our arms. Madame's hair was stretched into a tiny bun. No matter how I brushed with my white plastic hairbrush, like Marjorie's, my bun was never that smooth and small, so I wore a ponytail, a minor defeat. Mothers sat outside in the hall, pocketbooks in shiny white or black patent leather in their laps. My father came to collect me, itself strange and wonderful because I didn't get to see him every day, and I liked this best about the class. Madame's voice beat at us, *"Un* and *deux* and *trois* and *quatre,"* and I looked again at the clock, the white chunks of five minutes, and *five* and *five* and *five.* At the end of the lesson, the insides of my thighs clutching and hurting and my forehead tight from the pull of the ponytail, I checked the door for my father. Then he would come.

In the fall I started second grade at a new school, ten epic blocks further north, and my old school, with its unique banisters, fire-drill routines, Marjorie, melted away. I no longer took ballet. I didn't miss it or miss anyone. What I saw was me, my existence central, the starting point on the timeline. I met Jenny and Gwen. My teacher, Joe, flicked the light on and off to quiet us. When I noticed him walking toward the switch, my stomach would jump. Here it comes, and was I the only person who understood the ache of anticipating? I liked to slip out to the gray hallway, seek the bathroom. I didn't want whatever was next, didn't want to sort dry beans into egg-carton compartments. I didn't trust the lunches of *arroz con pollo,* nor the long tables instead of desks. In the stall I latched the metal door and sat, aligning the toes of my black patent-leather shoes with the black-and-white tiled patterns on the floor. *I am seven,* I thought. I lay on the tiles to cool my face. *My parents are getting a divorce today, and I am the oldest I have been in my entire life. I will always be older than I've ever been before.* I thought I knew everything.

I didn't think much about the dead little

friend, although my mother liked to bring her up; Marjorie didn't exist. Jenny and Gwen were real, every morning we hoped to be assigned the same table. I was riveted, documented them — Jenny, her narrowed eyes, the jut of her chin, the brown hair in a blunt cut to her shoulders. She showed me how to subtract three-digit numbers, how to carry the one, her hand on my paper as she slashed a line through the zero, wrote in a tiny, precise *1*. Gwen had string bracelets and the ends of her braids bounced against her collarbone when she ran. We raced each other in the park during PE, trying to let the other one win. "Is Jenny your best friend?" my mother asked. "Or is it Gwen? Which one?" Jenny or Gwen invited me over and I went with them after school. I stayed for dinner, sent home in a taxi. Jenny's mother unloaded groceries, fridge door held open with a big hip, as she asked us which words we'd suggested for the classroom's homonym list. Weight and wait, I said. "Good job," she said. Gwen's mother called me "lovie," just as she did Gwen. She let Gwen bring home the turtles over the summer and one year the bunny, too. The fathers came home, elaborate noises of keys and voices we heard from the pretty bedrooms, and the girls rushed out. Men missing from the woken daytime and the solid life of school — their role was to appear.

One day on the way home, my mother and I stopped into a soda fountain. She had come to pick me up from school, where she dimmed the other parents who stood outside our door, as we put our chairs upside down on the tables and gathered for dismissal. I walked next to her down Madison Avenue, tried skipping, walked again, took her hand and inspected it. It was very sunny. She suggested in her sunny voice, "Let's get ice-cream sodas." She ordered her special black-and-white, Coca-Cola with a scoop of vanilla fizzing it up. I got rice pudding. We sat at a table by the window, bright day on our faces.

I looked at the counter and there was Marjorie.

Marjorie, at the counter, with a woman.

How could Marjorie *be*? My departure from my old school had ended everyone. The school ceased. But — here, now — Marjorie was still going, being tall, fiddling with the button on her jumper. Separate from me experiencing her, she had continued; she had her own timeline, was her own center. I looked at my mother and shock flooded me: when my mother wasn't in front of me, she still *was*. New thoughts raced in, uninvited, an onslaught — the larger universe, experiences that were unknowable. I didn't know if I should keep eating my pudding, as everything had changed. The strange wisdom kept widening, ways of knowing altering the truth, and fattening mine.

Over vacation, I cried because I missed Jenny so much, a piercing hollow under my ribs — love! "So it's Jenny," my mother said. "Jenny's your best friend." After the holiday here she was again! She didn't die! As Jenny accepted the present I'd chosen for her, a zippered change purse beaded with shiny little shells, her face was passionless, my dawning sense that we might not feel the same strengths in "friend," but I pretended not to notice.

Gwen's was the first phone number I memorized after my own, her voice a thrill through the receiver, then my voice answering hers, as if we knew much more, had secret power to exchange. Her apartment had two floors, an architectural cocoon of white sectionals, white rugs, white walls. I would attend sleepovers there until I left for high school, depend on them. When we were thirteen, the summer after eighth grade, Gwen and I would go with a student group to France, adoring each other on the flight over, catching each other's eye, because each of us really trusted she knew what the other was thinking, and that the other was the only one who knew back. On the trip, new allegiances sprang up, magnetic twos and threes, and Gwen and I, without knowing we knew this, came to our end. High school would introduce new girls, permanently. But at seven, when we met, and at eight and nine and on until eighth grade, I would sit at the high white counter on a chrome stool as her mother buttered toast for us in the mornings, or I'd watch Jenny and her sisters tease their dad at dinner, the shared laughter in the same family tone. Each girl was a jewel, a clue that it was possible to have no drama at all. Boredom, they showed me, was an important form of love.

FACEBOOK

At Walnut Lake, Jessica Ribicoff and I were assigned to the same cabin. The first night, rowdy returning girls bullied each other, and above them on upper bunks Jessica and I made eye contact, confirmed safety. In daytime we walked the trampled grass, the woods and worn dirt paths, her freckled arm threaded through mine, or we laced our fingers into the chain link that fenced the pool, watching the older boys swim and hoist themselves out. We were always talking, crush confessions dovetailing, excited voices that raced and united. She stood next to me and we held in our stomachs when Greg La Rosa ambled by and said, "Hi." She explained marshmallow spread as we sat down with trays of Fluffernutter sandwiches. After lunches, we walked to the canteen to buy Pop Rocks. She made me a peach-pit ring, and I made her a peach-pit ring.

On my last day we said, "How can I live without you?" over and over. Jessica got to stay for the second session. I was crying, and she was, too, as we embraced by the cars. We were girls, we lived big. Our arms chained around each other's necks, our sobbing was pure. No lovers had been parted so cruelly, no bond had been severed so swiftly.

She wrote to me from camp, prolonging the dramas I'd hated to abandon — Mandy kissed Greg! — and I delivered to her my important news — "My new passport picture is gross." "Can you believe I've seen 'Star Wars' THREE TIMES???" We covered our envelope flaps in big-handed hearts and coded acronyms. I didn't think to confess true circumstances or to hide them, because I was unconscious they happened, wouldn't remember and assess them until many years later: in my mother's cocaine-driven rages, she'd grow violent, and she was hitting me; my father, divorcing again, had dismissed my stepmother and my beloved three-year-old half-sister with chilling indifference. In the letters I wrote to Jessica Ribicoff, outsider, I could assure myself I was starring in my ideal life.

A few days after I activate a Facebook account, the name appears on my laptop screen, so familiar it's almost physical pleasure, the six loping syllables of *Jessica Ribicoff*. She'd looked for me, hadn't forgotten my name either. I'm amazed, peering at her thumbnail photo, by how little she's changed — her crop of tight red curls, her giant smile, her freckled forearm. I'd know her anywhere. I friend her at once, and we trade rapid biography. We've both become artists, and we emphasize the coincidence, gratified by sameness. She's read the memoir I just published, and she sends me a piece of her pottery as a present. I'm startled an eleven-year-old has made such a beautiful, delicate bowl, and given it away. Of course she's not eleven. She's forty-one, has passed the same years I have. Jessica suggests we see each other, insists. She lives in Brooklyn, and I promise to call when I next visit.

She pulls up in front of the brownstone where I'm staying and waves me into her car. I'm deeply pleased to have the virtual representation inhabited, bright reality mixing with image and happy memory — curls, smile, vocal intonation. It's odd, though, to see her driving, as if she's kidding.

"Hi! Get in!"

"Hi!"

The car is battered, the floor scratchy with leaflets and pebbles. My foot kicks aside an empty Sprite bottle. Before I click the seat belt we're moving, and there can be no gravity to the reunion, no ceremony. Maybe it's as it should be, instant and girlish. We'll pick up from camp's last day. Jessica chatters as she jams the car down narrow streets and finally into a parking spot, unconsciously good at it. She's talking about her stomach problems. I've had some, too, I tell her. We both have! At the restaurant, which we glide into, I want for us each to know where the other likes to sit, but we don't, we can't. We're shown to a back garden. "Is this okay?" Jessica asks me. I ask her, "Would you rather be inside?" Then, before the waiter comes, she launches her daily story — a litany of phone calls from her mother, boyfriend woes, creative endeavors and the attendant money anxiety. She leans across the table, puts feeling into each detail, as if I'm conversant in her temperatures, her high and low, as if I know by nostalgic telepathy what's happened to her and what hasn't. I begin to feel I'm at the center of some impostor's mistake, and I'm embarrassed. "Why tell *me*?" I wonder. Who does she see opposite her? Quickly, I learn every rumination of her recent weeks. We both act like we *need* to know. For my turn she's nodding as I recount significant events, a checklist: know me. I mean to like this woman, the grown result of the girl I adored, but there's no room for the build, no interplay, as if we each stare at a posted video ad, projecting hungry wishes for a perfect friend. I watch her eyebrows, her mouth, trying to find the link between a random lunch partner and the precious memory-girl. We were friends, but the ancient, amber friendship has dictated nothing, left nothing behind but itself. We cannot bust out beyond this, trapped by a season's accident.

She starts to talk about camp, and my interest picks up, maybe because I will appear — the two of us will come back. Jessica has no memories of the pool, the sandwiches, Greg La Rosa. She tells how her parents left her there and she begged to come home. She had terrors at night and cried in the dark, trying not to wake the sleeping girls. No one wrote to her, she remembers, even though she pleaded in every letter home to be picked up. She remembers my mother, so fabulous and pretty, coming to get me and taking me away. She remembers I left her.

After the lunch, tired with performance, an act that isn't gelling, I'm eager to part.

We say good-bye on the sidewalk. I don't cross to the car with her, but we're both promising more visits, longer reunions. Isn't she feigning interest in me by now? Hasn't she, too, admitted that arbitrary overlap is all there is to us? Beyond the noted preferences and exclamation points of Facebook, we share only name recognition, and when I return to Montana I won't know what to write to the tiny thumbnail photo, smiling online. It's puzzling.

Back home I remember that after camp there was a last time we got together. In the early fall, when Jessica and I had missed each other for an eternity, our parents let us plan a visit on our own, and I went to Port Authority to meet her bus from New Jersey. My stomach was knotted with excitement until we were jumping up and down in the gate area. Then some mysterious, empty feeling arose, an unnameable not-there. We tried to whip up the bigness again, but school and real friends had filled the spots we'd briefly held, and we turned reticent.

"Want to go to the movies?"

"I don't know. Do you?"

"Or we could go to Bloomingdale's?"

"What do you want to do?"

At my apartment, with extra sheets, pillow, and blanket in my room, Jessica talked about her best friend in New Jersey — they took gymnastics together and liked to stage scenes from Judy Blume books — which made me jealous and bored. When my phone rang, Jessica looked at *People* on my bed while I talked to Gwen and gripped the tether to immediate life. I knew this was rude but didn't know what else a person did when she didn't feel connected anymore. We never saw each other again, until lunch in Brooklyn, after which I realized that Jessica Ribicoff mattered so much, will always, because with her I got to be a girl again in a time of seasoned fear. I can't leave this as a post on her Facebook page. I will write her something else instead.

Proctor Duties

I chose boarding school. My room filled up with neat stacks of applications. In our apartment, the phone's clamor, the television hum, the delivered boxes from the liquor store in the hallway, I felt erased by my mother, adolescence my violation. Anyway, she was moving to New Mexico, beautiful skies, better cocaine. She would sublet our apartment. I craved order and imagined that if I conceived of it, I'd have it. I would be glad to no longer monitor her druggy comrades splayed on our couch cushions for too many hours, their crumbs and empty glasses on the floor. I wouldn't have to assess for threat her charming frenzies or oblivious sleeps. I was twelve when I toured my first campus — the lawns edged, the library hours posted, the controlled bustle of the dining hall — and I wanted in.

The senior on my hall was called the

proctor, the word sturdy with earned clout. Abigail lived with the freshman girls, in charge of answers. She had a cast on her leg and crutches for the first weeks. Her door stayed ajar, her mild music seeping out as she tapped the end of her yellow highlighter on her open chemistry textbook, from which she'd look up, on call for us and our logistical problems. By day two, drawn to the most obscure promise of motherly indulgence, I flopped on her bed and fingered the lacy edges of her pillows. On her desk she had a photo, her family standing as a wall, many people gathered, and Abigail's floor-length dress matched those of the other women and girls. "That's my brother, that's my new sister-in-law, that's my mom, my nieces," she said, and named a dozen others. Her mother was "my mom," neither an event nor a burr. Abigail's voice betrayed no tiny spike, no tinge of buried trouble. I knew difficulties might be dressed up and disguised, and when a girl didn't reveal problems, I suspected her. But I hung around to hear her say "my mother" like that, "my mom," to inspect the support she presumed.

Abigail was my friend. That's what I called her. She didn't mind, if she gave it a thought. She talked to me, liked me. To be with her when she was hobbled, I stepped slowly, too, as we trickled down the stairwell. Other girls, her charges, passed us and called, "Hi, Abigail! Hi, Abbs!" She was game for my intimacy, the way I insisted on it, as she was game for squash and senior prank day, the way she captained other girls, able to direct and exhort everyone in the friendliest way, but her attention came to a stop. I couldn't penetrate her barrier, get more from Abigail, special treatment. She didn't hug. She stayed in her chair, drumming her pen on her thigh, as I cried, homesick on her bed or mad at a mean teacher. She'd been trained in peer counseling for a few days and could say, "You should see if there's a study hall," or "Why don't you sign up for swimming?" I marveled at her quick speech, its mimicry of the pep talks given to us by anyone in charge. I asked after her volleyball and her acned boyfriend. She was discreet but allusive, mature jokes about his body, his energy, which may have been about sex, but may have been about the sex that was not to be had because of youth and rules. When my mother spoke to me about sex, as she had since I was eight or seven, she headed into it, used wet, direct terms and elongated her anecdotes. Abigail would say, "We made out," a big grin, and that was it. She knew the dark places before curfew, damp grass and empty auditoriums. Something more was up, and I wanted her to know I could handle it, but she had Yankee distaste for explicits. In a state of peculiar gratitude and relief, I worshipped her.

I had closer, better friends that year, equals — cynical Jackie from the UK with her Cure poster, and studious Nell, whose brilliance was made clear the day she brought to English class her own Canterbury Tale in iambic pentameter. Like me, they were fourteen years old, occupied the east hall of the dorm, and attended third-form classes. We roamed campus together, discussed the same boys. But I tried Abigail on like her pea coat, which I coveted. I pretended to be concerned with her concerns. I took note of her Clearasil, her boiled-wool slippers, her tuck of books between crooked wrist and outer thigh, and, after the cast came off, her square walk, a product of multiple sports, cross-disciplines. My crush, fierce and devoted, was on her blond hair, carelessly flyaway, on her pink Fair Isle sweater with the white yoke. I had a crush on her competence, her busy fingers as she laced her lacrosse stick. She could make up a nickname for anybody on the spot, spout it in good humor. With Abigail, what *seemed* was what *was*. She wasn't sarcastic, hid no dark agenda. She laughed her same phlegmy giggle at everything — embarrassments, tragedies, coaches' names, final exams. Still laughing, she pulled her inhaler from the hip pocket of her wide-wale cords and sucked. Most afternoons, dressed in a sweat suit and track shoes, she returned to our hall in need of a shower. She'd pass my room, where I was stalling the taxing rigors of assignments or being careful with my LPs as I pressed them down to the turntable and calibrated volume, dorm etiquette, not too loud, but an anthem anyway: *I'm here, I have something to add.* Sometimes she tapped on my door — strawberry shampoo, plastic caddy. "Want to go to dinner when I'm done?" She protected me, I decided, especially in the first days, when I was at a loss, lost. The school had picked reliable Abigail for this job, had spread a dozen such seniors through the girls' dorms, and it was the right place for her but indifferent to me. I was perpetually unlaced, unmet, always crashing into my blunders. You *didn't* challenge the bitchy teacher, you *didn't* miss practice or skip out on study hall, you *didn't* masturbate in your single room with the door locked and your breath held. At least,

Abigail never did, ordinariness her emblem.

Once, she introduced her mother, who'd come up for a game. I grew nervous, as if her mother would divine my naked baby-sister crush, pity me. I shook her hand, then blurted, "How long have you known Abigail?" Abigail burst out with the coarse, rowdy laugh she usually shared with teammates. I was hot and foolish beyond foolish. The mother lifted a tight eyebrow, smiled emptily. Abigail never teased me about this, which meant a lot to me, a sweetness and sign of care, I thought. Probably, though, she forgot it happened. She did not dwell on discomfort, or much else to do with me.

She turned eighteen, which impressed us. She shrugged it off, left the dorm in a hurry with her lacrosse stick, walking with other players, all of them dressed in pastel shorts and docksiders, grosgrain headbands, gray phys ed T-shirts stamped in blue with the school crest. I wanted these things, these tokens of unity. I wanted to love a flat birthday cake in the common room with a dozen girls in pajamas and nighties, to honestly enjoy that, as if it could be enough.

In May, of course, Abigail would graduate and I would not. This ally would go, erased from school life. All year she'd let me tag along, so I knew a good portion of the senior class, towering boys with visible Adam's apples, girls with Audis they parked in a special lot, who walked across campus paired in sly adult conference. I hoped they'd boost my status, carry me off when they left, too, but the opposite happened. The seniors cleared out their gear and their trunks and departed in their blaze of vale-dictions. Quiet was left behind, distant mowers, slammed doors from across the quads, the *thwock* of tennis balls. The rest of us hurried to get through exams. I had few good friends in my own grade. My second year went badly.

For junior year I transferred to a different boarding school, and by chance I followed Abigail to Colorado Springs. I'd have my big sister again. My mother even phoned her and said, "You'll be a love and keep an eye on Susy?" "Sure," said amenable Abi-gail, who'd always thought my mother's af-fected style was a hoot.

My affair with the English teacher started midway through the year. I was sixteen and a virgin. He was married, thirty-four. He was risking much more than his job, he said, as he pressed shut the door of his office with one hand and stared down at me for our first talk "as equals." "You must tell no

80

one," he said. How unimpeachable, uncontestable he was. Papers from the Shakespeare class waited on his desk to be graded, mine among them. We had just kissed, I was triumphant and astonished. The month before — just a few weeks! — he'd teased me about my crush on him. He *knew*, but I turned my horrified exposure into a game, a magnificent challenge, and every week he came closer, our held glances pitched with danger. I drew him. In the last recent days, our silent, mutual certainty had kept me constantly aroused, unable to work, farsighted and distracted at the dining table with my silly friends.

In spite of my teacher's dire command and the way he trusted me, I had to discharge the sensation of knowing so much, and I called Abigail at her college dorm to whisper from the phone booth in mine. "I have to tell you something, promise not to tell, promise?" Abigail said "Yup," unconcerned. I could picture the shrug. She'd crack up at scandal without caring, she wouldn't ask for details. If she didn't approve, she never said, and, besides, I wasn't looking for an honest reaction. I was looking — or my teacher, after I admitted to him I'd told, was having me look — for an accomplice, and I asked to use her name for lying, for fake overnights and trips off-campus. If we had an hour, after the dorm mother signed me out to Abigail's on the permission slip, my teacher would whisk me to a remote campsite, or to a motel scattered with miniature cabins for an afternoon. "Sure," she said again. "That's a good friend," my teacher said, and I thought so, too.

Not everything was a lie. I still worked hard at school. Well, at my English class assignments. I divided the lie, my spectacular secret, from all else. I saw Abigail for real, too. We'd grab an early dinner of nachos or go to a weekend matinee. One Saturday, she invited me to spend the night, and I found myself back in dormland with her, a reassuring happiness. We had inhabited another long hallway, been surrounded by these same sounds of high, fast voices, the clatter of fire doors, the muffled flight of feet on industrial carpeting. The place reeked of synthetic scent, the fruited chemicals of so much perfume, shampoo. But I couldn't settle, and we were not the same as before. Abigail was no longer charged with my well-being, and our yearlong separation had exposed the absence of connection. With her college friends, she was preoccupied with ski weekends, car keys borrowed and returned; she spent money. She had a fake ID. She was not engrossed in petty duties, of which I had been one. I thought we'd talk about romance and sex, my consuming new interests. Answer my questions, Abigail. I need the big sister. *Have you ever done this,* I needed to say, or *should it feel like this?* I would have loved to confide in my mother, share with her the world she'd split open to me so early, but I didn't dare. I had too much to lose. Abigail, however, curated other topics instead. "You should really learn to ski," she said. Sports, grades, she focused on those. She'd never revealed the personal; I didn't know her. Our friendship had been an assignment.

We left my stuff, and she took me to a frat party, an off-limits basement dangerous for anyone, especially a sixteen-year-old girl, up late. But I didn't know to worry, made newly stupid by my unsupervised leap into the adult world. I got beer, let reckless boys squirt it into red plastic cups, someone passing one over to me. The beer tasted of rancid water, thin and wrong, but I gulped. The room was overhot. At the ceiling, through the transoms, lamplight shined the nighttime grass a bleary orange, and lit the concrete paths that rimmed the frat house. Things got louder, harder to manage. People yelled over the pool table, cues hoisted. Across the dim room, out of reach of the neon cast from the Coors sign, Abigail traded whatever with the roaring men and the other girls, lacrosse sticks propped, face masks on the floor. I waited on a sprung couch, holding the rest of my beer, shaking my head no to the guys. Their saliva burst into the air as they shouted, as their shoulders and chests flexed, puffed, wrangled. I wanted my friend to take me back, get ready for bed with me and talk, and we'd sleep and get up in the morning and go to brunch, but, nodding wildly, Abigail was backed against the wall as she cajoled and hassled the boys. *This* was her element? *Them?* I willed her to want to leave, but she didn't. I willed her to worry and come over to me, but she didn't. She'd forgotten I was there. She wasn't aware of the affection I'd pinned on her, how I willed her to be worthy of it, and how I hoped she'd notice the care I hadn't yet had.

THE ROOT CELLAR

Claudia gave me the number of a pay phone in the Safeway parking lot. That's the thing that made me concerned, seemed the tip-off that things weren't fine. She was living with roommates for the summer, didn't want to use the joint phone. I could picture her holding a grimy receiver, Mick's truck idling beside her. She sounded excited, or happy, some emotion that didn't fit. She had to get an abortion, she said. She was always enthusiastic.

I said I'd fly out to be with her, because that's what friends do. She'd been my best solace at boarding school. We'd just graduated. We relied on each other for reflection, company, mealtime allegiance. After curfew I sometimes left my dorm and snuck over to hers. I'd sleep over, our two bodies crowding and comfortable in her bed. I needed to be held that way, sistered. Claudia had a familiar manic looseness, let me laugh big and whisper big, and she seemed to greet me as a long-awaited permission. But she could also unbolt, threaten to break apart, and I worried. She left notebooks behind, screamed at her coach, seethed too readily when the riding instructor admonished the group after a lesson. "It doesn't matter," I'd say. "I love you." I offered her steadiness, perspective. "You're right, Sue," she often said, and I liked that.

I was planning to fly to Colorado anyway for a reunion with our English teacher. Claudia didn't know this. For the two years I'd been sleeping with him, was in love with him, I'd hidden it from her. I'd lied to her, deflected, invented alternate scenarios as cover with such precision I nearly believed them. In the solemn minute after our first kiss, the teacher grabbed my chin, forced my gaze, and said, "You most certainly cannot tell our friend Miss Claudia." She loved him, too, though not the way I did, not with such a desperate need to be chosen. She loved his guardianship and approval, made manifest in the high grades he assigned her. "You're involved in something now she will not understand," he said. He knew the girl-world trait of wrecked secrecy, and every few weeks he'd check if I'd told her. I never did. I didn't think that deception affected our friendship. I told her everything *else.* It didn't seem that I was living inside his mean ideas, shadowing his habits.

I first met Claudia the morning I started junior year at my second boarding school. The office assigned her to give me the tour, and she said, "It's a pleasure to meet you" in a formal voice. Then she released a peal of laughter, took my arm, and settled her own in the bend of my elbow. She was a confident guide, known by everyone. Here's the clay studio, the pool, the theater, here's your mailbox, the dining hall. We came to the stables, and she marched us in. "I just got this," she said, star pleasure, showing me a shiny saddle. Someone called her name, and she wheeled around. Another girl leaned out from a stall.

"Hey, *you*!"

Claudia cried, "I love you!"

"I love you *more*!" the girl cried back.

We returned to our path. Claudia rolled her eyes and said, "That's Julie." This girlish cartoon seemed a waste of powers. It was just two sentences, a moment, Claudia exposed as a little less secure than I'd thought. I intended to conduct myself as a woman for junior year, and I wanted friends who would do the same. But still, I liked

87

her giant welcome. Julie, it turned out, lived in my dorm as the senior RA, and by Thanksgiving she was my other best friend. We had privilege in common, childhoods of foreign vacations, winter sunshine. Claudia was intriguingly earthy, someone who could come up with a crude lesson on unions or women's rights, certainly more than I knew. In real life, separate from the performance for my benefit, Claudia and Julie didn't care for each other, masking dislike with pretty fakeness, but I could have both girls, move in two worlds. In the spring, when I was boiling with the terrific joy of my mighty secret and lost virginity, I confessed the affair to Julie. My teacher hadn't said I couldn't tell *her,* and she was involved with a faculty member, too, he thought. She's special, he said, the same way you are.

After graduation the parents left, the seniors drove away in their own cars, and I pretended to go home, too — "Bye, Claude!" — but went to Denver. My teacher drove us, knew the outskirts motel where we stayed parked for two unaccounted days. I was going to college back East, and we didn't know when we'd next see each other. He told me with love like this, we had no choice, *we had to.* In the airport he tightened me against his body. "Over winter break, at the latest," he whispered. I eyed the departure board behind him, restless as any teenager leaving familiar adults behind.

I'd already lied to my mother, told her I was flying to Colorado to see Claudia — we missed each other *so much*. I had to lie bigger now — lies stacking up on top of one another, needing close attention to stay organized — that Claudia wanted me earlier. I changed my ticket, arrived sooner than my teacher and I had planned. Out of the jetway, I saw Claudia tearing up the corridor, and I felt the eagerness I always did with her. Breathless, she hurtled into my arms. Her new boyfriend, Mick, came up and stood near, and I tried not to examine him directly. I didn't want it to seem like I was spying. He was a lot older than we were — older than our teacher — which I hadn't trusted in description, and I didn't like him here. The skin on his face was pitted, spots peeling with sunburn. She reached behind herself for his hand and leaned her forehead against mine. In a stage whisper she said, "I had it today!"

"But I was going to be with you," I said.

"It's okay. It was fast."

It impressed me that Claudia had actually been pregnant. True, my affair and its power to devastate, these spoke of the adulthood we were fiercely courting, always inspecting, but she had entered a maturity vaster and more purely female than sexual accomplishment, had surpassed me.

Mick walked ahead to the car lot. Claudia squeezed my arm and gushed nonstop, the way we used to come into the dining hall, our torrent of ideas, pretending to be oblivious of the boys, but we were so very, very attuned. She was talking about Mick, telling me things he'd built, personal philosophies he'd explained to her.

"We're going straight to the root cellar," she said. "I can't wait to show you." I tried to muster enthusiasm, although I didn't know what "root cellar" meant. She kept using it to refer to where we'd stay, and I pictured us climbing over potatoes to find a perch. I didn't want to get into Mick's truck; I knew I didn't want to leave the city. My teacher had my itinerary, and, aware I'd landed, he'd be pacing for me, dying for me, like I was for him. We were going to stay in a bed-and-breakfast. But first this. Claudia believed she was my reason for being here, so I had to make that look true.

We drove out of the city a way I'd never been and more than an hour up a sandy highway, higher and higher. My ears popped. I gripped the door's metal handle, was bounced in the cab as Mick took the curves with speed. Was he trying to get a re- action, did he mean to scare? He smoked a joint, spit out the window sometimes, showed no interest in our talk. Claudia was listing her family's Cincinnati summer habits, gleeful that she wasn't home. Mick's right hand played between the steering wheel and Claudia's thigh. She rested most of her weight against me.

When we stopped, Claudia reached across my lap, busted the door open, and pushed us out. "We can take a walk later," she said and lifted her hand, but her gesture was undecided, scanning a wide swath of land that showed me nothing but trees close together, no roads, no houses. I liked known space, classrooms, airplane cabins, motel rooms. What did she do up here, where nothing could happen? I followed. Mick had built the root cellar, a hump of soil, a door shoved into earth, which opened into dark- ness, coolness. The floor was untended dirt. In dusty recesses hollowed into the walls, dishes, cast-iron pots, and a bong sat next to oil lamps and matchboxes and little rectangular cans. It was like sleeping quar- ters on a boat, maybe. No, I couldn't compare it to anything I'd seen. It was all strange. I hated when Claudia knew a lot about something before I did.

There was nowhere to sit, no proper area, except for a table, which was crowded with clear, empty jars, lids scattered. We went outside again and Mick disappeared, a rustle of steps and then gone. I meant to track him, didn't want to be surprised, but he was steering clear of me. What did he want us for anyway? He was obviously close to fifty, or at least forty.

Claudia wore what I called her hippie skirt, and leather sandals and a white blouse that tied in the front. I was wearing jeans, cowboy boots, and a white sweatshirt with *Team* in fat, pink script outlined by pink glitter. New York irony; but instead the woods and paralyzed vistas mocked me. The wraparound silence left me small. Claudia walked us away from truck and root cellar to reveal the cook site, the logs and low rocks that served as their furniture, proud of the make-do, of the organic roughness, proud Mick had taken her in. I couldn't remember where they'd met, didn't want her to know that. We called the place "the compound," exaggerated teasing, but the trace in the word of military isolation made me uneasy.

"Are you smoking pot?" I said, parental.

"God, no. That's Mick's deal."

"You want to tell me about this morning? How it went?"

"Oh, the 'procedure'? Good, good, it was nothing. I mean, they said I'd feel tugging and stuff, but I didn't, and it seemed to go pretty quickly, and then it was done. We got something to eat before we came to get you." Her voice rose fast, broke high on *you*. "You're really here, here, here, this is so great."

I didn't know what "tugging" was supposed to mean. What else was it like, abortion? I'd barely encountered the word before, never spoken it aloud. What actually happened? "Are you okay?"

"Don't I seem okay?" She drew herself up and gave a flourish with her hand down the length of her body, a gesture of admiration I'd seen her use on the flank of her horse. "I'm divine!"

I'd thought she would need me, that I'd go with her and hold her hand or smooth her hair. But she hadn't needed that, or she didn't need that anymore, as if the abortion of the morning had been months ago instead. Confused by blitheness, I wondered if she'd made up the pregnancy. My mother lied for casual amusement, about anything, to anyone, so I stayed alert for it. But my best friend wouldn't make that shit up, not to me. Real friends wouldn't.

"So, it didn't hurt? At all?"

"Well, it *is* surgery, they keep telling you, it's on a million forms, but it's pretty fucking minor, that's all I can say, because I'm over it." She said, "You always expect a drama, Sue, but I'm okay. Really. Except they told me, you know what they said? I can't have sex for two weeks. Fuck that."

"Shouldn't you wait?" I followed those sorts of rules.

"Mick thought they're covering their asses, just, you know, so you don't come back in and blame them for not getting the whole fetus out, or something. He says they're always worried they're going to get sued. Anyway, no legal counsel will prevent *me* from having sex. Do you like him?"

"Yeah," I said, lying badly. "I don't think he likes me though."

"He's totally jealous of you, that's why. He said I was in love with you. I was like, who wouldn't be?" This was one of our routines, that we fit perfectly and were meant for each other, would end up together once we'd tried on and washed away the silly boys. But now she had a man. My lies so embedded, I kept forgetting I did, too.

"How's Ethan?" I said. He'd been her

sort-of boyfriend from the spring. She'd obsessed about him through April, May, into June, and we'd obsessed as well about my flirtations, tiny and giant, my several to Claudia's one, my flights, her fixation. We said we had senioritis, big-time — fuck finals! they can't matter now! — but this was my necessary camouflage, making sure my best friend didn't uncover my mistress identity. Now it was late July, five weeks of being high school graduates, five weeks of saturated longing for my lover.

"Ethan? He went to one of those, you know, his family has those summer places?"

"Wow, Ethan, Mick," I said. "What if they were in the same room?" I wanted to remind her of clean hair, smooth skin, Ethan's clean voice.

"I'm sure Ethan would drone on about the history of port taxes in the sixteenth century."

"Yeah, to make a point, what he was read- ing."

"And Mick would ask me later if Ethan ever got high."

"Ha!"

"And then he'd say he should."

"Ethan adored you," I said.

"No, Susanna. Ethan adored *you.*"

"Well, I don't know!" I said, but I liked it.

"I had Connor."

"And poor Kip, he was obsessed with you."

"Kippy!"

My teacher had told me, "Flirt with them," told me to act "normal." For prom I had Connor, and Claudia had Ethan, but we ditched them after we arrived at the fancy hotel. We danced with each other, sloppy arms and stagy affection. My teacher watched us, me, as he talked with the other standing adults.

Mick emerged from the dark of the root cellar, holding a blue metal coffeepot. A prop, I thought, for his Wild West. "Girls want coffee?"

"Yes! I'm starving!" said Claudia. "Are you, Susy?"

"A little. Sure." I'd seen no trace of groceries, no bags in the back of the truck, only shovels, a folded tarp, rolled-up chicken wire. Mick retreated.

That night, after heating the canned food over the fire and washing pots and plates in a pond, we went to our berths. I could hear them having sex, all of Claudia and none of Mick, and I couldn't tell whether she was objecting and crying, or enjoying it, which creeped me out, not being able to tell when I knew her so well, as well as I knew myself.

He didn't make one sound. I turned to the wall, wondering what he was doing to my friend.

Late in the summer, a few weeks before college began, Ethan called me. He was staying on the Upper East Side, a few blocks away. The city felt stopped and subdued, little traffic down Lexington, few shops open along Madison. Heat had canceled commerce. I welcomed his call.

"I should like to take you out for dinner," he said with his imitation of British formality. Claudia and I could never tease him out of this, which only made us smirk, watching the color flood his face.

"Yes, why not, indeed? Do," I said, but he didn't get it.

He arrived with half a dozen roses, which I left in the apartment, and we walked over to Third. Every phone booth, hydrant, and sidewalk square was glazed by heat, muted. Ethan reviewed his college worries, but his anxiety bored me, a step backward. I switched the subject to movies, travel, his family members who lived in the city. We knew it was conscious and strange not to mention Claudia. As he handled his wallet, searching for the right cash, I thought he was fairly sweet, especially when embar-

97

rassed. I kept trying to embarrass him so I could tell Claudia about it.

Then I took him to bed.

"Did you ever sleep with Claudia?" I said, as I closed the door to my room. I knew the answer but wanted him to say, wanted to see what became of the scene if we introduced her.

"I didn't," he said.

"With anyone?"

"No."

I wasn't a virgin, which put me in charge. I can't remember making love with Ethan, or remember birth control, or whether he left in darkness or daylight. I was thinking about Claudia, holding her off with one arm while I took hold of her semiboyfriend. In the kitchen after sex, Diet 7-Up cans on the table next to the roses I'd put in a vase, we said that we couldn't tell Claudia, we mustn't. We were both very clear about that.

That root-cellar summer Claudia and I phoned all the time, mulled our preparations and packing for college, where we'd be only two hundred miles apart instead of two thousand — not as close as we wanted, but close. She fluttered and didn't seem to know what she was doing, what to do, and this made me the one who knew more, who could calm her when things ended with Mick. I had our photo in a frame, the picture with our arms around each other, our faces splendid with a joke of our own cultivated vocabulary. Behind us you could see our former campus. I don't know who took the picture, because who else really mattered to us? She visited me in the fall, a weekend in my freshman dorm; and I took the bus to New Jersey to visit her, maybe twice, as I remember snow, and not snow. She walked me around, introduced me to dorm mates whose open doors we passed, but I wished for Sunday to hurry up, and I double-checked the bus schedule. We didn't understand how to tend our friendship beyond our common world. What could we talk about? I had failed to calculate the pernicious results of so much lying.

We went to brunch Sunday at a B and B, sharing the weight of my small duffel as we walked in the whipping white cold, snow and the crusted sidewalk breaking under our shoes. The dining room was close with adult voices and silverware, the low tones and the high silver notes. We were used to entering, to our unrivaled female power, but after we'd put the popovers and seeded jam on our plates, filled our cups with coffee, she talked in her half-decided way, her stops and starts, she checked to see what I thought; and I wasn't listening. I just wanted to leave. She needed so much, and I knew I could withhold it from her, take from her, because I had, which made me anxious to get to the out-of-business gas station where we'd wait until the Adirondack bus lumbered around the tiny corner and pulled in, and then I could put miles between myself and the rotten real me. From my bus seat I looked down as Claudia waved both arms, hurling kisses at the window, the teen drama for others to watch, and I silently pressed the driver into action. Please pull away, I was thinking, and waving.

The years after college we shared little. She couldn't afford to come to Montana, and she lived in Cincinnati houses I never saw, our connection less and less vital. "Hi, Sue!" "Hi, Claudia!" we burst out at the start of each call, excited and ready. History filled in for us.

"Guess what I heard on the radio! 'Our Lips Are Sealed!' Still have that Go-Gos cassette?"

"It's in the car!"

"God, and Juice Newton sucked," one of us would say. "Do you have any idea how much she sucked?"

Then the pauses. We were fading. We had our stories — the time we tried to order a pitcher at Pizza Hut, the time we pretended to be lesbians and *totally* freaked out those boys by the bleachers. We stuck with those.

Claudia had a new man, again older. He got angry, she said.

She said, "He tends towards violence."

"He's hit you?"

"Oh, no," she said. "He did break a wall." She was upbeat. They got married.

One night she called crying, but it wasn't about him. Her father had drowned. I'd met him over graduation weekend, watched him eat a hamburger, had seen his fingers work the laces of his buffed, black shoes. How could these words be uttered — *drowning accident* — how could they *be*? She raced me through each frantic frame, crazed. I wanted to say the good thing, to gather her uncontained sorrow.

"Whatever you need," I said, but what that might be was beyond my imagining. The scope of this experience was a blank to me. Again, she'd stepped into the terrain of significant event, major. For a while she called frequently, and it was the same call, stuck. She wore her father's flannel shirts and went over the accident repeatedly. I knew my job was to hear it repeatedly, but I drifted. Had I paid attention, she would have shown me a first real lesson about grief, its disorganizing confusions, its inescapable solitude. She talked stiffly of her marriage, their wrong-headed tensions, and at first I joined her agitated laughter about his AA meetings and his shoplifting charge, but I couldn't keep it up. I was worried about her, really worried. She got pregnant.

When her girl was walking, and we were thirty, she flew to Missoula. It had been many significant cycles since we'd seen each other. I was married, too, pregnant, and to both of us it felt important to herald together the start of this new phase. Touchstone, we said. That's how my husband understood her in my life, ready to feel courteous affection when he met her. I drove to the airport. She held her daughter's hand, bulging bags hoisted on her hip, a backpack weighing from one shoulder strap, and after our long fervent hug we walked at the toddler's pace to the car. I kept looking over at Claudia, hunting the antic, loyal girl, my girl. I couldn't adjust to her as a mother, her tranquility and command in the role, but she was a mother — calmed, attentive, adoring. As I made dinner, she played peekaboo under the table with her daughter,

and then the next night, rhyming and sing-
ing to her the whole time, she taught me a
recipe for enchiladas, coriander and shredded carrots to sweeten the tomato and
onion, which I make still. She shrugged off
her husband's danger, but he was the main
subject; we spoke in code to protect the
baby. We didn't mention the drowning. In
the morning, after thinking about her
trouble and risk and child, her fragile grief,
I walked out of my bedroom. "Stay," I said.
"Just stay, Claudia, you can live here, we
have the whole basement." It was the good
thing to offer, what the good friend says. At
the same time, I was thinking, "Careful, Susanna. You don't know how to follow that
through." Claudia, I'm guessing, already
knew that.

I woke in the root cellar, morning unable to
penetrate. I wanted day, wanted off this
compound. I pulled on jeans and went
outside to the big natural nothing, tingly
with Mick's silent surveillance. Inside the
dirty truck the keys hung from the ignition,
but I didn't understand the knobs and sticks
and extra pedal. We weren't going anywhere
until Mick wanted to take us down.

Claudia appeared. She said, "Do you have
any tampons? I'm bleeding." She was less in

love with the land and the event of my arrival.

"We could go down and get some."

"Swim in the pond, Claudia," said Mick, who had followed her, tin cups in hand. "It's natural, it'll clean you." She brightened and stripped off her blouse, dropped it and her skirt to the ground in front of the root cellar. White naked except for brown leather sandals, she grabbed my hand. "Don't come near us!" she called to him. "Susanna's very shy!" We burst into hysterics, because flamboyance in front of each other had always been required, egged on. Beyond his earshot she said, "He's quiet, isn't he? It's the pot, I guess."

"Are you, do you, is it good?" I said. "With him?"

"He says I'm the smartest person he's ever met. He says I intimidate him."

"Oh. Good."

Although swarming with pinprick gnats and mosquitoes, the water felt lovely as my shoulders dipped under the surface, the compound forgotten. I let the muck and silt push up around each toe, my fingers sifting the dark water.

"Isn't this worth it?" Claudia said. "No one ever comes up here. I can relax, I can breathe." She didn't look like she was breathing or relaxing. She never did. What's Mick's story, anyway? I thought. What's his *job*? But I didn't ask, afraid I'd betray my disapproval, which was weird, because usually we said everything. "*Total* honesty," we always promised. Bravery in front of each other, because of each other. Even if we were faking.

"You feel okay?" I said. "The cramps?"

"He was right," she said, dreamy. "They're gone."

We stayed another night. I fell asleep before I could hear them. Mick drove us down the mountain and dropped me at the house of a friend whom I lied about seeing before I went to the plane I lied about catching. "She'll give me a ride," I said. "Bye! Thanks! Love you!" They drove away, and I used a pay phone to give my teacher the address, and when he got there, grinning behind glass as he slowed the car, I told him all of it — the homemade root cellar and the dull food in cans and Claudia's creepy older boyfriend. My teacher shook his head and said, "I wouldn't expect our friend to make such poor choices. When will she know how much she has to offer?" We spent the next days in a motel — more anonymous after all, he said, than the bed-and-breakfast — where I was restored by wrapped soaps, wall sockets reliably inset, and the immense body of my lover bearing down on me.

■ ■ ■ ■

AWARE.

■ ■ ■ ■

ROOMMATE

Esther and I connected again, twenty years gone by, an exciting burst of solved mystery. Well, not mystery. Curiosity. From time to time I would put quotation marks around her name to search for her on Google. Driven and political, what great station would she now command, my first house-mate? She wouldn't still be wearing those dropsy cotton blouses and Indian print skirts, would she, but that was the picture I sought and expected, my life's own book-mark. I accrued bits of her personal file, outdated announcements, a string of cities, and I'd deduced she was a rabbi. This fit. Esther had been fierce with morality. But I never got in touch, an old intimidation preventing me.

I lived with Esther in an antique three-bedroom in Waltham, Massachusetts, an upstairs apartment on a long, bleak street. The house was gray, among other elderly houses of grays or blues, the block lined with aging cars. Although I stayed a year in this house, into a bleak winter, a summer, I remember late fall as perpetual: I walk home after classes, and the sky is darkening in metallic contrast to the orange maple leaves, the red-leafed oaks; I am becoming.

My friend Rachel lived downstairs — I'll tell you more about her later — and in the beginning I would stop at her door when I came home, before I headed up, hellos in the mahogany-paneled entryway. I was a little scared of Esther with her convictions and activism, her feminism, and docile Rachel shored me up. But I *lived* with Esther, which bid us into friendship, and we depended on each other with an affability that grew smoother, at least through the first months. We went to the supermarket in my car. We made a household and negotiated interlocking needs. We ate her lentils and yogurt, we drank my white wine. We took turns with chores — how central they were — washing the dishes, the rice pot, feeding the cats. Monday I'll do it, then Tuesday you. The two cats made tender parents of us.

Eventually, it was Esther who called me. She'd stumbled across my memoir at the library, the audio version I'd recorded, and she'd sped through a cross-country trip with my voice filling the car. "There you were, it was weird," she said. "Your voice just the same. And so many stories you never told me." Her voice, too, just the same — rooted in me with such domestic familiarity that within the first moments of the call I sensed where our conversation would lead and how we would conduct it. I was excited. As if we might find each other in the next room, the outside concerns excluded for the evening, I gave myself over. Remember the Christmas lights we strung over the bay window and never took down? Remember how the cats liked to sit side by side in the kitchen sink? "What are you doing now?" we asked, and I knew any answer would suit — "I'm a rabbi," or "Cleaning out the fridge." With resurrected intimacy, we answered in minutiae, as if the question were "What are you doing right now?" asked yesterday and every day, one of us sorting the mail in her coat as the other sat at the kitchen table.

I described my sons, their personalities, abilities, good company. She didn't have kids yet. She expressed amazement at my unlikely odyssey to Montana, admiration I'd stayed committed to a place, one man. "Fidelity was never your strong suit." I worked in an abortion clinic for several years, I told her. "You?" she said. I was proud and annoyed that this surprised her, and gratified that I'd grown into someone serious. She'd had a hand in that. Her startling example had made an imprint, and I wondered if any residual impression of me lingered in her life.

"What happened?" I said. "Us, when did we stop being in touch?" I didn't want to say "lose touch," in case blame was assigned, another old dynamic suddenly recalled.

She sighed, a sound that made me feel the Waltham floorboards under my feet. "I just remember that it always seemed like we would sleep together," Esther said. "There was all this flirting. And then I came to visit you in New York, and we had a fight, and I ended up going to Penn Station in the middle of the night. Remember?"

What? Even though I didn't remember everything clearly, I knew that this version was not among my lost memories. Esther had taught me how to share and cooperate, schooled me in seriousness. I was embarrassed to have a meaningful focus that was so different. I said, "Sort of," hoping she'd fill it in. What would we have fought about — although I had no trouble picturing us in

conflict, Esther's eyebrow raised to accentu-
ate her intractable judgment, her huge-eyed
stare that said, "You are accountable." What
I remembered was that Esther led us with
righteous certainty, and I often felt sheepish
and mistaken, as if I lacked conviction. I
admired her, but it had been hard to go on
feeling I was a disappointment.

The roommates of my life have been
women, and none lasted except Esther. The
snob at my first boarding school said to the
dorm mother, "I don't like *her,*" which two
days in I knew was anti-Semitic code, and
the dean moved her out. Courtney replaced
her, candied perfume in the red bottle and
her singsong giggle. She stood next to me,
the press of her bare upper arm to mine
when we wore T-shirts. This physical closeness tasted of home, the overheated way I
knew to connect. Courtney touched my hair
all the time, brushed her fingers on my neck
as she passed behind my chair when I was
at my desk. We shared clothes — Where's
your blue satin blouse? Can I borrow your
raincoat? Her shirts left sticky scent on my
skin, made me strange to myself. We sized
up the other girls, quizzed each other for
tests before breakfast. Courtney offered to
rub my neck one day and had me lie face-

down. She straddled the small of my back, and her thighs pressed in at my waist. "Take off your shirt," she said, the wide-open of her smile audible behind me. I did. She warmed her hands on my shoulders and under my hair, pushed at the muscles, and then she turned me over. I kept my eyes closed. She stroked first along the sides of my breasts, then over my breasts, her touch growing feathery, until with barest pressure the tips of her fingers circled my nipples. I sat up, put my shirt on, and we went to the dining hall. Aroused and uncertain, I said nothing and avoided her needy, penetrating look. We made it through the spring, but we didn't write letters after I moved to Colorado, where I would live in singles two years in a row. We weren't friends. Her attentions spooked me.

In freshman year of college, my mother arrived for an early parents' weekend and so poisoned my rapport with the school-selected roommate, the girl transferred to another dorm. You've heard that story. We'd been roommates only a few weeks, but over the next three years we avoided eye contact or shared paths, like dogs who scent the call to fight yet restrain themselves.

I lunged for intimacy, for the reassurance — *I like you! do you like me?* — but I always grabbed for it too soon, thinking that *a lot* equaled intimacy, and "a lot" never seemed like enough anyway. This made the girls quickly awful, at once too significant, and it probably made me awful to them, my alarming, unexplained hungers. We ignited, large, and flamed out.

I was a nineteen-year-old sophomore when I moved in with Esther, and it stuck, it worked. I'd torn a paper fringe from a flyer in the student union, arrived at the appointed time. Esther toured me around the apartment, sizing me up. She wore a long skirt over bare legs, the unshaven skin visible above her ankles. The place smelled of dissipated curry and cumin, perhaps from the night before. Afternoon sun revealed spans of dust in the air. Our tread made noise, a groan with each step. Esther pointed out "hardwood," it was an asset. And see the built-in drawers, the small closets we'll be sharing? She said the doors shuddered in their frames when the wind was high but I'd get used to it. Another girl, her friend, lived there, too. Esther was the one who collected the payments for the phone and heat, turned in the rent, the one who managed the kitchen rules and chore schedule. I wasn't a vegetarian, but she forgave that.

I got the sunniest room, in the front off

the living room and behind glass doors (I must have paid more). I brought boxes of books and a thrift-shop single bed frame for the box spring and mattress already there. For privacy I taped movie posters over the glass, a passionate couple mid-tango in *Carmen* and an image of a woman's gleaming, voracious mouth from *Choose Me.* Esther slept on the floor in a room off the kitchen, her mattress flooding the space. Her door was adorned with a hand-drawn poster from a folksinging festival. I also brought the brown rug my mother had chosen for my dorm room and the expensive vacuum cleaner she'd gotten her rich boyfriend to buy. "We need a vacuum," said Esther. "But how can you justify six hundred dollars for one? That could pay our whole rent for two months. That could feed people." I shrugged, aware I was inept at certain conversations, uneducated in circles beyond my own; but I wasn't worrying about my ignorance, I worried she didn't like me. "Well, but we have it now, it's really powerful," I said, hoping she'd forgive whatever blunder I'd made. We — we! New family! — also had a stately pantry, a deep porcelain sink, an oven with an archaic nameplate, the logo having since undergone many calibrations. We had push-button light switches, yellow linoleum with pale buckled seams in the kitchen. Things here had lasted past their fashion and outlived departed tenants. We had a bay window in the living room, a dilapidated hint of formal times in our livable shabbiness; an inherited couch, table lamps on the floor; my stereo on plastic milk crates. The shower curtain, suspended above the claw-foot tub on a circular rod, leaked water onto the tiled floor if you weren't careful. One of us was always annoyed as she wiped up after another. I could hear Esther's muttered irritation behind the bathroom door before she turned on the taps, and I'd feel guilty.

But I would be grown up here. *Our* bay window. *Our* shabbiness. Our dark stairway and jammed locks. We were giddy to put away groceries, to buy Comet and wipe it in the bathtub, to say, "I'm going down to do laundry." Once a month we spread franked checks on the kitchen table, and slid the calculator back and forth. Little by little, we trusted the other's advice. She said, "Is heavy cream what you buy if you want to make whipped cream?" or I held open the check register and said, "Do you think you're supposed to enter this here?" The third girl, a dancer, was often absent, but she left notes. "I watered spider plant,"

117

"Back Sunday." I can't remember any conversation between the three of us, but Esther and I chatted, companionable noise I counted on. At last I enjoyed the word *roommate,* its vein of *friend* implicit. Chat, though, was not Esther's real way. Angry with injustice, she was prone to extended statements and passionate insistence to get me to wise up. We didn't run into each other on campus. Esther might stay out late at a shantytown protest of apartheid, while I'd be fired up by a Renaissance art scholar; but we were engaged in a monumental and political act. We were Living Together, and we became loyalists.

Toward the end of the week, our schedules shed of immediate obligation, we developed this habit of sweet collapse. We lounged on the couch, the burgundy comforter pulled from my bed to cover our legs. We watched *Hill Street Blues* on my small color television. Sometimes, teasing when she liked an attractive actor, I could get her giggling, a spring bubbling up in her. She had a rampant, adorable giggle that just kept going, although it seemed she wished it wouldn't.

Esther was a full-time skeptic, to the point of bitterness. Not me — I was bouncy with social life, cheerful with sex, big on happy times and unbothered. This made Esther

118

skeptical of me, which I hated, anxious I would incur her disapproval. She prodded, nagging for changes I didn't care to make. "How can you not *care*?" she'd ask, disgusted yet affectionate. "Don't you ever read the paper?" One winter break I came home from Barbados, the annual trip to my grandmother's estate. The apartment was cold, unwarmable, and Esther, in a cabled sweater and wool hat, made tea for us and asked me leading questions. How much does each maid earn? Where does the staff live? Are they all black? She shook her head when I said, "But my grandmother's *not* racist!" She watched me start to realize this wasn't true.

Esther's emphasis on moral rigor was a downer. The too-small nylon uniform she wore the mornings she went in to Friendly's depressed me, as did her furious fuss when the manager told her she had to wear hose. She never agreed to eat out with me or that we should get pretty curtains for the living room, which seemed to me at the time a willful rejection of fun. I didn't track money; for gas and rent, for clothes, insurance and incidental student fees, for groceries, I received an allowance mailed each month by my father's accountant.

It became harder to watch television with her. "Not everything," I said, as she reviled beer commercials and women's fashion, emptying our evening of pleasure, "*means* something is wrong."

"Christ, Susanna. Look!" She grabbed the nearest record album, my *Like a Virgin*. Madonna in pink and pinker hues reclined on an anonymous floor and begged the camera closer.

"So what?" I said. "It's just a picture, Esther."

"It's not *just a picture* if it's the way we're trained to see women. If it's the only way women learn how to be seen."

We had a version of this fight fairly often, a tiresome reflex. She'd stomp to her room and I'd burst from the apartment to find my boyfriend and joke and fuck, anything I could do without having to inspect it.

I was aware of her body, of course I was, I lived with it. Proximity suggested intimacy in the student apartment, and physical intimacy pointed to sex. I remember seeing Esther at the sink in the kitchen, her back to me as I walked in, and how her thick hair dropped past her shoulders. This gave me pleasure, nice to come home to. I remember the gaze she'd fix on me across the table, and how I matched its intensity, defused her unnamed challenge, until we both cracked up. Her breasts were semivisible, braless under the fabric of her shirt. My mother had taught me that sex — sexual touch, innuendo, sexual acts, sexual interest — was the way to know another person truly, connection guaranteed. I didn't think this consciously, but it was in me, seeds scattered liberally under my skin. The narrow space outside the bathroom door, one woman in a towel wrapped under her arms, turning to slide past; the feminist discussions that alerted me to men's oblivion and shortcomings — all of that suggested that maybe we were supposed to become lovers. Esther barely tolerated my wolfish, sex-happy boyfriend who loped up our stairs. She and I lay on the couch with our feet in each other's laps. One of us dug her toes under the other's thigh to tickle and play. We played at every realm at once: house, family, seduction, education, marriage, united effort.

When Esther came to visit me in New York, I was living with my next roommates, Leah and Annie, three of us thrown by the vagaries of the *Village Voice* into a one-bedroom near Columbia. We looked like cousins, twenty-two-year-old Jewish girls from peace and privilege with good educations. Our copious dark hair set off the same tinge of yellow in our Ashkenazi skin, yet we were emphatically not a family. More like a campaign office for an absent candidate. Leah had the real bedroom, the prize for finding the apartment. I had the converted dining room behind louvered doors that allowed all sound to pass freely in and out. "Would it be okay if you turned that down a little?" we said at first, and then, later, calling between the rooms, heedless and impatient, "Please turn it *down.*" Annie, shielded by an inexpensive screen, slept on a twin she kept neat in the living room. She phoned home every other night, the good girl. She and Leah worked at the same company, departed together in the mornings. Leah would leave two thin chicken breasts to marinate all day in the fridge. They cooked together, one of them peeling broccoli stems as the other tended the meat. I ate ginger beef and cold sesame noodles at my boyfriend's before coming home late, or not coming home at all. I needed these women for rent, as they needed me, and we sought ways to not coincide. The three of us earned the same mean amount of money, worried similarly over subway safety, went to therapy, tolerated the broken elevator, crazy landlord, strife in the office. It was a biding of time, not that we would have called it that. We thought we were striking out with unique resolve.

It had been two years since I'd lived with Esther when she visited, and how epic those many uneven months since we'd dissolved our arrangement. I'd lived in France, moved in with my boyfriend (the one she didn't like), fallen in love with someone else, graduated, returned to New York. Dressed starchily, I'd interviewed for jobs; I'd filled out tax forms. I left the office late with the other interns for cheap Indian meals. I assisted a junior editor at a publishing house, where no one was a "secretary." My own missions the consuming memory, I can't remember what Esther was doing in that time, how often we talked. She sat with her legs crossed on my bed, inspected my tapes and books ("Don't you read anything beside novels?"), as she told me the details of her life, which I have now forgotten. Her same cynicism and indignation tired me, felt like the worn furniture I'd left behind in our Waltham apartment, for her to donate to a thrift shop or women's shelter when the lease was up.

But we'd fought? And so badly that she'd left recklessly in the middle of the night for

Penn Station to wait until dawn and her train? And that was it, we never spoke again, until now, tensions dismantled by twenty years' forgetting? My sons ran past my bedroom door and shouted to each other about what to do next — Come to my room! No, you come to mine! When I was done with this unexpected call, I'd remind them about math homework, get Jack to finish his piano practice. I'd start dinner. I'd learned to roast a chicken in the apartment I shared with Esther, to have it turn out well, the crisp, salted skin infused with the flavors of garlic and rosemary. I made this routinely for my family, and I couldn't recall what it was like to be decided by drama and argument, what it was like in our very early twenties when so much was effected by flash impulses, doors slammed. I had become the woman I'd been trying to be in that apartment. No: I'd become someone I had yet even to consider. In photo albums put together after college, pictures of Esther still show her in the sun on our constricted porch, holding up the cat to kiss his whiskers, rare frivolity; Esther in a row of women at her graduation, major passage. She'd invited me to attend, our roommate relationship nine months mature by then, almost a year. We'd been real, we'd been there.

When I moved in, Esther noticed I had a lot of opera recordings. She didn't know opera, she said, interested. A few months later we spent a Sunday on our stomachs, listening to *Don Giovanni,* the libretto open between us. The rug was scratchy under our elbows as we propped ourselves up. We played the first five sides of eight with meticulous concentration. The hours passed. We understood we were engaged in a sacred act. We rolled over and lay on our backs, not speaking. But some interruption that afternoon — my boyfriend came over, or I needed to wash my car, or she had to finish a paper — made us stop, and we left the last three sides for the following weekend. We postponed again, our infinite future of Sundays. We never finished, an essential note unsounded in our friendship, dramatic action suspended. That's where I left us.

HOMESICK

Everything was awful in France. "Junior year abroad" had arrived, reality instead of proposal and application, but my roommate's voice chained us to the States, her nasal rasp and pancake vowels unable to pull off French. She was nice, which I appreciated, but we had nothing in common, Linda and I. At dinnertime, Madame called us from our room — the once grand sitting room with high ceilings, now used for boarders — and we sat down to tough meat and what was left of the breakfast baguette. The crust scraped the roof of my mouth, scars for the next day. Madame's dining room overlooked a tidy park, but it was nearly winter, and she kept the shutters closed and the chandelier on through the day. To sleep, we heaped layers of faded batting over our beds. I turned to the wall, where at the slightest touch the brown paper with the gold fleur-de-lis pattern chipped away. I kept my hand on it as I whispered to it, "I hate you."

In the mornings Linda and I left the apartment and walked to the college along a generous boulevard. The shops were shut, but the cafés had cane chairs set out, and birds hopped among the tables. We noticed the impeccable women pulling the hands of their children, a scold and murmur hurrying them forward. The children's voices rose and broke against their mothers' in a French we couldn't hope to have, clipped, modulated. We wanted to tie our scarves that way, that easy style at the throat. But it wasn't easy. Nothing was easy.

At the school we trotted up the wide stairway to our respective classrooms. Light poured in from the windows that loomed at each landing, Americans on their ways up and down, commandeering the space. Nobody said that things were not as they'd hoped. Linda took French, to improve. I had history of French architecture, and the young teacher wore thin black trousers every day and a navy pullover with cuffs that came down over his wrists. Every detail was worth notice, meant something I did not yet understand. During class, I kept my notebook open and wrote letters to my boyfriend in Boston, explaining that *all* the

127

notebooks were filled with this sort of graph paper, the French interest in order as evident on the page as in the parks. We couldn't wait for Paris, where, we were sure, we would forget the musty routine of this provincial town and finally feel French. Linda and I were sent to separate arrondissements. I missed the ready companion and guard, the act of loyal care we had completed each night and morning.

I lived in the apartment of Mme and M. de Chambord, their two grown children, Hugues and Marie-Christine, and their dog, Orane. Hugues had the front room, next to the *salon.* Through the dining room, past the bathroom, Marie-Christine's room faced the courtyard, sunlight shafting in. My room, further along the narrow hall and beside the kitchen, was a sliver, as thin as an envelope. A cot sank under cotton duvets, and a desk was shaded by a shelf, where someone had left a dictionary. The tall window had two glass panels joined together by an ancient metal fitting. It looked out on the courtyard, too, but the gray side, with a glimpse of eastern daylight that grew thinner through the winter. There was a basin behind a curtain, where, it was made clear, I was to confine my toothbrush and soap. *"Bon!"* Madame said, as she pushed my suitcase into the room and stepped into the kitchen, busy on thick-heeled shoes. She clattered and slammed her way through her tasks.

With my door closed on the sounds I couldn't decipher, I sat down, an exhaustion of homesickness overtaking me. I cried with more effort than I'd done anything up to that point. I didn't know where I was, didn't know my new metro station, hadn't been able to follow as Madame peppered me with instruction before leaving the room — something about Easter? — didn't know what we'd have for dinner. Lunch, she had emphasized, one finger pointing at me, was not her responsibility. She'd mentioned their house in the country. Perhaps we'd be going, but I didn't know when. I set up tiny speakers and my tape deck and put in the Jacques Brel cassette I'd listened to back home. But I hated him now. So *French*.

Madame rapped on my door the next morning and told me to hurry for breakfast. *"Tout de suite,"* she said, coming down hard at the ends of her words. I dropped jam from a spoon on my toasted baguette and held a bowl of café au lait as she cleared things up around me. She showed me how to light the pilot light on the bathroom water heater, hurled the spent match into

129

the toilet, and then she left, the apartment bristling with quiet. I didn't know where Monsieur was. He seemed to talk only to the dog.

After the next strained dinner I fled the apartment and met Linda in Les Halles. Just the sight of her jacket helped, data my brain already stored. She'd phoned some others, people I knew a little — Frankie showed up, drenched in his new Drakkar Noir, Will from New Orleans, lanky Meg with her pop haircut, and Ben, deadpan sarcastic; and Miriam, whom I didn't know at all. We toppled into one another, shut the world out with our shoulders, scalded our hosts as we ate *pommes frites* and drank Stella Artois mixed with lemonade, a discovery perplexing weeks before, now so casually desired.

"We'll do this *chaque vendredi*!"

"*Il faut!*"

We were thrilled to use our French in real conversation. Maybe we'd be mistaken for French.

"Anyone know the word for 'pillow'?"

"*Comment-dit-on,* 'Who cares?' " We laughed.

"*Ça m'est égal,*" said Miriam. It was the first time she spoke. She was our exotic, living in a *pension* rather than with a family.

130

"You're so lucky," said everyone but Linda, who liked her guardians. They had cousins for her to meet, train trips they'd take her on. Will wanted to tell me about jazz, some Paris–New Orleans fraternity, while Miriam, on my other side, was rude about him in chaotic, vernacular French he couldn't follow. She leaned back in her chair, one skinny leg snapped over the other. With a cool, knowing purity, she was bitchy, which made her seem gutsy. We stayed out till three and I took a taxi home. I had not passed enough days here to feel money's value yet, to understand how soon it would be spent. The Haitian driver told me my accent was good. He smiled all the way to my neighborhood, knowing something but not telling me.

This was our group. Miriam and I would meet the others at galleries or for coffee after classes, but if I discovered a little park, a new plaza, I phoned only her, cultivating privacy. "I've got to show you this perfect place," I'd say. I put the franc Madame expected in the dish next to the phone. Or Miriam called me. "You're not going to believe this," she would say, "something else named for Victor Hugo." I'd jump in on the crest of her laughter so that we'd both be laughing the same way, both saying "Him, *again*!" We met on benches, my tired heart glad as she came across the raked gravel of the Jardin de Luxembourg. The gardens are beautiful! Why don't they have *gardens* in the States! She would give me the kiss on each cheek, take up my hand in hers, our bodies finding rest. We shared our information, tucked it away together, furtive. When she came to my place the first time she said, "There's me," and pointed at the group photo from the first days in the small city, that staging ground. The entire group was arrayed in tiers on the front steps of the college, forty helpless recruits. I was standing next to Linda, who had been my friend, or at least necessary. Three months later I could hardly remember her. Miriam and I studied pictures taken at the châteaux and the vineyards, at the roadside picnics, half our tour bus nosed into the frame, and Miriam was in them, sometimes not far from me, slim and straight in her gray trench coat. I hadn't noticed her before Paris, and even that first rude incarnation now seemed ghostly and gone, someone else, because now she was my *intime.* She liked it when I played with her hair, liked to whisper to me, and with her I felt indomitable, awake to every city surprise.

We both had boyfriends at home, fading from relevance. They had the same birthday, that must mean something, about us being friends. We both attended universities near Boston. We shared packets of chocolate biscuits as we walked, split long sandwiches of ham and Boursin, agreeing without a word on which sunny spot to choose, which bench. She knew a restaurant near school where you ate the meal *du jour,* a plate set in front of you. You paid almost nothing. Each of us had wine in a short, clouded glass. We flirted with two foreign boys who sat nearby, asked the one to teach us words in Dutch and the other to name German towns. They loved us, and we loved that. They wanted to see us again and, smiling, we walked away from them. I knew the weeknight soups at her *pension,* and she knew my uncharitable thoughts about ungainly, adolescent Hugues. Nasty secrets were glue. Throwing ourselves into the pronunciation of *Hugues* was glue. Miriam lent me *Talking Heads: 77,* which became my catechism, salvation in repetition; so she took me to see *Stop Making Sense,* which seemed to play all over Paris, any neighborhood likely to have a theatre where we could see David Byrne at 14h00, at 16h20, whenever we decided we wanted that. We must have seen it twelve times, our trance.

Eventually, exploring with Miriam, I came to know what I needed to know — the nearby *patisseries,* the metro stops. We liked *chaussons aux pommes,* we liked *pain aux raisins.* We carried bottled water and stamps, knew where to get cheap omelettes in places where they let you stay at your table. We came to feel natural as the grocer handed over plums in a thin paper bag. I bought cheese by the half kilo, grabbed my stiff metro ticket as the machine spit it out, pressed in the code for my building each evening. I no longer heard the clop-clop-clop in the late-night street made by my footsteps as belonging to someone else. Eventually, conferring with my confidante, I figured the age of each person in my French family, and that Hugues was embarrassed like an eighth grader by women, and that Marie-Christine snuck out every night with her red scarf knotted around her neck to go to her fiancé's. I knew to leave the butter on the table. I knew the family did have a country house and that they wouldn't invite me.

On my tight cot one night Miriam and I hustled and giggled about Mme de Chambord. Sprays of laughter kept shooting up.

"Shh, shhhh!" The center welt in the bed forced our bodies, our inside hips. We held each other's faces, her skin soft, like nothing else in the house. Our fingers in each other's hair, we were kissing light kisses, the edges of our mouths, until we kissed fully, the taste a stronger version of her familiar breath. Her tongue was a tiny point, sharp and fast. I felt her breasts against mine, and our yield, and thought, *Oh.* I raised the edge of her sweater and grazed her belly with my cheek. I didn't know what I was doing, but I ran my hand down the leg of her jeans, and up, and over the heat between her legs, tapping my fingertips on the surface of the denim. Like that, she came. Like that. I didn't know it was possible. I could make her come so easily, or at least she made me feel it was my doing. And with that deft tip of her tongue inside me, I came too.

In daylight we were established friends, *les deux copines,* but a new demand crept in. I had to account for my time, hours not spent together. "What did you say about me?" she'd ask, head cocked. She would be almost smiling, not friendly. We agreed the sex was a secret, which made it easy to ignore, until we were alone in her room, the lock turned quietly; or back at my family's apartment, hands over our mouths as we

135

came, Madame battering the evening meal in the kitchen next door. Since we maintained our identities as straight girls with boyfriends in the States, we had no problem when those boys visited. We pretended to forget how we'd be together after they'd gone, talking at their expense, coming at their expense.

No longer companion, moviegoer, art student, Miriam was the person who made me come. I needed this velvet hold more than anything, its crucial addition to make the rigid facades and planned gardens friendly. Out of bed, she turned petty over plans, whiny when she tired at the Musée de Cluny. She had to be cajoled at each turn, could brighten as soon as she saw a slice of *tarte*. Once, as we walked across the Pont des Beaux Arts, the Académie Française spread wide and white ahead of us, overornamented and exhausting, I turned my head to look at the water, and she drew in and cupped my ear to sing, "I've got a girlfriend who's better than that . . ." I was sick of *Stop Making Sense*. I knew I was wasting my precious months of Paris. I was wasting them standing at the turnstile in the metro, arguing over which stop we'd get off at, arguing over how long I spent on the phone with my boyfriend. We argued about disappointments that hadn't even happened yet.

I wished she'd go away, wished that I could have more friends, blend into groups instead of being sequestered, except I couldn't give up the skin, the tight tongue, the sating kisses. Our hands warmed inside unsnapped jeans as we lay in the dark. The secret wasn't lively anymore. We'd been through the stories of firsts, knew every opinion formed in France. I wanted a graceful extrication, but her whine grew shriller, her grip tightened. It was too much work to resist, and too lonely.

That summer, in the States a month, I missed French. Disoriented, I couldn't get interested in bland, local rules, things I'd known for years. My boyfriend and I moved in together, a first-floor one-bedroom in a town on the green line. But with Miriam, I had tamed a whole country! I missed the ritual of ordering coffee, school bags at our feet, the cubes of sugar plucked out of the bowl. I missed how we measured rudeness in the waiters and targeted the strangeness of others so we could ignore our own. The cigarettes outside cinemas at dusk, we'd done that, smoked, the stately blue box passed between us. *"T'as un feu?"* we liked to repeat, pretending absolute ease with the colloquial. My boyfriend was irritated when I made obnoxious puns in French, and I was irritated with him, his failure to laugh Miriam's short, derisive laugh, his inability to be *new.* As we had sex, I thought of her small, light body and of her breasts. "He doesn't even care about the Talking Heads," I told her on the phone, wondering if I loved him. I was homesick for the bite of her saliva.

At the end of the summer, I flew to North Carolina, and she was waiting for me in the airport. *"Salut,"* we said, but it was wrong. I was not myself. We were not each other. Never mind. At the house, she introduced me to her parents, and later we used the dark of her bedroom, trying not to be heard again, blocking out the footsteps and chair gratings from nearby rooms. "Remember Mme de Chambord," we said when we paused, "remember the *pension*'s fatty soups," our war stories. The next morning, she cooked breakfast with her mother, waiting for her to turn away so we could exchange cagey glances. As she slipped food onto my plate, she bent and gave my shoulder a silent kiss, and I shivered it off. I thought we'd be bold with our many willful identities, but we were two little girls, costumes abandoned. "I'm going to take Susanna to that place?" she told her mother. To me, she said, "It's the best coleslaw in the whole wide world." *"D'accord,"* I said.

She drove the blacktop, and as I looked out the window I couldn't see anything to notice, this American coma of dense, indistinguishable foliage, compared to the vital hues and edges of Paris, the careful forms, the exquisite plans, the shining architecture of conquering ambitions, where we, too, had stood out as vital and exquisite and symmetrical. The coleslaw was served in a scoop, as big as a baseball, sweet when I expected vinegar. In the afternoon she took me to her favorite spot on the kudzu-lined river.

"*What* is it?"

"Kudzu." She drew the word out a long ways, her native pronunciation.

"How do you spell that?"

We drifted on black inner tubes, one of us in an orange bikini I can picture vividly without remembering to whom it belonged. The pitch and throb of crickets worked on me like a sleeping spell, and when we got back to the house I noticed mud and scratches on my hands and legs, presumably from my scramble up the bank, as I'd followed after Miriam, after the fray of her

139

shorts against her tan legs. Both evenings, air conditioners at work, we watched baseball on TV with her parents before we excused ourselves to go down to the basement. They were Astros fans.

As I left, Miriam's mother gave me two pillowcases she had embroidered with my blue initials in thread still tight twenty-five years on. It's her I think of when I use them — the genial mother. At the start of senior year a few weeks later, I went to Miriam's dorm for a night. Because we'd done it before, because we were in the same bed, we had sex. I went down on her, she went down on me, but it offered no rescue this time, possessed no daring. I was thinking about the bookshelf my boyfriend wanted in the hall; I wanted it in the bedroom. She seemed listless, too. We no longer shared circumstances, our unsustainable French identities unuseful, cast down. We might never have met, or, if meeting — possible in Boston's collegiate stew — we might not have liked each other. After graduation Miriam left for the Peace Corps and fell in love with a Senegalese man, and that was the last I heard from her, a long, descriptive letter of dense pages about her wonderful new village in Africa and the wonderful strangers who had taken her in.

ANNABELLE UPSTAIRS

Annabelle was fierce about what was right. Letters were right, and invitations were right, and confidences and emergencies shared. She was soldierly about friendship: It must be like this, it will be like this. She sat me on her settee and leafed through the gilded album of pictures from five months before, explaining the Southern traditions, the rituals of weddings, the habits of her family. She was the third Annabelle in four generations on her mother's side. I went along, pleased to have instruction. She had a way of letting me know I had the right things coming to me.

Here's how we met: my boyfriend Jason and I were fairly new tenants in a modest Boston apartment building, slightly run-down, affordable. We noticed the couple at the U-Haul. Usually, we heard arguments in front of our living-room window, which was eye level with the sidewalk. The neighborhood was like that, a bit rough, and scraps of yelling would drift in, the sounds of car brakes, mad kids, doors slammed, so at the sight of two healthy people standing close together and smiling, we paid attention. He towered over her, but — their hair the exact same brown and their telegraphed understanding so complete — at first we thought they were brother and sister. A few weeks later the woman and I said hello by the mailboxes. I was on my way out, but I'd been hoping to run into her and we stopped a minute. She said they were newlyweds. I must have mentioned my birthday. The next week, on the morning I turned twenty-one, I opened my front door to find on the floor a tin of muffins with a tiny pot of jam. The note on heavy cardstock read

For your Birthday.
The strawberry tastes wonderful while the muffins are still warm.
Love from Annabelle Upstairs.

I'd never been above the first level of our building. Their door was ajar, and as I approached Annabelle pulled it open, holding coffee, one hand clasping at her white robe. "Dear Susanna!" She urged the mug forward, pressed my hand around it, and I was awash in celebration. Sunlight spilled across her tiny living room, but we didn't stop. She led the way. Her husband reclined in their bed, four spindled posters almost to the ceiling; mounds of white linens, tatted edges visible, and him in a white robe, too. She introduced us. "Peter, *this* is Susanna." She climbed up, piled her body against his, a look of such infinite gratitude and satisfaction on her face, it made me love her and hate her.

She gestured to the end of the bed, patted the duvet. I stayed in the doorway, only inches from them. Downstairs, her tin was on my kitchen table, our daylight gray, and Jason preparing to leave for the law library. She'd baked this morning, for me. I hardly knew her. Seeing me uncertain, she was gentle and laughing, "Come on, sugarfoot!" I struggled with this warmth, all this cozy invitation, drawn in and cautious. Annabelle regarded me from her delirium of marriage, of beginnings, of a pronounced and beguiling heritage.

Our friendship exploded, rampant and promiscuous. I was in my last year of college, gearing up for larger academic responsibility, but Annabelle was thirty, had earned a doctorate, had had the wedding. She knew no one else, in Boston because of Peter's medical residency. She had the bare knowledge she needed, her axis of home, hospital, work, where she was isolated with monotonous data entry. Daily, she urged me, "Come upstairs, come to our apartment," and up I went, into the foreign reaches of my own building. I was happy to take a break from my senior thesis, and from Jason, month four of living together in our off-campus apartment ("Do you think *you* could make dinner tonight?"). Her stately furniture was antique, all the way from Charleston. Although the pieces were absurd in our cheap building, I was clouded by envy I had to beat back, how she belonged to these objects and through them understood her own belonging. The cherrywood pedestal table, chairs to match, art, a breakfront, and a sofa with curving lines all cramped the rooms. She had a framed photo of herself in a wedding dress with her mother beside her.

In our first weeks — no, days — we confessed to adoring Hemingway, although as women we'd been trained to resist him, object. But *we* knew he mattered more than a temporary feminist argument! *We* found masculinity delicious and essential! We handed each other outrageous secrets, told what we liked in bed, or hadn't yet dared, raw details of Peter and Jason spilled freely at my kitchen table, frank sexual expression that I'd never shared with a friend so easily before. I loved her greedy whisper as she said "fuck" or "fucking," her plain revelry. She's like me, I thought. We explained the important women and sisters, described the scotched friendships, disrupted by rivalries, breaches, unmeant treacheries. Yes, yes. Our pure, driven intensity was too much for most people, we agreed. We were too much, we knew it — so we could be that way together. We shared our confusion about our powerful mothers, mutual permission to say the worst. Annabelle, intrepid topographer, had considered the daughter's dilemma and seized the power of distance and geography, and I felt allowed in my inarticulate ambivalence. She left Faulkner outside my door, a vintage cloth edition with no jacket, and collections of Keats and Ashbery. Her serpentine inscriptions began, "O dear Susanna," like proper letters, making the most of the endpapers.

We didn't see much of Peter. Weekday evenings, Annabelle flew upstairs and cooked a real dinner, which she sealed in containers and took to the hospital. Her generosity was fueled, to my astonishment, by consideration. Jason and I competed, sought ways to score. We loved fucking, but out of bed we waited to see who would do something for whom. Sometimes, returning happy from her quick trip to the hospital, Annabelle tapped at our door. She whispered the day's delights in my ear, her pride at Peter's success, as she waved to Jason in the room beyond. I wondered that this smart woman carried on this way, but I began to see that the duty gave her meaningful solace, compensation for Peter's daily absence, nightly absence. She went to sleep in that high bed, and he returned at three or four. They made love right away, she'd told me, or before she dressed for work. Once, from the stairwell, I heard them, a marvelous violence and oblivion from their apartment. I heard a rougher, more animal Annabelle, even more persuasive.

When we were together, Annabelle, Peter, and I, we were noisy, a heady unfurling of adventures, of tenor and soprano laughter. This movie, that book! Were you listening to the hearings? Isn't Greece wonderful, the honey, the ouzo, the *lamb*? Jason had since moved out, our intermittent nastiness finally full-blown and unlivable, and often, often, I went upstairs for Sunday breakfast, tea at dusk, wine in their pretty goblets. Passing behind Peter's chair as he talked, Annabelle would lean over and slide her arms down his chest until her chin rested on his shoulder. Her cheek pressed to his, both of them facing me, his long bangs fell into her hair, mixing chestnut and chestnut. I felt them, the force field and mutual possession, and her magnetic reach to gather me, although I wasn't clear whether I was friend, sister, or charge.

Alone, Annabelle always wanted more of me. I'd finish an answer, but she'd bend to me, one bare foot tucked under her on the settee, and say, "*Tell* me the rest." She made me think I had more, and in the beginning I was flattered. Then I felt I *should* have more when I truly didn't, and this wearied me. My answers weren't right. She'd chide me, pull nearer, her hand flattened at her chest. "I know what's *in* here, dear Susanna. You can show me." I groped for safety, reached for the edges. I wanted the ecstatic game and party, but also — Show me the invisible and the silences. Show me the complex task of *belonging*.

We walked together down Newbury Street. Peter had a rare day off, which Annabelle turned into festivity. Nobody but Peter made her laugh with freedom and mischief, and she was very giddy. Their divine flame lapped at me. We'd gone to a place they loved for a late breakfast of eggs Florentine. Now we walked in the sun, Annabelle in the middle, holding my arm while her rhapsodic gaze greeted her husband. Sexual franticness was always between them. We stopped into little shops, a makeup store, where I let the saleswoman dab shadow over my eyelids while Annabelle and Peter browsed with aimless pleasure, hand in hand. I owned hardly any makeup, and festive and expansive myself, I bought it.

Outside Annabelle said, "Well, sugarfoot. That's not a good color on you."

"It isn't?"

"No. You should wear more pinks. Don't you think, Peter? Plums and pinks on our glorious Susanna?"

"The woman in the store liked it," I said.

"Well, she's paid to say that, isn't she?" She pulled me closer by the sleeve, firm possession. "Never mind, we'll find you the right color sometime."

Once home I left the coppery pressed powder in the bag. Then the bag went into the cabinet under the bathroom sink. When I moved I packed the unopened shadow, and it traveled from one life to another until

I tossed it, but only after it had become perplexing clutter in a drawer, had lost its burnish of Annabelle.

After college I moved to New York. My father was growing sicker. His doctor walked me to a corner of the apartment and hinted at impending change. At first I didn't understand what he meant, and then I did. My plans would be altered. Instead of going to England for graduate school, I would stay, live nearby for his last year, be a comfort, learn him better. "Of course you will," Annabelle said on the phone. She believed in family decrees, the historical solemnities that told you who you were. She revered the power of matriarchs, and she adored fathers, understood the exact sort of softness they wanted from daughters. She came for a weekend, and she flirted jovially with my father, let him flatter her. I knew just that excitement but was trying to outgrow it.

When I fell in love with a new man, I brought him up from New York to meet Peter and Annabelle, and we went out to dinner. Noah was definitely a serious boyfriend, and in the ladies' room, Annabelle and I celebrated my efforts. On the return train I was sad, I told him, that I lived apart from her, my jubilant guide and champion, the one friend who fueled my burn and reveled in the feisty necessity of wanton spirit. He didn't get it.

Then, age twenty-four and thinking I knew what I needed to know, I decided to marry Noah.

Annabelle called me up one night. I gave her reports of my wedding plans, remembering each detail of hers — how her mother and sisters were dressed, the sprays of corsage against the chocolate shimmer of their gowns, how her mother had almost stayed in the background, for once.

"December, we think," I said.

She said, "Peter and I don't like him." Words died in my mouth. "Peter and I don't trust him." She told me I was headed into mistake, that I was acting out of fear about my father's health. "Don't confuse your men," she said, her tone firm. I didn't repeat this to Noah, but I went over it, growing angrier with her, a real wedge that threw me into distress. How could she? How dare she? Would I still call her my best friend? I didn't want to be told that unconscious anxiety dictated my choices. Later, when I left Noah — invitations, band, dress, cases of champagne, all canceled — I wouldn't have said it was Annabelle, because by then other problems had eclipsed that conversation, but I'll admit she'd seen harm imminent, and seen it long before I had.

Annabelle was the first of my friends to have a baby, and when she delivered, I took the train up right away. I didn't bring the baby a gift, wasn't clear on the customs. I brought presents for Annabelle: a long Victorian novel for her empty hours, a pair of delicate drop earrings, and a black lace camisole, "for later," I said. We'll fix this, return order. Sex will prevail. Annabelle showed no interest, eyes trained on her newborn. Peter leaned against the bedpost and talked to me. The box with the tissue paper was pushed to one side of the bed, waiting to be taken away. I was confused and replayed the steps I'd followed, looking for some mistake: didn't Annabelle want to be reminded that she wasn't only mother, that she would recover from the distended belly and glory again in the mania of a passionate body? That's what I'd want. I was offering her the recognition that a baby wouldn't define her. It seemed, though, that that was not what she wanted at all.

In a matter of quick, troubling weeks, we had little left in common, the friendship knocked from prominence. I let her talk through every shift, sensing that's what would secure our connection. I discarded content — ounces of weight gain and engraved silver cups sent by formal cousins — which I deemed irrelevant, and listened for Annabelle's charms and vigor, her erotic growl. She was drowsing in the big new love, the outside world gone. All her generous attention left me, poured over the child. I wish I could say I learned something — how much sacrifice of self a baby demanded, for instance — but I was listening for what was left of me in her life.

One evening I called. Peter was mostly at the hospital, his hours stepped up, and Annabelle was isolated. Poor Annabelle, I thought, who needs so much brightness, and the bigness of sex, and poems with glorious, unexpected configurations, everything I'd need: stuck alone in her apartment with a baby.

"Hey, it's me."

"Well, hi, you." There was effort.

"You okay?"

In a voice of awful stillness she said, "Something happened." She told me: It was a beautiful morning. The baby was a dream, cooing, kicking. They lay on the bed. When the kettle whistled, Annabelle tucked pillows around him and went to brew tea. I knew that teapot, another pretty and precious thing, handed down by the many women. She returned to the bedroom, and her baby's face lit up at the sight of her. She set teacup and saucer on the covers, leaned over, and smiled at her soft, new son. The baby gave a quick, regular spasm, which overturned the cup, and the liquid spilled out. "It burned him, Susanna." Annabelle said this slowly, as if having memorized a great text but unsure I would see every detail. I saw. She told about the burn unit, the scarring and the grafting. All the vocabulary was terrible. We both knew Annabelle had made a mistake. We both kept seeing that teacup upright, before it became the story of the teacup. I wouldn't have my first child for another seven years, but then the story would return to me. Then I properly felt its horror and grasped the passionate anguish of my old friend.

After her twins, Annabelle disappeared completely into the opaque realm of motherhood, to me a dusty replica of herself. We'd been friends about five or six years. I'd made the effort with the first child, celebrated the new birthdays, stuck the baby's photograph on my fridge door — the

sun spotlit his hairless head, his mother lying on the grass behind him, an arm around
his waist to prop him up. That direct Annabelle look into the camera of rigor and right
and satisfaction. But with the din and
demand of three children, Annabelle could
never return calls. Of course not; it was up
to me to keep calling, and, of course, I
called less.

I was visiting Boston one time, and I
phoned last-minute, excited to surprise her,
and she invited me over. Our reunions,
especially as they'd grown rare, carried a
necessary importance for me, benchmarks
as I presented my major developments to
someone who had been invested a long time
in my happiness. It was pleasant in their
new house, with the bright fabrics, and
generous space for the distinguished heir-
looms, and the framed wedding tableaux
set out on a grand piano. We were on her
settee, the twins asleep in another room, the
boy at fierce play on the rug, humming a
sweet babble that didn't distract me.

Annabelle patted my leg. "Tell me, Susanna. What have you done with your
Boston days?"

Friends, I said. Bookstores, movies, a walk
along the Charles.

"And what else?" This comforted me, our

old way retained.

"Well, what?" I said. "Oh, I know." I'd run into a boss from an early job. We'd had coffee. "And then he walked me to my car. We were chatting about the usual, his kids, his wife, and then he said, 'I really want to fuck you.' " I felt a queasy thrill reporting this, myself center-stage desirable and the boss weak with lechery.

Annabelle said slowly, "Why are you sitting here, Susanna, telling me this, this, this *unattractive story*?"

Easy: long ago you and I bonded over the blatant dreams in the faces of men. We knew we could assess their obvious longing as they eyed our breasts, our mouths, our loose hair, as they shifted on their feet to close the air between us. We knew the uncanny fever we inspired in empty classrooms, as our professors flattered our minds, thought *they* seduced *us;* the bosses made pliant and ours because of our unequivocal, unafraid eye contact.

"I cannot understand why you imagined I'd want to hear this," she said. *It happened to me,* I thought, dismayed; *you always wanted to know what happened to me.* We were quiet, the child's song bumping against my dim confusion. I kept hearing my voice say "I really want to fuck you," hearing "fuck" as if it were made of glass and rag and kerosene, a little bomb in my possession. Without agreement, Annabelle had dismissed sex, disowned her wonderful "fucking," and I didn't know where that left me.

When my first son was born, I sent out the announcements, and soon Annabelle called. We lived a country apart, her Cape, my Rocky Mountains. I couldn't remember how long it had been since we'd seen each other, years of her kids' stages and dogs acquired and divergent tastes formed. Her eldest was in first grade, her twins out of babyhood. As before, she knew vastly more than I did.

"Peter and I were talking," she said with determined pleasure. I could picture the engaged face, and with a tiny excitement I sensed I'd recaptured her interest. "We wondered if you would like a very *big* box of pears or a very *little* box of steaks." I stuttered, could find no comment. "What would you *like, dear* Susanna?" She meant to celebrate, but my mind was stiff with distress at what I'd done by becoming someone's mother. I knew Annabelle wouldn't get this, her own right family habits secure enough to make her sure of her many roles.

Pears, steaks; big, little. Annabelle's choices, when I was feeble with exhaustion. I sought the answer she wanted, wanted to be what she wanted, and then didn't give a shit.

"I don't know," I said.

"Now, come on, sugarfoot, what do you want?"

"I don't know."

"Well. You tell us when you do." The warmth was gone, as if my not choosing was intended to wound her. *I've failed her,* I thought; my home, I felt, was already stuffed with failure. Suddenly formal, we said a strange good-bye.

A couple of years ago Annabelle called out of the blue and plunged us into our impressive conversation of novels, criticism, exhibits, her need to know, my compulsion to tell, our respective passions reinforced. We were guided by the terms of the youthful friendship.

"And your father," she said. "Is he well?" He was well, had never succumbed to the possible emergencies of his health. "He must be terribly proud of your book? Is he?"

"Oh, Annabelle, ha. He told me I'd written *The Magic Flute.*" I was flat with this. My father hadn't mentioned the contents of the memoir as he pointed out parallels of operatic structure. He congratulated himself devilishly on the genius of his interpretation.

Annabelle was ebullient. "How wonderful, Susanna. Don't you see? He compared you to *Mozart.*"

I couldn't argue with that.

BLIND DATE

The way Louise looked. That was the first thing people mentioned. My father described her looks after he hired her. The supreme paleness of her skin, her red hair in bright contrast. Her wrist, as it emerged like a stem from a thin cashmere sleeve. Limbs, height, long spine. Then her translucent eyelids, shut for emphasis as she pursued a thought. Late in our friendship I found this annoying, the way she became cloistered and rare, but while I loved her it was endearing.

My father always hired attractive women, intelligence required but beauty expected. He told me he would have seduced them were he not in the wheelchair, and married, of course. Infidelity was common practice in our family, reflexive, like reunions are for other families. But by now my father was paralyzed, couldn't make a move. Couldn't make his move. He watched, he enticed.

Louise was in her early thirties and also married, about ten years my senior. She'd finished her MFA, then been sent to my father by one of the old goats who passed pretty, sharp writers around. To tell me of his day when I phoned, he'd say, for instance, "Louise took in a kitten. It's Louise's fifth wedding anniversary. Did you know Louise lived in Istanbul? I urge you to go to Turkey." He loved saying her name. By the time he introduced us, we'd been pushed into an arranged sisterhood. Willowy, pale, she was astonishingly unfamiliar as a specimen. He spoke to her with rakish games and double entendres, and I felt like leaving the room.

Becoming friends with her was not hard, and I knew it pleased my father. Expert at the beckoning, Louise seemed to sense that she had a responsibility to bestow herself on others. She was accustomed to our gratitude. I'd come to my father's apartment, where he edited the magazine, and I'd wait as she followed his last bidding, as she put away letterhead and galleys, wrapped her long neck with a scarf, got one arm into her coat. My father, seeing me wait, would keep her a few extra minutes, a last flirt, a final tease. She'd be laughing good-bye and *good-bye* as the front door closed and left us in the hallway, elevator button lit. There, she turned her shimmery gaze on me. By doing nothing, she promised elegance. I noted the merino blend of that coiled scarf, that she squeezed lemon juice onto her avocado salad. I read the articles and authors she spoke of reading. We talked each day, less and less about my father. What are you doing? Where are you going? "Would you like to come?" she'd say, sounding like I'd won something. We went to movies she suggested; walked dozens of city blocks, found specialty bookshops, and she gave me *White Noise,* which I devoured so we could discuss it. We had drinks in downtown bars, the tantalizing disorientation of Tribeca at night, where we'd be joined eventually by her husband, Bert. Bert was a gauze around Louise, less than her. He worshipped her, too, I assumed, and I approved. My father loved to hear from me those particulars of her life he had no way to see, and I loved to deliver them. He mentored her writing and thinking, but I could tell him what it was like to watch her buy shoes, to watch her accept the seat offered by an impressed man on the subway.

"My father thinks you should take voice," I'd say to her. "Oh, that," she'd smile, her private galaxy, but nothing more. And I wanted clues to him. I had begun to consider his promiscuous mentoring, the young women who arrived and sat near and left with their arms full of books. He complimented their boots, noted the tiny buttons up an ankle, took an interest in their ambitions. Still childish, I fell short; he had a genius for including me in the conversations so that he could point out to Louise what I had yet to do. She defended me, another reason she was my heroine.

I knew only a little about her. She was not forthcoming and used her privacy, a treat held apart from a puppy: she'd married right after college, then moved to New York. I knew she lived in Brooklyn in a second-floor apartment she described with maddening opacity as "small." She had nephews. I pondered each discrete item of information, assembled the fascinating woman. I mimicked the flutter in her face, imitated her cadences, as if I might enchant myself and transform into her, which would demonstrate how deeply I knew her. I'd do whatever she suggested.

"You remind me of me," Louise said, after meeting my boyfriend Noah. "I feel protective."

"What do you mean?" I said, pleased. She hadn't liked him, I could tell, and I wanted

162

her to say something outright. "Protective of me?"

"Of the two of you, as a couple." She closed her lids, a smile half there, and she sort of shook her head at the ceiling. She could make me disappear. What if she'd said, Don't make the mistakes I made? Then I could have said, What mistakes, what mistakes, and coaxed out her details. We could have gotten somewhere, grown.

She finally asked me over for dinner. I'd never been to Brooklyn. No one in my family, as far as I knew, had ever been to Brooklyn. I was a little scared I'd get lost, away from the reliable graph paper of Manhattan's upper streets, so I met Louise after work, and she took me to the subway. Downtown she said, "We change here," and shuttled us through the passageways. We came out at Court Street. Twenty-five years later, when I disembark there, it's still hers, Louise Street. She pointed out the regular stops of her life as we walked — a public library, a Lebanese bakery, a toy store for presents. Her friends had babies. I decided I'd get a coat like hers, camel-colored with a tapered waist. I would buy baby presents. Finally we came to the slender building, where we climbed a flight, and she unlocked the apartment. There was Bert, setting the table.

In the close rooms, Louise was as formal as she was anywhere. Her lithesome hands, the empire in her posture, that conscious grammar. I sat on their bed, which occupied the front room. I said, "Can I see? May I look at your pictures?" She handed me an album and went through to the kitchen to pour wine. "You act too?" I said, looking at her college productions of *Godot* and *Lear,* Louise dressed artfully, her height and elbows and the new-penny color of her hair all dedicated on stage, her pallor a radiant moonlight amidst the grayer actors. "Oh, not anymore," she said. "Bert directed those."

I said, "Is that how you met?" and she gave her private, reluctant giggle.

After the dinner Lou and Bert walked me to the subway like a departing babysitter, the evening term expired. How could I get my life to be like her life, dinner for two on the table, a pepper mill, fresh candles pulled out of a drawer, a serious job where my intelligence counted? I hugged Bert and thanked him, hugged her longer, even as I could feel that thin stiff body release me.

I wouldn't let myself know my boyfriend

was a loser — an actual loser, at gambling — but my friends knew and tried to signal me. Annabelle in Boston had said outright she didn't trust him, a blow to our friendship. I tried to think of Noah's gambling as a course he was completing, which thus would come to a scheduled close. I marvel at that foolish, inexperienced girl — me — absolutely directed by vain hopes. Can't you see, I want to tell her, that this will come to nothing? Anyway, my father encouraged him, speculated with his erudite charm on the effects of gambling — "You've read Dostoevsky of course?" — or he'd describe Monte Carlo in the '50s, planting his cosmopolitan nostalgia in my Midwestern boyfriend. Was I meant to worry, or was I meant to laugh?

One day, in the park for a walk, Louise said to me, "You guys seem like us. It's just — It's just . . ." She had a careful concern, which made me consider my plight seriously for the first time. And hers. What did she mean? She and Bert were in step. There was no strain I could see.

"Yes?"

"Do you want to meet Will?" she asked. "He's single, and he's great. You're worth a great guy."

"Well, I know, thank you, but —" Noah

and I had just paid a key fee on an apartment on the Upper West Side. We were moving in together. But Louise wanted me to say yes, and her intention and desire were impossible for me to resist. I didn't know how to stay myself.

I met Will at the Lincoln Center fountain for the adulterous blind date. We talked, naturally, of Louise. Her rare looks, her golden confidence. I got him to tell me things about her from before I'd met her. She'd run marathons; she'd led choirs to competition victory. Of course victory. We sat on a concrete bench, where I thought about kissing him in the open, baiting discovery. Louise loved him, treated him like a brother, so I'd love him, too, step right into an affair, if he'd do it. Will wasn't interested, wounded from rehab and getting sober. Over dinner at a fake-Southern barbecue place, he talked of petty trials at his job. He was the unhappiest person I'd ever met. Nothing like Louise, who could close her fluttering lids, render trials as inconsequential irritants.

I think Louise threw Will into my path so I'd stop watching her, just for a little while. She left Bert. I didn't know this was coming. One day she phoned to change lunch and explained, as if she might as well mention it, that she was moving out. "You're what?" This was a shock, our friendship redrawn in a cold instant as absent of the real confidences. I'd been trying to copy a phantom, had never had access. I'd been planning to become her, eventually, once I stopped following Noah to the backgammon parlor, stopped yelling on Broadway as we made our way home; once we made a little money. I would own long scarves, stand straighter, be supported by praise and esteem.

So she shunned the marriage and started to drop her friends. I thought she was dropping people who didn't like her lover, a movie director; but she was shedding skins, I realized. She was becoming the next person. Panicked, I did not want to be dropped and upped my interest in the director. I came to his opening night. We stood as a threesome, acting out pretend conversation. When he went to the bathroom, she described sex. "Passionate mutual interests," she said, head back, eyelids tipped closed, and a gush of laughter escaped her. She was not the elegant Louise I copied, not with this uncharacteristic candor. Fuck you, I thought. Come back, I thought. But she wasn't really talking to me.

She must have taken the director to meet

my father, who would have been jealous and punishing of her, while flattering the lover. Soon she left the magazine, and he hired the next attractive woman, my next un-achievable sister.

Louise slipping from me, I was there for Bert. We could keep her going. I was careful not to equate our abandonment, but I wanted my extravagant loss hailed, too, a friendship death to his marital death, if not quite as traumatic. He should know that none of his friends, *their* friends, understood his sorrow as I did. Louise, who had claimed all our focus, and we'd given it over, was missing. We were disoriented, aimlessly investigating her disguised heart. We met in restaurants, recalling countless meetings, when we'd been the three of us, the four of us. A short while after Louise left Bert, I left Noah, willing to forfeit the apartment. "She was right about him," I said. "Maybe she's right about me," Bert said, and I soothed him. For months we went on, evenings at small-scale theater productions, earnest phone conversations that lasted past midnight, Bert's tardy arrivals at bars — he was gravely late, which had driven Louise mad, and they'd carry on a quiet fight for his first few minutes. I would watch her distress rise, hated that. Then she'd bat away conflict with the lilting laugh and puckered eyelids. "He should behave better to you," I used to say in private, imitating her worldly concern for me, and she'd agree.

Bert offered to make a dinner. Baking had saved him during the divorce, a relationship to dough and heat that he could master. He turned out one tart after another, caramelizing pears, shaving apples that became crisp browned layers in the oven. When he invited me to his new place, we were by then closer friends than I'd ever been with Louise. Anguish and real rejection, Bert and I found, fed intimacy far better than worship had.

I stood on the platform as the subway left me there. Bert's directions seemed complicated by excess details as I crossed streets, but then the brownstone appeared, confirmed the effort, and Bert answered the garden-apartment bell. He'd kept the cat, who dove behind the sofa. We were pleased and smiling, our mutual interest something we had built, that belonged to us, and I handed him wine to celebrate new starts. Without her, his habitat was fastidious, stripped of manuscripts and brimming folders, no lilac-silk bathrobe on the back of the bathroom door. He had pens in an earthen cup on the upright piano and cookbooks alphabetized in the kitchen.

The dinner was a wooing as he set out grilled lamb chops and braised vegetables, took his time. We would sleep together, we both knew that. I took my chair and he stood, mixed a vinaigrette for the baby greens — walnut oil and champagne vinegar, my first taste of them. His pear tart and brewed coffee. We'd been heading here, our remarks increasingly sly, giving us excuses to bump shoulders, or slide into each other, my head resting against him at a play. I knew the smell of his coat and also the stronger, more complex smell of his T-shirt, couldn't recall how Louise smelled. In the kitchen I stopped him from the dishes, turned him to me and kissed him, a question answered, like kissing Louise, or what remained of her. After we made love, he walked me to the subway entrance, where we kissed a solid, triumphant kiss, and I went home. Our affair lasted a few weeks, more evenings plotted like the first. I learned Brooklyn's Sunday streets. Sometimes we were happy and silly, other nights just plain glad to be touched. How hard we were working not to mention her. How hard we worked to tend the faint red ember that was about to go out altogether.

EVIDENCE

Working for the movie producer, I occupied a furnished house on the bay in Sag Harbor through the week. I can't say I lived there. The producer, who didn't want to leave the Hamptons, had rented it to be his office, and I was a sort of domestic assistant, tending both the professional duties and the several homelike rooms. He came in the mornings, killed his engine in the driveway. He had the *Times* and the *Wall Street Journal* under his arm, poured himself the coffee I'd made in the kitchen, then sat at his enormous desk, scripts and magazines spread around him. I was his D-Girl — scout, basically — and I read screenplays and short stories and typed coverage on an electric typewriter set up in one of the bedrooms, the door open so I could respond to him.

It had all developed fast, the parting from one job and familiar colleagues, a leap in salary, the unconventional setup to indulge the producer. On weekends, I shuttled my cat back to my studio on Christopher Street in the new Honda Civic the production company had staked me, moon roof open. Some acquaintance, hearing I was out in the Hamptons, told me to call Debra after I was settled. I'd need a friend, yes, a way to occupy the black lampless evenings of rural winter, when the fax machine had been turned off and the essential tasks finished. A couple of weeks in, I called the number, and Debra invited me over that night, her spontaneity an excellent indicator of a new friend. If I had a bottle of wine in the shabby kitchen, I took it with me. I followed her directions, slowing at each intersection to read the street name, as I mapped my temporary town. I pulled in behind a black Volvo wagon. This woman, I'd been told, had a baby, a career as a writer, which I wished to have, and her husband was an architect. She'd said to come to the back, the glass door that slid open on a deck. I could see in before she saw me.

The kitchen glowed with lights at every level, recessed in the ceiling, hanging in a modern chandelier, tucked under glass cabinets above the extra-deep counters. Debra hung my coat, took my hands in hers, chatting, chatting, she never stopped. Her daughter, not yet a year, sat up in a high chair and worked at the tangerine sections Debra set in front of her. The baby flung the segments to the floor, laughing, and Debra sectioned off a few more. Babies were new to me. At once Debra was telling me local tales, as if in my first days I would have assumed my village part and accumulated pertinent questions. That man at the post office? The bartender Thursday nights at the American Hotel? "You've seen *him,* you can't miss him! You're working for *who*? Oh, God." She didn't *know* him, no, but it was a *really* small town, you'll see. She loved any detail about my boss, his obscene house under construction, the woman he'd just married, she'd gone to Smith, was she nice? We speculated on his fidelity, past and future.

Her husband, Dean, arrived and hung up his coat, kissed Debra, kissed his daughter. I saw them fit, and I tried to determine my place with them now that we were four. I took a chair next to the baby and began to hand her the fruit, wipe at her cheeks with a damp napkin. I let her play with my bracelets.

Debra made spinach sautéed in nothing but minced garlic and a flick of oil in a cast-iron skillet. She pulled a fish from the oven, decorated it with preserved lemon, olives, bits of fresh tomato, and from a green glass decanter with a metal spout she drizzled olive oil over it. She set down a bowl of new potatoes in their skins, spotted with parsley. Her thick dark hair was held off her forehead by her constant wrist, flicking up, sweeping back, and at the same time she separated a potato from the bowl, cut it roughly with a fork, and blew on it before she gave it to the baby. I was enchanted by her gestures, the evidence of domestic longevity. They had an oversize wall clock, as regal as a train depot's. Their giant range hulked in black and chrome, burners alight as she finished the food. Each room in the house spilled toward every other. Off the kitchen a wide pantry passageway was provisioned with Le Creuset pots and lids, tins of steel-cut oatmeal, lined-up snow boots, piled catalogs, baskets with polar fleece scarves and vests. Everything looked to me like proof of people entrenched and powerfully able.

I went home with a piece of Debra's almond cake, and I ate it in the morning with coffee, wishing to call. I waited till later.

"Thank you for dinner."

"That was *so much* fun. You're great with

the baby."

"What are you doing?" I wanted to be invited again. She asked me for the following night, and I muffled my disappointment. It seemed to me I should be in her friendly house right now.

Weekends, back in the city, busy with my reverse life, I almost forgot her. I'd go to dinner at my father's, where we talked about him; I'd meet my stepmother early Sunday at the flea market; her expert hand shuffled rose gold lockets and vintage clothes. "Now this would be good on you," she'd say, pausing at a jacket, walking on, leaving me to retrieve it if I wanted it. I went to the movies with my sister or met my aunt for waffles at a diner. Monday mornings, I started for the Hamptons, zipped up the Long Island Expressway, heading to Debra, who waited for me, for whom I laid out the eccentricities of my family. She'd analyze everyone, explain why someone was like this, someone like that. I found this helpful.

In Sag Harbor we saw each other a lot, daily, or nearly. When she phoned, I said yes, sneaking out on the chores my boss meant for me to do, if he wasn't there. I jumped into her front seat when she pulled up. I didn't want to miss a choice observation. She drove us to the beach, exotic for its chill and emptiness, and related local escapades and crises. She took me to roadside stands for the last fall produce, her car humped up on the sandy bank of the road. We went to the bakery, where the pleasure of hearing her voice as she picked out ciabatta and rye, her breathless ups and downs as she asked playful questions of the baker, was enough, better than bread. Or I waited in the car, I didn't mind, the baby asleep in the back while she ran in. A couple of times, she came over to my house-office for a beer, chic in black turtleneck and dark jeans. With the copy machine imposing on the living room, the visits didn't last long. Instead, she encouraged me to share her pretty life, join, and I did, feeling visible in my want. I wanted her friendship, her things, her smart talk, her tales of voluntary exile from New York City. Sometimes, arriving for an early weeknight supper, I'd find another of her friends in the kitchen. Debra introduced us, and I'd settle in my usual chair, say little, waiting for the woman to go. Once Debra had seen her out, she'd come back to me, indiscreet with backstory she had to have me know.

In her double-sink bathroom, I inspected the labels of the Kiehl's conditioner and

Dr. Bronner's shampoo, sniffed its strong peppermint. In the baby's room, I touched the white wood rocker, imagining scenes I never saw. Debra nursing at midnight, diapering, Debra in the shower at 6 a.m., quickly shaving her calves before she ran downstairs with damp hair to make coffee. She was so brisk and lovely, her voice as light as a girl's, but something rough behind it. We'd play on the rug with her daughter, the evenings growing blue then black beyond the giant, modern windows. Her mother phoned often, her "Sweetheart?" on the answering machine, and Debra would jump up and take the call in the kitchen, her voice almost the one she used for me, between us. I tried to imitate it for the baby, get breathy and sure. I could hear her congenial argument about a *Times* editorial or baby care, short phrases of family shorthand. "Susanna's here," she'd say and end the call, return to the living room describing the many fond knits of relationship that bound her, secured her. My mother kept me on the phone for hours, an evening's commitment, and she'd drain every private thought out of me, every intention and idea. I could never recover the unwavering self as neatly as Debra did. I could never have said to my mother, "Not now, I have a friend here" without feeding her a saga, or becoming part of the outrage she would show the next person she called. "Sue hung up on me!" At my rental, when I went back at 9 or 9:30, the air was stale, the sheets cold. Every morning I'd clean up breakfast and empty the litter box and make my bed with the drab bedspread before my boss came over to land in his swivel chair and place his boots on the desk, which ran the length of the picture window. He got the view.

At Debra's, the house wrapped in close firs, I had my spot at the table, a slice of imported salami in my hand, talking as she produced wintry meals of Portuguese stews, chopped chard with butter, roast beef. Everything tasted wonderful, well salted. We mixed argument and affection, each insisting what went first on the washed lettuce — the kosher salt, no, the olive oil. When Dean walked in we pretended he could settle it, and he pretended to, sometimes in my favor, sometimes in hers. "I *told* you!" "You see!" Tipping into each other, we held eye contact like longtime friends, my hand warmed at her waist.

"Susanna's eight years younger than me," she told Dean at the table, pointing at my face.

"Where were you eight years ago?" I said.

How did you get here, build this?

"In New York and married." She smiled at her husband. "But not to you." She'd already been in one marriage, had worked in the city, thrived but in another way. The history startled me, put in place, then discarded. I didn't really want to hear. When my mother talked about London in the '60s I'd feel the same: I hadn't existed yet, so forget then. Now, now, Debra was *this,* what she'd always been meant for and what I counted on her to be. We'd been waiting to come together.

My job ended. I had to leave Sag Harbor, clearing my effects from the office where I'd slept four nights a week for most of a year. I dropped off the key at my boss's carriage house. Across the gravel his main house loomed, the taunt of sudden money. I drove to Debra's, where we stood in the driveway in tears, the little girl on Debra's hip, her hands grabbing at my hair and at her mother's. We vowed to make the effort, knowing it would be difficult. For a short while I lived on Cape Cod, where a monumental blizzard that winter affected us equally. Before phone service went out, she reeled off the news, the halted plows adrift, the streets erased under snows, and I missed those streets. Then I met Christopher and went to live in Montana, she got down to writing a novel, Dean's practice thrived. We kept up, sometimes a frantic e-mail exchange over a whole day, sometimes a single, knowing line. I missed her with an intensity I couldn't convey to Christopher, who'd met her twice — not enough to *know* Debra as I felt her, the delicious daily companion but something else, too, her competent vibration. Our calls became shorter, the time between them longer.

The last visit I made to her, I'd taken the bus from New York out to the Hamptons, Daniel a toddler in my arms, board books all the way, one after the other. My lap was dark with his pee as we climbed down the bus stairs. Debra, leaning against her car across the street, laughed to notice the damp and ran over, delighted, kissed Daniel. At her house she washed my pants. She fished through a couple of deep baskets in the laundry room, plucked out a Patagonia hat that her daughter had outgrown and put it on my boy's head. "There! Perfect!" I felt his anointment. She wore sheepskin scuff slippers, so now I wanted a pair. "Where'd you get those?" I asked. She wore thin sweatpants in dark crimson, chic somehow, and when she leaned low to retrieve a bowl

181

from a cabinet, a line of colored lace and mesh was revealed against her skin. She stirred everything in me, made me whole and happy, though I could not have said why.

"Are you wearing a *thong*?"

"I know! Thongs, *right*? But you *have* to trust me. They are fabulous, the most comfortable thing ever."

She showed me her workspace, a desk that hadn't been there the last time, where she sat every dark morning and wrote for two hours before her daughter woke. I did that, too. She told me about the novel and the agent who'd sold it based on the proposal, what good friends they were. I didn't have an agent. She had a new fiery purpose, which made her more luscious, yet it distracted her. She listed trade details with the confidence of someone already sick of them. Her attention wasn't the same, when it had been on me, and mine was also different. My son's curls were visible in the sun as he bobbed around her backyard, and I watched him through the open glass door as he followed her much bigger daughter. I said, "Oh, wow," and "That's great," and tried to offer pure support, but I was flooded with the old news from her kitchen, the old wanting of everything she liked and bought. I badly wanted her to be as I'd left her, and at the same time I wished to be home in Missoula, where I had a clock like hers on the kitchen wall, where I had thrown catalogs into a basket by the back door, because Debra did that and it made me happy to evoke her, though I didn't look at the catalogs, never ordered from them. She took me up to her room and went through her closets. She gave me an expensive V-neck she didn't wear anymore, clingy and dark green. She let me try her M•A•C lipsticks. "Viva Glam, that's it," she said. "Everyone needs at least one Viva Glam." We walked with the kids into town, the slow, distracted bumble, where we went inside her favorite shop and she tried to talk me into buying the thongs, exorbitant trifles. I couldn't afford them. Daniel and I slept in her daughter's bunk bed, me on the upper in whimsical sheets, patterned with the alphabet. In the morning I said, "Where do you get these?" and planned to buy them for my house, my son. Always, the two children were everywhere between us, and she threw open cabinets, made us food. It was hard to keep a thought going.

When she was stuck in her novel, she phoned and asked if I'd help her. This thrilled me, and the heavy packet appeared the next day. I read with a pen in hand and ticked and drew arrows, rallying my best thinking for her. I sent back the manuscript, and a week later another padded envelope arrived, pink and purple tissue paper festive inside, and I pulled out five pairs of the expensive underwear, Debra's glamour and élan. The next time I was in New York, I happened to pass a boutique that sold them, and I went in and bought myself two more pairs, the cost on the receipt tribute to Debra's big ways, her unchecked permissions.

One day I noticed we hadn't spoken in months, and I left a message. We needed to recalibrate an imbalance. No response. I left a few more. After several days Debra called and in a tight, odd voice that contained no echo of our intimacy, said, "I'm going through something and I have to disappear and you have to trust me." I hadn't the faintest idea what she meant. I pondered her words, scanning for a break in her womanly code.

We arranged to meet in Sun Valley, the mutual particulars of schedule and travel coinciding for a long weekend, our two families together. We hadn't seen each other in five or six years, which didn't matter, really, in parent time. We each knew without hearing how the other spent her time, what the back of the other's car looked like, how weekends were ruled by soccer games or recitals or school fund-raisers. Her family got to the condo late. I'd waited up, and I leapt for her as they came in tired, their many bags bulked in the entry. I pressed forward to grab her, shoulders the same, the soft black sweater under my touch. "God, at last!" we were saying and rocked together, the stored excitement out. "Oh my God, I've missed you." In the morning, we drank coffee and built a fire. Dylan — that baby — was fourteen, knees and legs, and long hair coiled up in a stretchy head-band. She kept her earphones in and left uneaten bagel on the kitchen counter. I'd seen her sprawled in the center of Debra and Dean's bed. I knocked, and Debra called, "Come in!" She stood midroom, said, "We're doing this face peel!" The mask made a green plastery skin on them both, and Dylan sat with one long loose leg over the side of the bed, stroking green varnish onto her nails. The bed was a littering of vampire paperbacks, CD jewel cases. They were talking at the same time, stumbling over their amusement. Debra tapped the cake on her face, handed her daughter a washcloth so Dylan could wipe hers off. "There's still some on your neck," her mother said. To me she said, "You have to try this, do you know Lush?" I couldn't help making a note of it.

They jostled each other, picked sweaters out of open suitcases and threw them back, tossed shoes around. Debra went in and out of the bathroom, they didn't bother with whole sentences. "But, Mom, *Mom! Listen,*" thoughts bursting as half phrases. "It was this *awful —*" "I told you," and Debra looked over at me to let me into the conversation, but I didn't want in. I hovered like someone waiting for a tip. She was alight with intense love for another girl, another devotee. It's her *daughter,* I thought, but in me it surged: not fair. The bottomless wanting and no woman to answer it. I knew to get out of there, and closed the door.

We left Dylan in charge of the kids, and the two couples went to a restaurant. I'd just published an essay in a magazine, and I was telling them about assignments, the sudden splurge of an awakened identity. I was proud to share this with Debra, to follow her.

"Why can't I have that?" she asked Dean. "That's the career I want."

"You had that," he said. "Now you're doing something else."

"Look at you guys," I said. "You're so together." My husband and I were barely interested in the other one, except in our united daily persuasion of our children.

"It comes back," said Debra. "I know you can't believe me right now, but it really does, and *you'll have lunches* together, long talks again, when both your kids are in school." She gave me a look: the sex. "It's so much better."

"It's true," Dean said.

If Debra said it, I believed it. If Debra had it, I'd wait for it.

I kept wanting to ask about her disappearance, that weird halt in our connection, when she'd suspended our contact. Had this figured in their cozy renewal? I thought I'd wait till we had privacy, but her splendid chattering, her bubbling, never waned. There was no chance, and when I imagined what truth I might hear, I found I didn't want to learn.

The next day she and I planned to go to the thrift shop I'd told her about, for the cashmere sweaters and couture coats cast off by last season's wealthy skiers. Dylan wanted to come. "This is great," Debra whispered. "She hardly ever wants to do things with me anymore." In a clumsy row the three of us walked into town. The girl had been lovable strapped into her high chair, unable to join our talk, but now her silence commanded us, her mother trying to undo it with bright questions.

At the thrift shop, Debra pulled things off the rack for her daughter, and Dylan sorted through clothes for her mother. Each with an armload, they went behind a curtain, sharing the tight space and narrow mirror of the stall. I heard Debra exclaim, Dylan object, the giggling. Her ankles flashed and disappeared and reemerged as she pulled on white jeans, ski pants, velvet trousers, kicked them off again. Not those, oh, that's nice, let's get that! I waited in a wicker chair, clothes on my lap.

Debra's hand, the wedding band, appeared at the top of the curtain, grasping the rings to move it aside, and as she started to back out I saw them caught facing the mirror as one body, one in front of the other. It was over, Debra undone from me, outgrown. She had a daughter to wear her skin creams and earrings; she would not enclose me again with devoted attention, and I was worn out with forcing my ruin and longing upon woman after woman.

Debra and I never shared real life, not for a

minute. In Sag Harbor, I had acted a village role, a temporary assignment. She drove into the city once, and we had an elegant lunch in midtown, but she'd come to the restaurant from somewhere, and had to be off again straight after. She never saw my apartment. We didn't even walk a block. We didn't share quite the same era, my eight-year lag part of our security. And when it came down to it I didn't care what had prompted her weird, sudden silence. Her hugeness happened not with me but inside me. For a time we used the phone, and we had the one resort weekend. At the end of that visit we told each other how much it had meant, what a good and necessary next step this was, onward, but it was not that. It showed us the way out, opened the late-night door at the end of the party for the good-byes. We didn't say the good-byes. No one would have.

Two months later, success came to me and upended normal life. I gathered my closest friends on the front lawn for impromptu champagne, then over the next few days phoned others far away, but I could not call Debra. This news, I sensed, would not fall easily into place. "She'll hear about it," I thought. "She'll call." She didn't. Months of a silent friend became a year, which, I re-

189

alized, didn't feel exactly bad, a recognition — mutual perhaps — that Sun Valley had been our finish. I'd check in with her, I decided, when I was done writing the book, but I didn't do it, held back by nervousness and unsure which of us was waiting for whom. A year later my name appeared in the *Times*. I could picture Debra's oversize kitchen table in noble, seasoned oak, Dylan gone to school, the empty, pleasing house. I pictured the white cup, Debra with black coffee as she sat to look through the paper, and she would have turned the page and seen my picture. Maybe she didn't recognize me at first, the publicity photo a structured fake, but at the sight of my name she might have made a sound, felt glad. Wouldn't she call? I imagined the paper spread open all day, set out for Dean to see when he got home.

So much time has gone by that for me to call her, or for her to call me, would signal a dead child or a divorce, rock-bottom emergency. It would sharpen focus on the finish of our friendship, embarrass us. Who wants to explain? Simply, we do not know each other. The friendship fluttered heartily, then diminished, then stopped. I wear her V-neck top, prize her unique crackle, prettiness, talent, breathy confidence, womanly chic and charisma and the smooth appearance that she knew what she was doing, but Debra herself only echoes. I still contemplate the gap, those cold, dropped months when I had no access to her mysteries. The friendship shines but stays put. That's different than missing her. I doubt she misses me. There's no evidence to say she does.

Nina wrought a petite medallion out of gold, stamped with *40* in her strong, antique hand. "Wait, you made this?" I said on the phone, as I examined the minuscule perfections. She said, "I make one for each of my women friends when she turns forty." I was touched and grateful. Her bounties came in these unexpected ways, always meticulous, her talents upon talents private until she decided to reveal them. It was hard to turn the focus to her. I thought that's what we shared, a deep certainty that someone's interest might be a trick. We both knew how to make others feel entirely special. I wore the tiny disk the whole year, proclamation on a short chain, the precious metal in the dip of my throat.

We weren't yet friends when I left New York in 1993, and it was distance that sponsored us. She had just married someone in my social crew. He'd met her beyond our bounds, and they went one afternoon to City Hall, announced it to us later. She unsettled the rest of us, her careful regard, the imperious flavor in her brisk voice. Did she like us? Would we ever know? Her fine hair angled close to the back of her neck, cut boy-short. Nina had pared herself to bare elements: shades of black against white T-shirts, square-toed black shoes, clean jewelry. She used no makeup. Absent adornment, her naked strength shone through. She had a sleek portfolio, the flat canvas strap across the front of her plain, smooth T-shirt. You could tell the cotton was excellent.

We were immersed in the toughest sort of fairy tale, daughters in a bind. We knew the term *stepmother* was a stand-in, an excuse to prevent *mother,* aloud. That word made us shiver, teeth gritted. But Nina and I didn't back down. We said "mother," tasted bile. When I visited New York I met Nina in small dark restaurants, midafternoon, her freelancer's schedule convenient for both of us. We had miso soup or salads of cabbage and cucumber, white vinegar. Aware of the midnight strike on our time when I'd disappear back to Montana, we sped through talk, cramming in as much as possible. We sifted the rubble of our relationships with our mothers. What we both wished of our mothers was to leave them. You have no idea how much this mattered, our solemn admission, the assured company in case we ever did it.

We noticed the parallels in our marriages — the forceful and decided women in charge, our quiet husbands, gentler than we were, gentler than most people we knew. We needed them, and they really needed us. It was nice to find a woman who felt burdened as I did by her own extroverted behavior and vivid personality, by her own compulsion to manage. We congratulated each other on how we made life work for the husbands. We chose the off-white paint (Benjamin Moore, Nina advised), we took the sick animal in, our relationship with the vet already secure, cultivated with care. We sent back steaks that were overdone.

She and her husband came to Missoula. It meant a lot. Few of my New York friends had bothered. They arrived by car, goofy and happy with the time they'd granted themselves for a cross-country trip. It was delightful to see her like this, a bit of the urban carapace abandoned. Or, rather, intentionally set aside. We made them dinner, showed them into the guest room, took them out the next day to the one Indian restaurant, at last in the company of someone who could say with me, But it's not *really* Indian food.

She lived in Chinatown, adroit at navigating the sloppy fish markets, ice loose on the pavement. She hurried, chin forward, her fast stride fixed. She organized us all when I was defeated by fatigue, picked Pho Viet Huong on Mulberry Street, told us what time. Her husband would come from work, our old friend Rob from Brooklyn, sometimes with his wife. I arrived from the Upper West Side with Daniel, three years old, whom Nina adored. She ordered from the large pages taped to the wall-size mirrors, tremulous hand-written English beneath Vietnamese characters, seasonal fish, seasonal pea vines I'd never heard of. We ate the exquisite salt-and-pepper soft-shell crab. She knew to move the water glass out of Daniel's realm, and she played with his little plastic panda on the table. Daniel explained himself to her, and she looked over to beam at me. Nina was my smart, close, calm family, as if we could erase the true histories and organize elements as we wanted them. We conspired in reinvention.

Nina trusted herself but not others. I knew the burden of impossible standards, also felt narcotic relief at being the expert organizer, the self-reliant worker, the responsible one. I imagined we had turned that similarity into intimacy, and into an affectionate in-joke. Once we were talking about sheets. They have to match, they *have to,* we both said, and recognized perfectionist allegiance. When I make the bed, the white tones in the quality cotton pleasing me, the corners secured under the weight of the mattress, and the turn-down snapped, I always want to call her to share the satisfactions.

Nina and I broke up once, before we did finally. The first time, we laid it all out, swept the record clean, promised. We were professional about it. She inspired this in me. When I'd needed order in the most desperate way, from the slump of new motherhood and baby shit, rank trash, she was a clean corner. Although I couldn't find my clothes and hadn't had a haircut in months, I could dress up my voice on the phone for her, sharpen my delivery.

Then, while I was writing my book, we'd

had a long quiet. Almost finished, I felt the return to regular life nearing, and I called, hungry for one of our hourlong talks, wanting to say, "I'm back." Able to cover vast ground, Nina and I could never talk briefly.

She was cool, strained exchange. Terms had altered, but I couldn't tell why.

"What's going on?" I said.

She sighed. "You're the one who benefits from the friendship." She said she was tired of it. This news scared me.

"I try to pay attention to you, you don't let me." I sounded like a baby. "You deflect," I said. She agreed. Nina was very good at turning the eye from herself, our joint focus on me, and she'd always known, gently, that this made me nervous. She knew as well as I did the fearsome power in the word *self-ish,* had lived a childhood in its cold shadow, but she used to reassure me that she liked our fast-talking energy on me and my life.

I said, "*Nina,* you must know you're incredibly important to me." A voice in my head demanded, *prove it.* "You know that, don't you know that?" I wrote her a letter, wanted to make it up to her. Just tell me how. I steadied my hand on the paper, trying to keep my inked lines as elegant as hers. Things were okay for a while.

197

■ ■ ■ ■

She was pleased to provide and laid out my former city in 'well-chosen strokes to feed my homesick longing. She sent surprising presents. A PalmPilot, still with its casings and plastics and immaculate box, although she'd used it for a year. Her stylish wrapping jobs, the confidence of understatement, were legendary, butcher paper and a vintage-looking label she'd designed herself. When Jack was born I asked her to design his birth announcement, and she made a card of superb beauty — strong flourishes, clean lines, gravity and simplicity, conscious she addressed a holy task. She Fed-Exed the art to me with instructions for the printer, recommendations for the card stock color and weight. Once she sent a huge package for Chinese New Year, a dragon-head mask to delight the boys, tiny firecrackers, weird candies, red envelopes with money. She brushed off thanks.

In her loft I admired the sculpted brushed-chrome magnets from MoMA and the silver chairs from Design Within Reach. She'd had her dresser made — she knew what she wanted it to look like, sketched it precisely, had it constructed and installed in the bedroom. She brought the vision into being. Shape beauty, she dared me, whatever you want.

We had unused French in common, excellent accents. For work Nina traveled to Russia, Holland, Iceland. I drank up details of her travel. We said we'd go to Paris when the boys were bigger. Let's wait till Jack is three. She wanted to be with my children, and I was grateful, as I felt trapped, the world closing down. She was kind to me then, considerate and patient. She sent me a book about visiting Paris with children, wrapped with her precisions. We had that conversation when Jack was six months old, and three felt impossible. It was a spring day in 2001, which I remember because by October travel seemed never-again. We never did go.

On the morning of September 11, Nina went up on her roof, for some other reason, and was standing there. Then from her distance of eight or ten blocks away, she kept watching, standing. I imagine her stone-still, her designing, elegant mind stilled. I reached her that night, going through the frantic list, finding every New

York friend. "Are you okay? Where were you? Are you okay?" I had monitored a dozen strange temperatures. In our brief talk I felt ice in our exchange, trauma's slur. I couldn't grasp what she needed to convey. This was the beginning, I think, where we started to break down. Bigger than us, of course I see that, but I failed her. After that, she was less and less a part of her neighborhood, until she'd had enough of the acrid air and the snapped phone service, the chemical tang, and the central, inescapable toxic memory; and they moved to Brooklyn.

I guess the end of us is marked — *40.* The tiny gold medal I wore the whole year we were at our closest is in with my other jewelry. I'm forty-seven. That's a long time to not be friends, to be unsure of the mistakes and what I failed to fix, to wish I knew. I left my mother, broke our bond. Nina grew polite with me, didn't want the details, and after I published the book about it I never heard from her. I try to sort through the pieces. In her strength and command I didn't see fragility, thought that was only mine. It never occurred to me the elegant friendship could end in shards.

KINDLING

It isn't easy, in a small town, to not know people anymore. You must rely on external forces or drastic change. Christopher was the one to tell me that Claire was moving away. He'd seen her at Food Farm. "Somewhere in Oregon, I don't remember," he said, as relief softened the hurt I still felt at the sound of her name. I was glad — no more vigilance in certain neighborhoods, no more heartsickness at certain cross streets. I felt freed.

Claire's reasons for ending us made no sense to me. They mattered hugely, but I was unaware. At the start we had shopped for groceries together, exchanged baby clothes, shared late-night calls, her voice a smooth and constant comfort. We went for walks with the strollers when neither of us could stand our babies' faces another instant. Our husbands disappointed us, our sons filled us with the deepest awe. We shared tales of the ravaging parents we'd fled, and we lived six blocks apart. Everything a friendship needed for kindling and fuel was there.

I met Claire at a playgroup. I hadn't felt like going, but forced myself and the baby out of the house, anxious to escape the tedium. The group met in the daylight basement of a nonprofit that helped struggling parents, teaching life skills, providing phone numbers for social assistance agencies, poison control, day care facilities. I came in and then found myself on the floor on my knees, unzipping my son's coat, unlacing his boots. I never got my own coat off, disrupted by his wants — another toy, another cracker, another easing through life's strange currents. All the currents were new to him, and he made them new to me.

Aware of the other mothers as unique piles of fatigue, I settled against the wall. We made a ring around our babies, who grabbed and lurched and startled each other. It was almost funny, but we were all too watchful to laugh. A woman managed her toddler with an extended hand as her other arm cradled a newborn. I was horrified to see a fresh baby, then grateful. How far I'd come in a year. One boy was dressed in striped overalls and work boots, just like

Daniel, but his step was surer, his grasp more refined. I looked around to pick out the mother who had chosen for her boy the same clothes I had that morning. Such awareness provided solace in the otherwise numb endeavor of slaving for someone else. Her thick ponytail sat low on her neck, her face long and pinched with sleeplessness. She kept her eyes on her boy, spoke to him in short intervals, "Robby. What do you have, Robby? Do you need me to undo that?" I sensed her competence. Well, that's not true. Everyone seemed better at this than I felt, and I credited each woman with proficiency. I hated them all, fought the club, and needed them desperately.

At the group the following week, choosing the spot beside her, I learned Claire's name. She'd lived here a year. I could smell aggressive laundry soap, proper care. We discovered we lived not far apart, and, one day soon after, we took our boys and a picnic to Rose Park, where hardly anybody went. It was always windy there, and as we sat face-to-face on the bench, we had to speak up and push hair back from our eyes and mouths. We weren't comfortable, but we stayed. A few yards from us the boys found things to do. Usually, when I said I was sick of my difficult mother, friends wanted to talk me out of it, but Claire told me she'd severed contact with her family, that was the way, to preserve herself, to forge her life, to save her son. I think you'll understand, she said. She told me her secret, something only her husband knew and that I was never to tell. I promised, solemn with the gift of confidence. I'd found a way in with this strained, sober young woman. We'd made a sacred bond, if scarred.

She came to my house, or I went to hers, establishing the easy exchange that would define our friendship, our lives as mothers. We still regarded the word *mother* as outside of ourselves, a dubious costume. Her house was tidy and tucked, like an unopened file cabinet. Clothes hung on hangers, compared to my baskets of ignored T-shirts, towels, and pajamas. The wall showed a series of trains Claire had painted, very nicely, and I wished I'd painted something for Daniel, although I didn't paint. We sat on the floor. Daniel seemed to like Robby, so I would like Robby. The boys batted pieces of train track around, sometimes linking up, more often not. Parallel play. One of those terms, we agreed, we never used to know. We described our husbands, joking without mirth at the mess our marriages had become. We were coming to understand how helpless we were in this new age.

We both worked, and we both split parenting duties with the husbands, the child always with one parent or the other. Claire and I were not able to relinquish our sons to the peculiar influences of other children or to the hidden histories of unknown adults, their oblivious violations. We hardly saw the men, felt married to each other. It's odd I can't remember Claire's exact schedule, as if some once crucial information of my own has been erased, my middle name, my childhood address. I still feel her, remember her thereness and necessity, and how much I liked her for her woe and frankness, and then loved her. Obviously, she would have other things to say about the friendship. In the slow afternoons we'd relate the tiny dramas of vaccinations and rough nurses, or speculate on those rotten mothers who ignored the explicit instructions about car seats. We went to Target for diapers and cereal, one cart, the babies strapped in side by side, making us laugh as their phrases and random expressions interlaced. At the fabric store, we sorted through the discount flannels to sew into baby quilts. We took the boys to China Buffet, grateful for the foods under the heat lamps. The babies could toss rice on the carpet, handle sticky dumplings. So tired, we didn't care about additives and too much sugar; we wouldn't have to clean it up, expend our waning strength. She knew Daniel had to avoid eggs and corn, and I worried on our outings about the dogs that scared Robby. We measured daytimes in minutes, nap durations, radio schedules. If Daniel woke at 2:30, it was too early to call Claire for a walk and I'd have to wait. At 3:00 we met, our soft hellos, our automatic, repeated walking circle of the neighborhood, the shared minutiae all that distinguished that day from the mess of days before. At five-ish, one of us might say, "What's in your fridge? Want to come over with the boy? I've got salad, I've got some ham." She called both of our sons "the boy," and I loved that and did the same.

Claire brought me a chocolate cake one birthday, granting the day's single moment that observed me instead of my child. How flattered and thankful I felt. She brought pumpkins over for the boys to carve at the kitchen table and showed me what to do with the knife. Each week Claire, who'd signed up for a food subsidy, received so many eggs and so much milk, she would make giant pans of flan, two at a time, and bring one to us. My husband didn't like custard, so it was all for me, gorgeous with burnished caramel.

Once or twice, after the boys' bedtimes, Claire and I went to the movies, but we always came straight home after, our time economized for the sake of the families we were building. We took that seriously, a reverent calling. Good night, thank you, she'd say climbing out of the car, See you tomorrow. We'd never met in a downtown bar for drinks, we'd never caroused through the jewelry displays at the mall. We had not done anything silly.

For Daniel's second birthday, Robby was the guest, chaperoned by Claire and her husband. The six of us gathered in the living room. The parents made the usual remarks of relief that we'd escaped our original families, come all this way, lucked into one another. It was always like this with them and us, quiet anemic parties, attempts at family, but Claire and I were getting used to it. It was the best we could do, and she knew that about me, and I knew that about her. She gave Daniel a wooden stool she had painted with beautiful blues and stars. Around me, I held the love close, of my husband, child, and indispensable friend.

■ ■ ■ ■

With the boys almost three, Claire and I talked about whether or not we'd have second children. What did the husbands want, we wondered, sort of. We debated the advantages. I began to be certain I'd do it, didn't reveal that, and I didn't mention to her I'd started trying. That was between me and Christopher. When I told her I was pregnant I felt her careful withdrawal. She called me less, and she mentioned another friend. They went to the fabric store. If the situation had been reversed, Claire pregnant instead, and without me, I would have felt abandoned, and maybe she felt that. I don't know what she felt. She came to the hospital after I delivered, happy for me, and she cradled Jack, six hours old, smiling down at him. She seemed less herself, but I was blinded from labor and sudden baby, and everyone besides him was dimmer.

We went away together once, us and the boys and not the husbands. Without overseeing their paternal attempts, our unconscious surveillance, we could breathe and loosen. United in thrift, we picked a cheap cabin a couple of hours away. I almost remember us doing this, but those amnesia years swallow the particulars, and I can't picture my friend in the morning, her hair undone, her voice still low. I cannot picture the rings on her hand or her favorite mug for coffee, or remember if she drank coffee. We knew so much, reaching into each other's lives by the handful, but never like sisters, never for fun and cheer. The friendship existed to save the mothers.

By the time Daniel and Robby were five, our shared life had unhooked, one hook at a time. The boys attended different schools, and our schedules had changed, new routines and new jobs. Claire wore white fitted tops and crisp skirts, her time no longer spent on the kitchen floor or a basement rug. Her family went on vacations, and sometimes I wouldn't hear from her for a week after she got back, each of us respectively busy. But I didn't miss her. I knew I had her.

Just before Daniel's sixth birthday party we had a lunch date, the rare two of us. Jack was at day care, Daniel was in school, and I was in a good mood, released. We met where we often had when Daniel and Robby were little, at the Catalyst, which kept high chairs and a milk crate full of dinosaurs, where the staff never protested the time we'd taken to linger, the request to replace a dropped spoon. We'd gone there when Jack was nursing, a calm place to keep the baby calm, and she'd held him so I could butter my bread, spoon up my soup while it was hot. Today I was talking about the party. I'd rented the carousel, and Daniel had chosen a few kids from first grade to come and Robby, of course, his main friend. She could drop the boy off, I said. Can you believe it, she said, that we can actually drop them off now? I couldn't believe it. We didn't need to monitor our sons' experience all the time, guide their way. We watched out for less, had pardoned more of the world by then, forgiveness our slow, uneasy work. Through lunch Claire detailed ways she was reconsidering her parents, thoughts flying. She was launching into new territory, which included a fresh recognition of her strengths, which had always been obvious to me. I remember feeling excited. She had done hard work, faced so much. We were light.

We hugged good-bye. A few steps away, I remembered tickets for a play and called out the invitation. Great, she said, also walking away, pulling her keys from her bag. Pick you up Tuesday, I said.

A day later her e-mail came.

I can't be friends with you anymore, it said.

You shit on everything important to me, it said.

I could feel the water I'd just sipped run into my gut and spin. Everything grew huge, a carnival of mistake. There was more, a litany of my faults and falseness, and that first hour I reread the note countless times, trying to build sense out of it, connect her words with the reality I had presumed we shared at lunch one day ago. Yesterday. I had to read again, because shock kept snapping the thread of a sentence. I phoned and left a message. Please call me, please. We can talk about this, I said. I left another message. What about the lunch? Why didn't you say this at lunch?

But she wouldn't return my calls. Another e-mail followed a few days later, declaring finality. She wiped me from her life. I felt nauseous all the time, and crazy, and doomed. How had I failed at this, at her, failed so utterly? Was I really as callous and arrogant as she said? She would have nothing to do with me.

On the afternoon of the birthday party I constantly checked the carousel entrance, looking to see if Robby had arrived, predicting she'd have her husband drop him off. But Robby didn't come. That friendship, it seemed, was also over. Daniel didn't register it, young enough to slide affections around. It hadn't occurred to me that she would pull her son away, yet I allowed for relief. A few summers earlier, on a day of appalling heat, we had walked our boys down to the river, setting out towels on a spit of gravel near a shallow side channel. Naked, the boys ran into the water and climbed on the fallen logs and rocks. "My penis is bigger than yours," Robby told Daniel, and there was a wicked streak in his voice that I wanted to shield my child from. How dare you, I thought. How dare you, you little shit. But we laughed about it, Claire and I. Hadn't I listened to her calm, measured voice as she bade her child be nice? What had we forgotten to do?

So our friendship ended. We were severed. In the wake of her decision I couldn't draw a deep breath. It undid me, like losing love in my twenties — when one man could pronounce his word — but worse. How could I know us and she know some other us? I reread the two letters, my only pieces of her new plan, trying to martial any hints into a reasonable argument. I cried all the time and kept saying to Christopher, "This makes no sense." I had never liked the bearded irises that grew ominously tall in the shade of her house. We'd sit beside the plastic pool watching the babies, as the flowers bloomed looking already spent, waving their decay around. I think I'd used that word once, *decay*. Was that it? Had I offended her like that? Her flowers? "Susanna," Christopher said, "It's not the *irises*." I called up other friends and demanded they describe me. I walked myself back through each memory, as many conversations as I could, searching the most recent months for the rupture she'd known was coming. The Susanna she described was not me, was not even a part of me. A few weeks before the lunch, I'd written Claire a reference letter, and now she told me I blocked her progress at every turn. I had championed her, admired her artistry, appreciated her cakes, and now she described me as competitive and condescending. Her version of me was a terrible thing, a chill slinking creature that made its way into my head and settled. I no longer had Claire for a friend, but I had the me Claire jilted, and we kept each other mean company.

Christopher and I were in the middle of buying a house, and in the initial excitements and anxieties, I missed my good friend, missed sharing. I missed her eye as I regarded the antique mullions of the windows, I missed her kind, practical help as I scrambled for child care on the day of the closing. I wished I could show her the stove's fanciness that overwhelmed me, confess I felt I didn't deserve it. I missed her as I set up my desk in a sunny corner, wanted her to know where I'd be working, how perfect. I had to remind myself that we weren't friends. It was difficult to learn.

I dreamt of Claire for months, grief's debate, and I saw her everywhere, the popular profile of her car a small terror. Sometimes, thinking she stood a ways off on the sidewalk, my heart would lunge, and I'd fill with the hope I could put things right and guide us to our normal place. Sometimes, a cold dread sank me, and I wanted to hide, to outrun the inevitable encounter. But there was no encounter. Once, attending a concert, I glimpsed her forehead, her hairline, in a crowd. Yes, there was her husband. The lobby mass shifted, and I caught sight of the whole of Claire's face, bright with discussion, almost unreadable: I had never seen her happy.

A few months later I received a note. "I'm finding it impossible to stay mad at you. I heard you bought a house. I'd love to come see it." But this was too late. I had been wrenched and remade by her rejection. I couldn't risk my reality overtaken by another whim. She couldn't undo this. We were no more.

When Daniel was in eighth grade, I had to go to the high school with him one morning for an early orientation. Amidst a swarm of kids and parents, he and I were locking our bikes outside when a calm family sailed past us. First the father, then the mother said a warm hello, their teenager between them, taller. Hello, I said, the ready smile of small-town errands, a gracious reflex. Then, in the next empty minute, the gnaw of the forgotten in my brain, I realized that the mother was Claire. She'd moved back to town without my hearing of it, and, transformed by time or maturity or both, she was no longer someone I recognized.

■ ■ ■ ■

Awake.

■ ■ ■ ■

WE TURN INTO MOTHERS

I know people whose social lives continue twenty years on from their senior-year dorm suites, who keep up with intimates and every lesser acquaintance, attend any wedding, people who gather with family, campmates, high school exes. They look forward to reuniting, plan summers. They depend on the traded favors of past times. I never did any of these. Either it took work when I was already taxed, or I'd abandoned the version of myself old friends expected, or I'd cultivated new interior landscapes where these people could not fit. So I have just one friend from college, Rachel. We met when I was a freshman, eager with new starts, and she was a senior. Incredible to me, we've lasted and lasted. We became friends who had a past together. Old friends. Also incredible — we have foundered now, our roles much changed, our grip unsteady.

The day I met Rachel I'd arrived early for

the first session of a writing class. Everyone was excited and talkative, as we'd all been chosen for this workshop. One woman was already seated, hunched over her neat white paper. Her hair curtained her expression. The rest of us stood around until the teacher came and made his chair known, and then we picked the spots that advertised our characters — shy, ambitious, arrogant, self-assured, afraid. I chose a seat across from the woman with the hair — Rachel — and watched her slide her fingers over one strand after another, a nervous repeat. I was attracted to idiosyncrasy, understood it had invisible origins.

After the teacher's credo and the introductions, Rachel, never looking up, pierced other writers' work with self-effacing wit. Her own work was beautiful and surprising. Over the weeks, she and I came to talking, a few words, a few paces together out of the building and down the steps before we parted. She wore suede gloves and a coat with a raft of shoulder pads, hem to her ankles. She aligned the buttons and fastened them before she stepped outside. I never saw her hurry.

One day, as someone read aloud, we made eye contact, then looked away, careful not to trigger indiscretion we couldn't take back. Class over, I suggested lunch, and she said, "Well," a reluctance in her voice that spread nervousness in front of us, like an open newspaper. I thought she was worried about other commitments, exams, et cetera. "Come on," I said. "Half an hour." We went to the dining hall that served falafel. When I lifted the pita, as we assessed the good writing and the mediocre, it fell apart, sauce soaking through. I rolled up strips of bread with sprouts and chickpea crumbs, and the sauce slid down my fingers. Rachel ate in discreet bites, no mess, considerable food left behind on her plate.

Within a few weeks, she was essential. Racing around together on the T, she showed me Cambridge, poetry bookstores, shops for vintage clothes. We made up stories about strangers, about ourselves. We ventured to Boston, ordered half carafes of wine late night in the North End, brought home cannolis from Mike's Pastries. Movies starring Barbra Streisand or Prince bred in-jokes that lasted for months. It was the happiest sort of time. I invited her to come with me to the empty house on the Cape, long in my family. My gentle grandmother had spent each summer there since the early 1950s; and for six midsummer weeks, barefoot, bathing-suited, my sister and I would live with my father in a house across the street, which my grandmother had bought for that purpose. That house was gone, my father having sold it within months of inheriting it, as if a sentimental stink might dog him. Or he just needed the money. The structure still stood but had been turned into an expensive B and B. My grandmother's house, though, was preserved, maintained by her responsible daughter, who rarely used it. I explained all this on the drive our first time out there together.

Rachel gaped at the opulence I was used to as we entered the house, thin gray handle on the screen door a known happiness in my fingers. We came into the lemon-oiled dining room, delicately crammed with grandfather clock, nineteenth-century breakfront, Windsor chairs. Rachel touched the brass candelabras fit with white-wicked ivory tapers, turned the cut-crystal decanters my grandmother had been handed by her decorator. In silver dishes on the sideboard, mussel shells showed their mother-of-pearl and pinecones gave off their ancient air. We both loved old-fashioned beauty. We both loved the enormous pink roses woven into the black carpet. Rachel asked, What's this, what did I think of the ornate barometer, the antique sextant, the series of oil portraits? "Are these your relatives?" They weren't, but they fit the house.

On the dunes, wind pounding us, the gray sea stretching out, she let her voice grow loud, surprised at herself, then breathless back in the car. And she loved the late-afternoon return to the enclosure of the guest bedroom, where I'd given her the four-poster bed, the pink coverlet and pink pillowcases, silky with three decades' care. Happiness became her, although it did not seem to come easily. We made fires, we made hot milk with nutmeg, added teaspoons of Kahlúa as if we were breaking rules. She thanked me for weeks after we got back to school.

As if flirting, I coaxed her closer, and she didn't resist or disapprove, granting me room to behave as I liked. We couldn't have been more different. I admired her ladylike deliberations and composure, the faux-Victorian drop earrings, the impeccable white of her blouse, and she seemed to enjoy my assault on her primness, as I flaunted a wickedness she wouldn't allow herself. I did or did not write my papers, didn't turn things in on time, skipped consecutive days of physics class. I was dating Jason, a happy, vigorous sort of business. We made love everywhere, in the back office of the radio station, in the basement of the library, met at lunchtime in his central-campus room, in my room after midnight. I told details to Rachel, scandalizing her, thinking vulgar delight was a tonic. She could use frankness! As we passed the library, for instance, I'd give it an exaggerated glance, and she'd stammer, crack up. "I can't believe you, Susanna. On the *floor*?" I wanted a trade. Come out with your mysteries, I thought, waited. Now tell *me*. I told her of the affair in high school with my married teacher. Now what about *you*? I wanted to know what made her go quiet, what accounted for the tics. But the more I revealed, the sharper, cruder, worse behaved I was, the more detailed her questions of me. I flourished with her interest and kept talking, as she retreated further, donning that fine invisible mesh of the attentive observer. Whatever it was I wanted of Rachel she could not release. Not every friend has to say everything, know everything, I told myself. I calmed. What we did best together was give Susanna the stage she craved. Rachel did not fight me for the spotlight.

To escape phys ed, I'd signed up for ballroom dance, and I convinced Rachel to join me. "You can be the girl," I promised. I grabbed around her waist. She gave in, pulling back her body, also smiling at my plea. "Okay, okay." We surprised ourselves that we were good at this, because I was not graceful and she wasn't athletic, but in each other's arms, crucial complement, we were terrific. The opening bars of "In the Mood" made their permanent groove in my brain, carved muscle memory, and I still feel my fingers curve around Rachel's hand as she set it in mine. The third week the teacher told everyone else, "Watch *them.*" We grinned, arms lifted, and ate up the room with our fox-trot, then our waltz.

For Thanksgiving, Rachel took me home to Connecticut; my Honda, my gunned gear shifts, her hand rising to the dash now and then. We played a Woody Allen stand-up cassette until we were gasping, I almost had to pull over. I'd never felt my body so fully occupied by free delight and hilarity. I talked about Jason, our reflexive breakups and predictable reunions. She kept her eye on the wheel, on the road. Let her watch, I thought. Let's see what she does with recklessness. She didn't say much about her parents, except biography. She named their hometowns, her father's enlistment dates, kept herself out of the way, a narrator detached. When I talked about my parents — the brief mention of my father, the marathon confusions of my mother — I rolled out whole stories, contempt and resigned comedy my high-wire act over more conflicted emotion.

As we arrived, her mother emerged to greet us in the driveway. The house stood over us. I'd been unaware of suburbs, the shush and halt, the way everything was settled by legible street signs. Her mother took us through the garage, into the hallway that led to the kitchen. We were to do nothing, she was saying, except recover from our hard work. I loved the whiff of lawn mower fuel, and chicken roasting this early in the afternoon. This was a foundation, this was *a house,* with a mailbox and a mat that curled around the base of the toilet and a bird feeder out the kitchen window. I inspected it all, an exultant anthropologist. There was a sewing room and a screened-in porch. The front doorbell, which I tried, went *ding dong.* After supper her father sat in the TV room, and I went in and asked him to show me the old army pictures and Rachel's baby pictures. I was excellent with parents. Rachel stayed at the table, pulling at her strands. "Wait'll you see this," he said, energized, hunting through a cabinet. He put a home movie in the VCR, fussing with the controls and his reading glasses, and I called to her, "Look at your tiny red barrettes, I remember those!" She wouldn't come, I could not involve her.

At night I tossed off sweater and T-shirt, stood, upper half naked, rummaged for my pajamas, and Rachel reddened and turned away. She put a Lanz nightgown over her head, let it drop from her shoulders, and slipped her clothes off beneath the flannel, a trick of modesty I'd never seen, even at boarding school. In her bed, we whispered, still a habit from the time not so long ago of sleepovers, voicing the hopes darkness invited. Before we were up in the morning, I heard a car pull in, the trunk thump shut, a screen door open and spring back. Her mother called to us, "Girls!" and I got right up and went down to see what was happening in the kitchen. Bags of groceries brimmed on the floor by the fridge. Her mother chopped carrots and red onions into tiny dice. She whipped them with a strong arm into the cream cheese for our bagels, which she'd sliced and toasted. She set one before me as I slid into a chair. Rachel came down later, fully dressed, and didn't eat.

We didn't leave for walks or shopping. We

stayed in the house and let it govern us. Hour after hour in the TV room, "Funny Girl" and "Annie Hall." I loved the green- and gold-flocked wallpaper along the stairs, the comfortable, sloppy kitchen with the stacks of Entenmann's boxes on the crowded counter. The sounds of her moth- er's business seemed to inhabit each room, bills being ripped open, drawers closed, the radio dial adjusted. What was that, I thought, watching every move. What does that do? Her mother, as she talked to me of redheaded cousins and recent bar mitzvahs, washed onion skins down the disposal, flip- ping a switch, not even looking. Sunday I was depressed to leave, to resume the seri- ous chore of study, and I held on to Ra- chel's mother, who insisted I come back; and I would come back many times in the next five years. Rachel kept her distance, coat buttoned and messenger bag held close. She accepted quick pecks from her parents. Once in the car, she said, "They love you." I thought she was talking about me, my success, but she meant them, what they required. She was inspecting some mechanism, trying to understand them, and I waited, but she didn't say more.

In the spring, my mother brought her new

boyfriend to Boston for the weekend. "He wants to meet you!" she said, and I knew he'd heard the same. My mother liked to promote her plans before anyone involved had reviewed them. When I asked her to slow down, or when I said, "Really? He really wants to come to Boston?" she'd say, "You're going to adore him, I know it." I hated the sense of being molded for her uses, set up for her parade. The boyfriend was rich, so they stayed at the Ritz-Carlton, glamour on the Common. Just a few towns apart, my mother and I could share the instant thought. Mostly, we spent the time together, but when I wasn't with her, she'd phone — The girl on the local news, look at her teeth; the color today of the Charles River, what do you think? Call me back. In a weekend, I learned the Ritz phone number and the name of each polite concierge who answered and connected me to her suite.

I asked Rachel, patient and keen to observe, if she'd come to brunch on Sunday, meet my bubbling mother of the legendary misbehaviors. In the tranquility of the elevator we looked around — this other Boston, old elegance, how unlike our functional campus, our cheaply built student housing. Down the serene hall we found my mother's door ajar, her voice audible, that fake-sexy whisper for the room service waiter or someone on the phone. It didn't matter who, boyfriend, sister, hotel manager. "Sue's here!" she said and hung up. I moved into her outstretched arms. Her overdone affection was meant to impress my friend, initiate her. Rachel swayed by the door, unwilling or uncomfortable to step onto the wide-open of the carpet, as my mother flung greeting and inquiry at her. Rachel gave shy answers, lowered her head, and her hair fell forward.

Maybe the rich boyfriend, who would eventually marry my mother and move her to Dubai, dined with us in the hotel's restaurant, but I don't remember him that weekend. After brunch, where my mother had ordered fresh-squeezed orange juice for all before we'd been handed the menus, we returned upstairs with her — she was big on being escorted, and she'd probably promised me some money. I was dying to review her with Rachel, let another's perspective calm me, organize me. My mother, in the open-doored bathroom, peed, flushed, still asking questions of Rachel and interrupting herself as she used the sink. She emerged with a wooden hanger, hotel robe trailing from it. The breast pocket, embroidered *Ritz-Carlton* with the logo of a lion's head, made an electric impression of blue against the bleached toweling. "Feel this, Sue, come on." She lifted my hand and stroked it over the terry cloth. Rachel watched me surrender. "Heaven, isn't it!" said my mother. She offered Rachel a sleeve and said, "Feel," which Rachel did. Anyone instructed by my mother obeyed. "Rachel's got great hair, doesn't she, Sue? You've got *great* hair, Rachel. You know that, don't you?" She pulled at my satchel. "Here, open up." She bundled the robe and shoved it into my bag. "What about Rachel? Rachel, love, do you need a robe?" She went to the closet, scanned the floor. "We have two? Yes! And a shopping bag!" Rachel looked at me, checking how to play the game, or if this was a game. "I'm okay," she said. My mother skipped to the bed, grabbed the phone, was insisting to Housekeeping that the suite had *only one robe* and she expected another *right away.* I shrugged. I was used to it; now you've met my family. On the way home, Rachel said, laughing, "I can't believe you just stole a robe from a hotel." "They can afford it," I said, pleased by conspiracy with my truant mother, a way of being that was as natural and expected for me as the morning bagels and special cream cheese in Rachel's Connecticut. From time to time

Rachel would ask if I still had the robe, and I said, "Of course." (It was very well made.) I wore it every night for years, enjoyed its pilfered luxury until it fell apart. That's how Rachel knew my mother, prancing thief, irresistible, delinquent fairy godmother. Rachel didn't see how weary I was of the dedicated, upbeat badness, of the permission I was always asked to bestow, of the temporary luxuries that were never earned. I didn't know I was tired of faking.

That summer I moved into Esther's apartment, which was above Rachel's, the gray house a mile from campus. Rachel, who had graduated, lived with a chemistry student from Colombia who was engaged and a young chef apprenticing in Boston. Every weekday morning Rachel went into the city, temping at design firms and PR agencies. *Nearby* was the right proximity for us. I loved Rachel's antidote to my life's early disorder, but her carefulness, those tiny perfume bottles she kept lined up, her white linen runners embroidered with little violets atop her dresser — it could be too much for me, airless.

Rachel laughed at her preferences and idiosyncrasies, a sign of health. She liked being teased, let me. She dated no one, never even looked — another idiosyncrasy? She blushed over Prince when we saw *Purple Rain* at the second-run theater, a heat in spite of herself. It seemed there had been someone, one camp summer, some kissing, but she said only enough to conjure the faintest sort of disappointment. I didn't know — and by now she was one of my closest, most enthusiastic confidantes — if she was a virgin, such a key topic, the words *virgin* or *virginity* most of us managed to fit into every conversation. She modeled modesty. I threw myself into the outrageous orgy of Jason, not caring why Rachel let me keep talking about him.

For fifteen years Rachel and I went deep with our mutual ways of seeing and reading, mutual comic pleasures, love of art, Italy, all that, and we laughed so hard, with love, at our stark differences. After my graduation, we'd never shared a city again — I in London, she in LA; I in LA, she in St. Paul — but if we found ourselves in New York, a weekend coincidence, we'd catch up at top speed over rushed coffee and I'd come away revitalized by forgotten happinesses, by being known and unconditionally loved. Our voices lapsed into younger, sweeter versions. I liked who I was with her, who she let me be, looser, giddier, indulged. We corresponded with devotion, letters, frequent calls — she always sent antique cards and small meticulously packaged presents for birthdays, new homes, episodes of turmoil — lipstick in a shade I liked, thoughtful that way. I counted on how she held me in her heart.

When Daniel was three, and I was thirty-four, I went to visit her in El Paso, where she'd moved for a job at a magazine and met her husband. I'd missed out on the particulars of the courtship, which fell during one of our inconsequential periods of less contact, our respective focus more intense on our own necessities. He was nice. Apart from their wedding a few years earlier, before I'd had a baby, Rachel and I hadn't spent a full day together since college, so I suffered the travel with my toddler and didn't mind the effort. I wanted to see her in this new place. I hoped she was at home.

Rachel's mother had died some months before, news that ran me through with sadness, but far away with a baby and still weakened by a first bad year of postpartum depression, I couldn't get to the funeral. As I deplaned in El Paso, as I forced apart the stroller's clasp on the jetway and settled my son, tucked his stuffed sheep under his unconscious hand, I wanted to make up for that, give Rachel belated tenderness. And I felt grateful that I'd be with a true friend who was excited about my son's central, redefining role in my life. Rachel always asked me to tell everything about him. She understood that he *was* me, I was him. Motherhood was like new oxygen now, a revolution. Friends were being sorted out, who would endure and who would recede, but with Rachel, who had lasted so long, there was no question. She was already part of me.

No: what I really needed to know, to rewrite, was my previous definition of the word *mother.* My own mother would not serve, and I had backed away from her. Rachel, who'd seen the mess I'd come from, proudly called me a good mother. She would see in my son my concerted efforts, the placated anxieties. She would help me be proud of myself.

In the airport, something was wrong. Rachel took no time for the hug, stepped out of my reach. Where was our click, our *way*? Her gaze jumping, she repeated questions about baggage and travel. She'd purchased a car seat for Daniel, a gesture I appreciated — I tried to say so — but it had to stay wrapped in the plastic, she explained, so she could return it after we'd gone. She was preoccupied, I didn't know why, as I struggled to reconfigure my mood, my needs and old happiness.

"You okay?" I said in the car.

"No juice in the car, okay, Daniel, no getting it dirty? No juice?"

Daniel said, "Juice? Juice?" He said it to himself the rest of the way.

Rachel worried, Was he thirsty, could he wait, would we have to stop? He's fine, I said, it's fine. She didn't notice me respond. She switched worries: he might chew on the plastic, swallow it. The hospital, she said, was not too far from the house. Nonsense concerns jostled in my head — What did she mean? *How* far was the doctor? Her worry rocked us back and forth. I stopped trying to protest. Just let her be what she needs to be, I thought, a discipline I was trying to practice with everyone, and with myself. At the house, it'll be better. She drove a maze of short back streets, paced by stop signs, our journey abrupt and slow at the same time. We could not sink into our usual pleasures. We couldn't get anywhere.

We stayed inside the house, the windows sealed. A constant hum announced the air purifiers. She worried about our room, that Daniel would suffocate or choke, that the Texas heat would desiccate him. "He won't choke," I said, a firm rebuke — *Are you listening to me?* But her conversation was with herself. Everything here, she said, was susceptible to fading and inevitable deterioration. "I can't even sit on the patio." Her husband spent a lot of time out there. I missed the Rachel who danced, who recited our movie dialogue, and I wanted to kid her out of these strangling anxieties, but it was dawning on me, with a dense sadness, that this was a task beyond any friend's purview.

After I'd settled Daniel the first night, we sat on the couch, our backs against the armrests. Her husband was out and the house was still, except for the tremor of the purifiers, which ran under our feet. We ate good pineapple sorbet she had taught herself to make, and I was impressed. I asked about her mother's funeral. She sped through details, a numb account of guests, aggravating missteps of the rabbi. "I miss her," I said. No maternal presence ever forgotten. I hadn't seen my mother in more than a year, since my son was eighteen months old.

The last time my mother had visited Missoula, toppling with overexpensive presents for the baby, her manias dictated and tangled by medications, she seemed to forget me before the ride to the hotel from the airport had ended, single-minded in her need to score painkillers. I was trying to list plans, but she asked if I knew a doctor, any doctor, who could see her right away. She asked again, then again, musing about medical expertise in Montana. *Addicts are like this,* I thought as I drove. Stupid you, I said to myself, always ready for her to be some other way, the vain wait. Each visit, every time. Children of addicts are like *this,* accounting for the tiniest disturbance and new twitch, but hopeful. Amassing hurts, but hopeful, hopeful. My mother didn't care to leave her hotel. Her back hurt. She called me twice a day to her room, where she took my baby, set him on her bed, pushed her face into his so that he had to turn his head to escape her ravenous gaze. Nine prescription bottles were bunched on the bathroom counter, various pharmacies. I hated that each time I went to pee, I counted them.

Then I knew my paradox: I could keep hoping and get nowhere, because we'd always be like this; or I could change myself and end us. So, a few days in, I rallied terrified courage and told my mother to go. I didn't want her anymore, like this, conniving and addicted and rioting, would have to face the broken heart instead; she switched her ticket and left, unimpressed by my dilemma. But I understood that I'd reached some new kind of finish, and whatever grief awaited me at the deprivation of a mother, I'd handle it. I'd have to; I was done.

Rachel that first night ignored my fondness for her mother. She let me praise and reminisce, and then tears streamed down her face, her hands up to cover herself.

"I'm so sorry," I said, thinking we shared.

"No," she said, "you don't know." She made an angry disclosure I'd never heard in the years of our friendship. What she said was private, and so quick and bare I was hardly sure of it. Busy soaking up her mother's mothering, I'd missed my friend's pain and trouble. Rachel had disguised them, as she'd returned our happy focus again and again to me. I set down the dessert and reached my hand for hers, but she ducked, picked up the bowls and disappeared to the kitchen.

Rachel took us out each day, thoughtful excursions she planned for Daniel — the zoo, the Border Patrol Museum with the old cars and uniforms, and she snapped pictures of him, found his delicious purity with her lens, what I always wanted others to see. But each trip stuttered at her over-wrought interaction with an ATM or a public bathroom, her sheer worry. On our last full day I wanted to walk Daniel around the neighborhood, see the pink desert willow blossoms, but Rachel tried to talk me out of it. The pollen count. The aridity that aged you on the spot, dehydration inevitable. The strangers out there, you just never know. I felt confused, as she darted among excuses. I tried to identify the problem to solve. Finally I realized that she didn't want the door opened and unman-aged air to balloon into her living room. I began to want to hurt her with my energies, use whatever was at my disposal to make her notice me. It was an ugly thing to confront in myself, but I was worn out with trying to respect the manufactured plights, accommodate them. The college desire to shake her up a bit, bring her a little reckless fun, had shifted into a mean mission, a nasty impulse. I grabbed Daniel and walked out, leaving the door open. Years before, Ra-chel had met my transgressions and youth-ful stupidities with affection, ardent curios-ity, even delight; now I could not interpret her anxieties. I balked at such outright panic displayed, and, unable to help her, I judged.

Her formless anxiety was prefacing my

thoughts with fear. I had to get outside, breathe that suspect air deeply, encounter other people. She would hover at the bathroom door as I stayed with Daniel, who was potty training. He couldn't shit for four days, until we were on the airplane. As I wiped his bottom in the cramped lavatory he said, "Why doesn't Rachel like poop in her house?"

After that, the friendship stalled. The conversation the night she cried seemed not to have happened. I didn't know how to move in this mire, be heard, nor how I could ask for more details or offer help. We spoke less and less often. Her wounds were unadmitted, impenetrable, and she was mute on matters of grief and loss and anger. Articulating mine had become my life and work. I needed to forget the visit so that I wouldn't feel how close she was to some weird edge from which I couldn't rescue her.

Rachel got pregnant. I wondered how she'd withstand the bodily mutiny and uncertainty. She didn't talk about the pregnancy, but right before labor she called, and she was scared. Real and scared, in a real voice. I'd never heard her like this, no jokey dismissals or vague, unmerited fear, and my hopes lifted. She wasn't barricaded.

Close your eyes, I said, imagine a peaceful place, where you are relaxed, and we thought of the Cape, described its beauties, the stretching ocean. "And that pink bedroom," she said. But she knew things would go wrong.

She called in the morning. "I delivered," she said. She didn't mention a baby. She insisted she had nursing problems, first this one, then this other. I was sympathetic, but for several peculiar minutes I learned nothing of the baby, growing scared to ask, anxiety planted. The next day, another flat conversation, little mention of the new daughter. I debated a call to the nurses' station and finally made it. "I know you can't talk about your patients," I said, "but I wanted you to know one of them's in trouble." The nurse said nothing. "She's, I think she's at risk. I'm concerned about her ability to bond with the baby. Postpartum depression." I knew that darkness, remembered not asking for rescue.

"We'll see," the nurse said, unimpressed. "Thanks for calling."

I saw, with the monstrous recognition of treachery, that I'd pushed beyond welcome or right. What an infraction, what a breach. Rachel was closed to my help, away in unnamable traumas that, I had determined, were rapidly racing to the surface. I believed I wanted to help, my clumsy method undermining my good intentions. I wanted for Rachel what had not been done for me, when I'd suffered my first maternal months of gagged despair. I loved her, my longest-lasting friend, wished her to be happy, peaceful, but more important than our friendship, there was now a little girl, poised for a mother's unreliable mess to engulf her. Susanna's anxiety versus Rachel's. I felt, urgently, that mine had to win. That little girl, that little girl.

"Something's *wrong* with her," Rachel kept saying to me, or musing out loud. I ended every call more aggravated, less concerned. Rachel carried the girl back to the doctor many times, back to the ER, to be told that nothing was wrong. "See? She's fine," I said, tight and desperate for her to calm down. "Should you call La Leche League maybe?" Then, three weeks later, emergency bloomed in full force, and the baby had open-heart surgery. Rachel and her husband spent their nights in the NICU, collapsed but alert, waiting. Rachel's anxieties rallied into this one certainty. One couldn't argue with her anymore.

When her baby was two, recovered and

thriving, Rachel brought her for a visit to Missoula. I'd bought new towels, which I washed with new sheets in unscented detergent. I wanted to make Rachel comfortable, to let her rest in my welcome, even though I knew she'd protest comfort, find a way out of it. It was as if she had grown allergic to ease.

"Oh, Tillie can't eat that," Rachel said within the first minutes, staring into the freezer, which I'd stocked with blueberries and waffles. Blueberries, she pointed out, were corrupted by pesticides — their large surface area. The waffles had traces of egg, and Tillie only ate low-fat yogurt, this one brand, she'd have to go to the store later, where was it? She set her daughter on her lap at the table and clamped an arm around her waist. She pushed away the plate of red grapes, explained avocado gave the baby hives, asked had the lentils been washed first? "Spit it out," she told the girl, who'd got hold of a piece of fusilli in pesto and stuck it in her mouth. The food appeared at the tip of Tillie's tongue, and was swiftly dispatched by Rachel with a piece of paper towel. She was very sober as she asked where the garbage was.

The worries and instructions were constant, too much. I didn't understand the multiple serpentine explanations, or believe them, felt hostage to worry. My friend was scaring me. At night, Christopher and I wondered if we should call her husband, check this with him, her tightness and alarm. We'd noticed that the child couldn't be bothered with food, that she turned her head repeatedly to her mother's breast, waiting for Rachel to unbutton. Rachel would sigh and scoop her up and disappear for an hour, or two hours. Once, I came into the guest room and saw her fretting over her breasts and the baby, and it was the tensest scene of nursing I had ever witnessed. Tillie didn't seem to be there.

But you don't call, when it's your oldest friend, her family. Any minute, you keep thinking, things will right themselves.

It was the last of the three days. We packed up the car to go to the airport, Rachel's ladylike bags trim with hidden zippers, Tillie coaxed into the car seat. I was at the wheel.

Rachel turned in her seat to face me.

"Ready?" I was tense.

In that rare and real voice Rachel said, "Do you think I'm a bad mother?"

After days of thoughts that felt so treacherous, I was aching. I was blind and beyond reason. If I could get through to her, if I could make her see —

I said, "Yes."

Rachel looked at her lap. I felt disgraced by the ringing "yes." I said, "You just, you seem to be struggling. You seem afraid. The world isn't . . . I want, I wish you could enjoy this. She's fine, you know. Could you — Do you need help? So you can experience the pleasures in this, not just all the fears."

Later I wrote her a letter. "I know I don't really understand everything you're going through. You need to deal with whatever's going on." "To be honest," she responded, "you write me that letter every time we see each other, and I'm sick of it."

I do? I thought, as I tried to remember past letters but couldn't. Okay, good for her. We'll make something new, gloves off. It didn't happen.

She did not impart to me details of the help she found. Why should she have? I wasn't being a friend, I was a bully, even out of concern and love, unable to stifle my ancient terrors, to ignore history's lens of a crazy mother. My own obstinate parenting rules, my choices to protect my sons — they might have looked a fretful mystery to the outside world. Her newborn had had massive surgery. I would never know what that had wrought, what that changed in a mother's breast.

"Why are you still friends?"

I was at another friend's house, having a drink and reviewing the visit, trying to puzzle out the intensity of my reactions to Rachel. The question bothered me.

"We just *are.*" I explained Rachel's sweet temperament, her sly scrutinies, our shared cultural humor. During the visit, we'd been in the car, a trip to the grocery store that had momentarily calmed her, and I'd looked over at her deeply familiar face, felt the abiding river of affection between us and what a gorgeous, teeming history that was. Yes, our history, I'd thought, our *knowing* through all those years, knowing everything that happened, and with whom, and which challenges changed us. That's not a small thing.

"I love her," I said, but I couldn't think of one thing I still did to show her.

"I can't believe you told her she was a bad mother." This friend didn't have kids but she knew you don't do that, ever. No one does that.

Rachel never confronted me about calling her a bad mother — I doubt she forgot about it — and my own shame made it difficult to revisit the moment, confess error. I don't know how to repair the mistake. She knew me well enough, loved me enough, perhaps, to understand I didn't mean her, that I wasn't talking to her. Perhaps she understood that our interior traumas defined so much of our characters that we could never bridge some essential chasm.

Rachel's father died. She didn't call me until weeks later, and as I absorbed the news, terribly sad to hear, I was even sadder that we had no more clear course. We were unsure of our closeness; maybe I didn't deserve her family news. Our long, bountiful intimacy had slid into awkward, sporadic connection. We have not yet found our way back.

If my mother had said, "Do you think I'm a bad mother," had spurned the shoplifting, given up sexual compulsion and coke, if she had managed herself in order to see who her daughter was, if she had asked from her sluggish highs, from her devilry and madcap seductions, her thoughtless, childish wreckage, *Am I a bad mother,* I would have answered. She would be buttering a raisin pumpernickel roll in a beautiful restaurant, or tying the sash of her hotel bathrobe in a sunny bedroom. *Am I a bad mother, Sue?*

Yes. Shut up and sit still so I can unleash my exhausted certainty: you are a bad mother. If only I'd known how to fit that defining anxiety into its proper place.

ORPHAN GIRL

When I met Mary, she was too sad to speak, but I didn't know that. I was twenty-seven, and I thought she was shy, a shy woman, when my focus was anyway on men, maleness. Mary was married to Christopher's grad school friend, Clay, who could fill any room to its corners with oratory, and loved to. None of us could get a word in. Our first evening, dinner at their cabin, Clay shooed back the dogs and gave Christopher the clasp and release of men's affection. We all shook hands. We'd been in Missoula two months, broke and not writing our books as we'd planned, just working at thin jobs, when Christopher heard that his former friend was here. I liked them. I liked the dogs who rushed the doorway when we arrived, and the academic shabbiness, worn rooms littered with books. We all knew these sorts of rooms, our faint kingdoms of creative sprawl.

Mary kept their baby daughter on her hip as she took corn bread from the oven and ladled out pork stew, set the four bowls on the table, which was arranged against the night's window and lit by a small lamp at one end. She stretched her neck away, unconscious and practiced, when the baby grasped for her pendant earring. The boy, age four, bumbled near his father, who focused on us, his newcomers. Clay was still standing after we'd sat down, a wine bottle ready in his grip — the flavors, he exclaimed, of the excellent green chilies and the best hominy, you're gonna love it. Mary tucked the baby into the high chair and pulled it close. He berated movies, musicians, novels, and made us laugh and long to one-up him, as if that were possible. He ranged over subjects — the grading of the dirt road that passed their cabin, James Joyce in Zurich, the politics of game licenses, the upstart shock of the new Target built out by Costco. He said, "We first got here, and that area was wide open. Farms and fields." He meant when they'd met as undergraduates two decades before. They had left for bigger cities, but this town called them back, and Clay was ready on any civic topic. For months after meeting Clay and Mary, I thought of Missoula as his.

In the next two years the couple was regular, if not intimate, in our lives with spontaneous dinners and weekend hikes, picnics on the river with the Bitterroot Mountains massing beyond us. They told us about better fishing spots, demystified local idiosyncrasies. "You can drive in Montana with an open bottle?" "Yup," Clay said. "Gotta love it." Both were artists, and Clay made their scant money. A book contract, a teaching gig. I talked writing with him, and I was writing, too, newspaper pieces and movie reviews, although it would be ten years before I'd produce a book. His book came out. Christopher and I, envious, congratulated him, and meant it. We'd seen his duty and discipline, knew he'd earned this. Every morning he retreated, leaving Mary to run their affairs. A photographer, she had curated collections and shown her work, although she was now occupied with children and household. If pressed after dinner, she might retrieve a flat box from under the stairs and lift off the lid, her old prints, while Clay changed CDs at the stereo. She flipped fast, and I had to make her go back. I absorbed the pictures, giant color portraits of strangers' cluttered bedrooms but with no people, spirit echoed by eccentric private evidence. She had captured some worthwhile loneliness, and I wanted to investigate, but I also wanted to flee, find boisterous warmth to temper the ghostly absence.

Clay and Mary were moving away, and we were sad. Our first friends, the first we had come to know as a couple. Their child was the first child we'd delighted in. *"Actually,"* the boy would say, his face grave, "ferns were the triceratops' favorite food." "How about the *Tyrannosaurus rex,* did he eat ferns, too?" *"Actually,* he was a carnivore. He ate dinosaurs." We'd house-sat for them, taken care of their dogs, spent the days they were gone cloaking ourselves in their concerns and testing joint life. Christopher and I were not living together. He needed slowness, so we'd been laying out careful plans for *one day.* The first night we stayed there, as Christopher paced the creek, I wandered inside, considering responsibilities I would have if we'd established all this. I stood in the boy's room with my hand on the railing of the toddler bed and imagined him waking, the morning window casting light on his blanket, and how he would rise in these blue dinosaur pajamas, the cold floor, come to breakfast and his parents' voices. That was the time Clay and Mary forgot to tell us the dogs' names. One of them had a tag, the commanding, rangy male, but the other, a smaller tagless female, ran far into the woods on our walk and could not be called because we couldn't shout, "Dog! Dog!" She didn't come back until the next night, our day lost to anxious waiting.

Clay and Mary bequeathed us their cabin. In a great gesture, which seemed of mild consequence to them, but would effect a most significant change for us, they gave our names to their landlord, who shrugged with easygoing indifference and transferred the lease. The day we moved in, zigzagging across the gravel from the borrowed truck to the empty house and back again for another box, we said, "We should put on Steve Earle, we should make pork stew tonight, isn't it time we got a dog?"

It was impossible to accept our full right to a place where we had been hosted so many evenings, Clay's mournful, masculine soundtracks, his masterpiece of paella, the patter of their son's ideas. Mary stood *here,* whisking the cream before she served chocolate soufflé from this oven, and Clay cajoled, pronounced last-call witty sarcasms as we stepped through *this* door into the cold

October air, the April air, at the end of those nights. On the drive to my place, the lit cabin receding, we praised the creek and stove and run-about dogs, the artist life, Clay and Mary's fine example of family.

Clay and Mary left things behind, and those became our daily things, old chairs, some kitchen stuff, stickers on the fridge, extension cords and *New Yorkers*. We put our bed in their bedroom, showered in their shower, used up the lightbulbs. The cabin — main level and downstairs, ten-sided and entirely fronted to the south with huge windows — was heated by two iron stoves, and Christopher chopped wood every day, the axe left after him in the stump, on call. Strips and strings of kindling skimmed the bare floor, debris grainy under bare feet. We bought slippers. We bought another broom, kept both at hand. Mary, I remembered now, had swept after the first dinner, the baby fussy at being set down. At Christmas we could only think to put the tree in the spot they'd had theirs. The windows at night reflected the inherited bulbs, our light blinking dim red, dim yellow, and green as we made love on the sofa. Christopher was made so happy by moving out of town and five miles up the canyon that, although I preferred accessible activity, city society, I embraced the solitude, too. Living together, we instituted new habits, our habits. Agreements about grocery shopping, about how to angle the television. We were the ones now who talked about the graded road, the unplowed snows, the unruly brambles of pink wild roses that narrowed the driveway. When we eloped, I called to tell Mary. Our marriage, not a beginning but a deepening, had been sanctioned in these rooms by theirs.

In Mary's first independent hours, her little girl in preschool, she started to take pictures again, told me a little about it. While we talked on the phone, I'd stare across the cabin to the wall where we'd hung the photo of hers we'd bought. It was a large print of children at play, close on a young girl who sat on a rock, higher than the others, her face turned from the camera and hidden, damp greens, blonds and blues. Mary said she was photographing the densest, lushest Southern growth, massive, lurking fronds, the screens of invasive kudzu, what should not be there but had taken over to erase the known reality. She exploded the prints to enormous size to show the finest threads of close, leafy vein. When I saw them, I saw so much voiceless green, closing in, and through the foliage a bit of white plain sky. How sad she was, it dawned on me. Sadder than she could say.

One day, when we'd known each other three years and were separated by two thousand miles, she said, "My parents were killed in a plane crash."

"Oh my god," I said. Phone silence wielded its solemn tyranny. I said finally, "How old were you?"

"Seven." I pictured my friend as a child.

"What — Then what happened?"

She'd been sent to live with her aunt, her kind uncle, many cousins, like a girl in the books I'd used to love, when I'd wished in my own childhood for a magical release. Each time my disorienting mother went away, I'd wanted a plane crash, hoping she'd never come back. Mary had been that fabled orphan, sent to a farm where the animal need and constant activity overruled tragedy. And no one talked about the accident. No one, she remembered, asked how she was or remarked on her life's abrupt arrest. Faced with such large and real loss, I didn't know what to ask.

"Yeah, it's okay," she said.

How could I have not known the very thread-and-needle of her character? I told Christopher, asked him, "Did you know?"

I'd let only my own experience define her
— the warm dessert in ramekins, an incidental photograph, her children's clamor,
Clay's teasing. "But this," I said, as I revised
her, added in trauma. This changed everything. This *was* everything, wasn't it? No,
he hadn't known. Clay wouldn't have told
him, the times they went fly-fishing, taking
Clay's muddy Jeep. They didn't get near
death or damage. They talked fishing, an
infinite examination of spring run-off on
the nearby rivers, hatches and nymphs, the
cold-day habits of browns versus cutthroats.
The few times they went to the Silver Dollar on Railroad Street, light yellow beers on
the scarred oak bar, they didn't talk about
women or anyone, unless someone had
published. They did not review the past,
which they'd shared in classrooms, growing
into the men they'd become. Clay kept
them on course, as men.

I was happy Christopher had him, their
once-a-month occasions, because he didn't
attach easily. He left that to me, although
my voracious appetite for people startled
him, and he was baffled at the energy I had
for varied relationships and heavy confidences. Introverted and keen for solitude,
he let me be the flash, our outward engine.
I loved to hear people talk about their

changes and despairs, sudden loves and tortured histories. For Christopher, though, the parallel male could be welcome; or unmissed.

After Mary told me of her orphaning we didn't mention it.

Clay and Mary returned. They bought a roomy house a few blocks from ours (we'd moved within city limits when I was pregnant), central for parties and music jams. There was a drum kit in the living room and a piano in the dining room, canvases painted by successful friends. Mary put unusual colors on their walls, burnt mustard and autumn green, and kept the pink '50s bathroom as it was. Her giant prints hung here, glassed and framed. They had terrariums, frogs, finches, fish, a cage with a heat lamp for the kids' snake. The kids' friends bubbled in various rooms. They got a new dog, a giant, who collided with arriving guests and always had to be put out back, Mary dragging at the collar as Clay poured the drinks. Clay had claimed the garden shed as an office, speakers mounted on the wall. He had a real job and complained affably, sighed, "That's the price of Missoula, man. Everyone's willing to pay."

I didn't talk writing with Clay anymore.

He had many more books, had come out into the literary world proper, and this made me shy, with an envy mixed in, so sharp it could constrict my throat in his presence. It was unspoken between us, he was one sort of writer and I was another, and out of social grace and genuine affection we avoided exploring that. Clay wrote about broken couples and the hard outdoors, in third person; I was trying to write about my family, a revealed experience of myself as a girl, what became of me. I wrote to uncover something, and I hadn't found out what. I couldn't risk Clay's rhetoric if we talked about writing, his good-natured, entitled coercion.

Mary and I grew closer, spent unstructured time together, stopped by each other's doors. When Jack was born, she loved coming over, just to hold him. Years can go by like this. Years did. We seemed to talk of everything, the mundane and the serious. I met her siblings, one after the other, as they visited; I came to her openings; we traded copies of good novels. Mary invited my children to her kids' birthdays and put a glass of wine in my hand when we arrived. The year Jack was not yet two, she made sure there was a party favor for him, even though he wouldn't have noticed. But we never went near the disastrous. I was proud of my maturing abilities with boundaries, respected privacies better instead of interpreting them as rejections. I did not demand the secrets, left agony alone.

Hard trouble came into my marriage, private confusions. Christopher and I were dealing with them, but it was slow, aggravated work and I grew oblivious to my friends' matters. One evening Mary asked if she could come over. She sat at the kitchen table and talked about Clay, said they had troubles, new distances. Her news was hard to take in, a surprise in the midst of my own problems. Then, after a frantic season between them, their marriage ended.

Mary stayed in the house, and the kids went back and forth to Clay's apartment. We never saw him. No more grilled meat, impromptu parties, brown bottles of local beer on the kitchen table, no more Etta James turned loud, with Clay's intractable opinions the comfortable boom over us all. Mary came to me, a sudden solidity to our friendship, and I welcomed her in the middle of dinner, or late at night, or when I was writing: of course come over. I took her in my arms, her collapsed sobs. I would be the steady, needed friend, would not bother or dismay her with the concerns in my marriage (anyway, we were headed toward repair; I felt irrationally disloyal). Trained by years of therapists attending me, I knew unadmitted sorrow, its deep well, and I knew how to listen. I witnessed her devastation, her harried spirit, and she felt accompanied as I hoped she would. Absorbed, she did not notice my shock, as I realized how vaguely all our years and conversations had only hinted at a couple's bargain. Again I revised her, added crucial, invisible information. I watched every dark stage — anger, objection, ravagement. She called in despair when the divorce papers came through. She was walking from the lawyer's office to her car, holding them in her hand. Calm, helpful, I waited for her realignment.

I hadn't been through divorce, but I did understand loss as an inescapable refrain, the not-having. Our parents — hers dead, mine impossible, daughters left to blister in the elements. Always, we talked about art through this, art as the third party in our sad congress. A big book of Kertész or Brassai or Cindy Sherman on her coffee table, I'd open it, and Mary, unable to help herself and still crying, would look close and consider aloud the composition and depths, the arrested image. We revered the uses of the hidden self. Even upset, she would have to stand, couldn't stop herself, and reach from a high shelf a more obscure work, so that she might show me the connections, the force of influence. Then tears. Then wine, and wine and tears, and sighing into the exhausted end of the evening, when I promised on my way out to call the next day. "You're a good friend," she said, patting my arm, distracted by sadness. I was.

That year she forgot my birthday. I didn't want to mind; great friendship should transcend the petty. In contrast to her seismic ordeals, what was my brief event, regular and yearly anyway? Except I did mind — all these days and hours of being here for you, I thought with high school petulance, and you *forget* me. About six weeks later she stopped midsentence. "Did I forget your birthday? I did, didn't I?" "That's okay," I said, acting adult. "I'm sorry," and she was, and I felt better, but I stopped being so available. It didn't occur to me that this was actually a more authentic way to engage.

I wanted everything out, swept away. A mania of decluttering had come upon me, a revolution. My closets were wide open, drawers pulled from their beds. Stuffed garbage bags waited to go to the thrift store, piled at the front door. I was in a madness to unbind myself from objects. For two years, shaping a book about my mother out of intolerable memory, I'd been immersed in private history, debris collected, organized. The tiniest specifics, the interior agonies, had been recast as art.

I'd finished the book and needed my living self back. The written self had to be dismantled and the writer disarmed, so I could be in the world. I put my deliberate hand on every object in my possession, as if climbing a rope ladder from an inky mine. I decided whether to keep a thing, throw it out, give it away. I couldn't stop talking about it, boring my family, but Mary was interested. In eight, nine, ten weeks of daily work I'd decluttered my house. Not just a broken turntable, an ugly rug, clothes that had fit me briefly, but I'd also cleared the back of the car of the torn atlas and cracked CD cases; the makeup drawer of ten-year-old lipsticks and sour-smelling foundation; the rattling excess amidst the silverware. I tossed books inscribed by my married English teacher with his suggestive euphemisms. I sorted twenty years' worth of file folders, shredded a decade of credit card statements.

"You did? What else?" said Mary. We sat in her living room.

"I found one box filled with phone bills from my apartments in New York, in the eighties."

"You're kidding."

"I had two *dozen* copies of my high school literary magazine!"

And the elegant but harmful clutter, more difficult to consider, to discard — the antique writing secretary from an ill-matched boyfriend, the guilty booty of a shopping trip with my grandmother. The tiniest clutters, safety pins and buttons mixed in with dimes and a flash drive and a loose watch battery in a cracked saucer on my dresser. I felt the unhaving as moral nakedness.

"I want to be surrounded by nothing."

She looked around the room. "I hate this house," she said. "I feel bad every time I walk in."

"Let's declutter it! I *want* to!" I *had* to. Her eldest was in college now, her teenage daughter hardly home. She let me. I came the next weekend with sponges, trash bags, and a clamp-on spotlight, and we descended wooden steps to her basement, the bottom of everything, and began. We worked for ten hours. We covered ourselves in the fine litter of memory, sharp mistakes, outgrown baby-hoods. We forced our bodies up the steep stairs over and over, hefting warped boxes, broken trikes, single skis. We swept away the mouse droppings and bleached the floors. We wore masks and coughed. We named and examined and sorted as we uncovered one more moment of her life, five more, a hundred more.

Mary thanked me a lot. She liked that I was there. I had torn through my belongings in private, but I realized, helping her, that I would have welcomed aid or witness. So hard for me, trusting help. I'll do it alone, I'll do it myself. It was easier to be the hero who got credit for changing the air inside her home, shifting her perceptions, than to wait for rescue, afraid of inevitable disappointment. The second day we worked in her bedroom. We cleared away the divorce paperwork, the wedding-present lamps and Clay's books, hauled out the stuff he kept saying he was coming back to get. I missed him, too, the best of him, but I hoped she'd take the space for herself, speak up. At the end of the day she gave me a small oil she'd painted, strong, abstract colors, and I hung it across from my desk, where I see it now.

"Do you think you could come over?" Mary

said. She'd gone back for a master's degree, and she was in her studio, preparing for an important review. She didn't have much time. "I could use your perspective." I went to the old building on campus and found her workspace. She had scraps and photos pinned to her wall, arranged without much arrangement, an artist's process visible. It was, as I could recognize from my own work, the laying out, before sense is made or the artist grasps her own intentions. But, her presentation ten days away, she required emergency coherence, and she was panicked. "What'll I do?" she said, distraught and unreachable. We tried to sort through the images, objects, muddles, tried to extract some narrative, but her wreckage blocked progress, and we arrived at dead ends. "Well, thanks," she said. "You always help." Not this time, I thought.

Mary didn't make it, the review postponed, and I thought of her jumbled studio, the debris of ideas and starts, how she labeled it hopeless, went quiet. She could capitulate to chaos, a certain restlessness that could drive her friends crazy. She hunted in circles for her keys, couldn't be counted on for directions. Deadlines and expectations didn't help.

Once, some years after the divorce, Mary invited me over, an evening when her kids were with Clay. "I want to make dinner for you."

I refused. "Why don't you come here?" I said. I would feed her. She was alone and I was ensconced and enfamilied, dinner prepared anyway at my house. Her effort on my behalf would put me in the uneasy role of being beholden. Wouldn't it? No, said Christopher, there is also one more gift to give a friend, after the gifts of listening, helping, decluttering, calming, there is another gift. You can let her care for you. People need to do that, too. You'll see.

I accepted. I stopped myself from bringing both wine and flowers, opulence my safeguard. I chose a few stems of tigerlilies, to please her astute eye, and let her pour wine, quench me. She'd set plates on the table in her backyard. There was small traffic in the alley, dogs, garbage cans being arranged. The sun was at fence level, and we shifted our chairs to see without glare. As I tried to settle, she kept jumping up, going inside and coming out with the forgotten — the bread, the platter of asparagus, then the lemon, another bottle, while I held myself in my chair, allowing our roles to switch. Conversation felt awkward to me, but Mary, a long-dormant freedom alive in her face, was easy. She laughed at herself, asked me questions, asked for stories of the boys. With no trouble, no panic, she pondered her increasingly distant breakup. I forced myself to quiet my habit of advice and overview. Just be, Susanna. Just be with Mary.

The next spring Mary had her thesis show. I hadn't seen her work in all that time, a whole year, consumed with my own major events. My father had died, I'd been away for weeks. I went with Christopher and the kids, in late afternoon. We walked into the few small rooms of the university gallery, the reverent space mastered by an artist, by art, clean walls glowing under useful spots.

One room contained her series of small photographs, each of a single object belonging to a friend. Each picture — a bowling-alley matchbook, say, or a doll's shoe, or an old watch — was accompanied by a brief quote from its owner. Mary had illuminated one detail, rather than gathering up un-wieldy collections. Some of the pictures and epigraphs were funny, some poignant, some simple and capable. The boys were inspecting a photo of an ancient franked train ticket, Amtrak reds paled from the '60s. I went into the second room.

Around the time my father died, Mary's aunt died, too, the woman who'd raised her. The family home was excavated, possessions distributed from the Midwest, sibling claims honored. Mary had opened old trunks, pulling them from remote storage. She lifted out the dresses, the contents of a closet to which her slim mother never returned. Petticoats, dancing dresses, day dresses, topcoats, floor-lengths, nightgowns. A whole wardrobe, some pieces stitched by hand. Mary's teenage daughter was bigger than the woman who'd chosen these clothes, been zipped up in them. Mary took them, enlivened by new material. She set each dress upon treated paper, then left it under glass for hours in the sun; natural chemistry to bring forth hidden elements, the veins of the fabrics. When she removed the glass and the dress, washed the paper with water, an ethereal impression remained. Repeated on the gallery wall, giant pages were arranged in quartets imprinted with the life-size shape, even the weave and the pattern, of tulle and taffeta and silk and cotton, wavy ribbons from sheer aprons, prim, crimped collars never to be ironed. A skirt fanned out across the width of the papers, as if on a dancer's body, mid-twirl. I stopped before each silhouette, the blue-white residue of her mother. These cyanotypes were unlike Mary's earlier work, a shocking leap, yet all her work was in them, an artist fully gathered, and I knew it. I knew her. Over eighteen years of care and slow knowing, the deliberate construction of friendship, I had witnessed the elements colliding inside her, reorganizing. I hadn't known I was witness to this, just knew her, loved her, cared what happened.

When Mary arrived at the gallery I was on the verge of tears — about her, I thought — and proud. I gripped her, everything between us intensified. We sat down on the gallery bench. She held my hand. I could offer Mary no more than gape and wordlessness. I knew her, the many shapes and directions of her, could feel all she had brought to bear in the making of such work. How startling to feel — to actually know — the scope of her loss, its roots and defining duration. I remembered the silhouettes of the mammoth Southern plants; the haunted empty rooms; the ongoing, anonymous grief she'd captured in her series of roadside crosses stretched over Montana, markers for the victims of car accidents. I fathomed,

I realized, the complete narrative of her work. Disaster, desertion; rescue, comfort. I'd listened to the conversation of an artist with herself. She was not silent. She roared, mourned. I told her this, or something like it, garbled by emotion, and she looked at me. "Susanna," she said, in tears, "you've done the same." The two of us shared friendship, motherhood, wifehood, woman-hood, and even more — an unsayable volcanic core. We were orphans, and all this time we'd been trying to figure out how to make that beautiful.

NAKED

My acupuncturist kept talking about Flora, this amazing massage therapist, gifted. Sylvia sorted her tiny needles and chatted, her middle fingers pressing along meridians until she found a point, pierced me. Flora painted, Sylvia said; she had an instinct for gardens; she wrote poetry. "You'd love her, and she'll adore you." Sylvia, who'd been proctoring my physical well-being for some time, urged me to book a massage.

Flora resembled my father's mother. Looking at her petite, stocky body in the first meeting, I kept losing my place, drawn back to the lost comforts of that grandmother, dead in my childhood. Flora could have been fifty, she could have been sixty. There was something perpetual and elemental about her. In a blue flowing top over white pants, she was fit, easy in herself, a seaside-goer. Although she talked in a honeyed accent, her Tennessee roots or

South Carolina, I felt certain we shared some genetic link, which made me happy, and I asked about her people. She told a lot. She made eye contact and leaned forward with confidential joy. I have always been a sucker for women like that.

I courted mothers, but I had to pay them. Money was the headline to the relationship, the guarantee that I hired a mother's affection. The past few years, as I had broken from my mother and tried to purge her influence, I accrued professionals, women who soothed and tended me, arranged my hair, adjusted my spine; women who asked me to undress and left the room. Per the contract, I'd remove my clothes and lie on their tables, wait for their hands.

I lay down on white paper for Susan, the nurse practitioner. She scraped an expert Pap smear and looked thoughtful as she palpated my breasts. She reviewed my nutrition and sleep, my hormones and sexual health, for as long as I wanted. For Barb, the aesthetician, I left my clothes in a heap on a cushioned stool. I put on the thick robe that hung above, snugged it at my waist, then lay flat. She sanded her palms from my knees to pelvic bones, her face intent on her work. I was her task. We knew what was going to happen. After she waxed my legs she moved to the head of the table and peered at my brows. She worked upside-down, stroked on warm wax and yanked it up again. "How are the boys?" she'd say, not listening, which gave me the room to answer with words but not depth, no invest-ment. When I started yoga, I noted Gera-lyn's silver toe ring and the health of her taut, muscled back. I bent my body to copy hers. At the end of the first class, she lowered the lights and instructed the class in her soft tone to sink into our mats, cover ourselves with a blanket, deepen our breath. My eyes were closed, and I could hear her feet pad across the carpet. She crouched beside me and whispered, "Would you like another blanket?" I nodded, shy at being made special, and hungry for it. She left and returned, dropped heavy wool over my ankles and unfolded its weight up my body. She took her time, conscious hands as she smoothed the blanket under my chin. I never opened my eyes. Tears traced the sides of my face as I tried to be still and receive. My body called, "more," as she lifted her hands away.

Seated across from me in a tiny office bedroom, Flora said, "Tell me, what's going on for you?" Such authentic interest alone could move me, and I outlined for her the body she'd meet in a few minutes, its injuries and tensions, the chronic plagues, the new discomforts past forty. She listened, another kindness. She knew the emotional world was made manifest in the body. Yes, yes, I thought, as I eyed the table, which was draped with clean sheets in pale colors and a cotton blanket, turned down. Touch me.

She left me to undress, and I folded my clothes. I wanted to stay aware, to absorb all the care the money and the hour would allow. As requested, I removed earrings, rings, necklace, hair clips, made myself blank. I settled into the sheets, a place to begin again. This is what I was always seeking.

Flora tapped on the door. "Honey? You ready?"

I liked the asking, then the waiting.

I propped myself up on my elbows to watch what she did, as she uncapped vials, mixed oils. "Lie down now," she said, a quick pat on my head, and I set my face into the cradle. Flora pushed a shallow pillow under my ankles, adjusted this and that. Barefoot, she circled the table, her fingertips in contact with my back. I read their warmth, that there was nothing insistent in their pressure. This was just her work. She set her open hands onto me, over the tripled layer of cotton. I tracked her solid, standing form in relation to my prone, self-consciously relaxed body, and how she inserted her body into the space we shared. I was, as ever, on guard, aware that no boundary holds.

The massage lasted beyond the hour I'd paid for. I was always careful never to want more than was allotted, but Flora kept on. When she finished, I was deeply worked, sore with it. I scheduled another appointment a week later, then added another for the following week. I didn't care what regular visits might cost. Like the right therapy at last, it called.

The next session was gentle, the next a pursuit deeper in. The next, we'd agreed to the bargain, my skin to her hands, her hands to my body, our mutual education. We worked together, as I undid my physical pieces for her, one by one, and she attended each thoughtfully. This calmed the psychic churn, something I could never manage on my own. Each week, returning, my body revealed the gentle shifts she'd encouraged. *Look* at your hip flexors, she'd say. Much more range. See how your vertebrae have spread apart? Each week I left her office in need of rest and water, clarified and properly attended.

While she worked, she asked for history and talked about her own, her varied life and its many incarnations. The exchange was balanced, her, me, her, me. She took an acute interest in the book I was writing about my mother, asked questions that probed the relationship, that pondered creativity. Many times after Flora I went straight to my desk, stirred and awake. We examined her troubles and trials, her several marriages and what she still missed. We both accepted ancient foolishness and dangers, laughing at ourselves, sometimes so hard she'd stop the massage to sit and catch her breath. I confessed secrets of my marriage, laziness of mothering. She showed me the poems that filled her notebooks. There was always another era I'd forgotten to explain — oh, the day I delivered! — or some life chapter she hadn't yet covered — farming on a kibbutz! — and, eyes closed, I absorbed her competent touch, soaked up her voice, her Southern cadences rising and dipping. They rocked me.

For a year we went on weekly. Flora was a therapist who could be a friend, without its being weird. We said we should go out for coffee, but we never did. We said, come look at my garden, my tulips, but we didn't. In such frequent contact we couldn't help but keep close track of each other's lives, enumerate regular habits and constant truths — "How was the dentist?" — and I involved myself in her concerns more deeply than I did with most good friends, but a tacit clause in the contract prevailed, boundaries insisted on by the money, guaranteed, and we kept to the office at the top of the stairs in the converted Victorian.

One day I was on Sylvia's table for acupuncture, as Flora gave a massage to someone in the next room, and my agent phoned. I'd been expecting the call, too jumpy to benefit from the needles. Sylvia and I mostly were chatting, which she indulged when I was agitated. She handed me the phone and stepped out. The book had sold. When she returned, I was still on my back, stunned, and I burst into confused tears. She called Flora in from the hallway, where she was stocking linens. The three of us celebrated with triumph and disbelief. They held me, hugged me. They saturated me with praise and sent me out into the world.

It was an afternoon two months later, August heat trapped in Flora's tiny upstairs room. She had the shades down, darkness a stand-in for cool. It was stifling.

I lifted the sheet off my skin. "Would you mind if I just didn't have this?"

"Lord, no," she said. Each week she'd seen me in naked sections, a quarter of my body bared at a time with evident borders. "You do what you do, honey."

I kicked the sheet to the floor, exposed all. It startled me that I didn't mind, that I'd assessed the risk unconsciously when usually I was so very aware, exhaustedly so. Flora's capable hands went to work, re-signing our invisible contract. I lay still and softened muscle as she pushed into my flesh. Both her hands took hold of my thigh, and I gave her its weight, abandoned inten-tion, dropped my will. Like a meditation that slips for a mere second into transcen-dence, I allowed the rapture of this woman's love, felt fully loved. The instant sprang away, disappeared, but it had undone some-thing. I tried to come back, to focus on the boxy room. She moved to the calf, shin, the foot, which she held, waking my toes with the pads of her thumbs. She came to the head of the table, where she buoyed my head's weight in her hands and pressed her palms and fingers against my scalp. My mouth felt lazy. Flora, usually a train of talk that couldn't be halted, exhaled and sighed, no words, and we shared stillness, the efforts of our bodies adding to the close heat. Raising me from the shoulders, she slid her arms under me and gathered the muscles on either side of my spine, held me up, and I surrendered. Each breath was a risk, her forearms strong under the wings of my back, new courage, a brave submission.

Flora, always attuned, felt the give, the shocking change. She swept her touch along my shoulders and arms, the soft sides of my breasts, down my legs, over my knees, onto my feet, holding and releasing, holding. I watched her face, the black eyes she turned often to mine. I looked at the ceiling, yellow sunlight striping the walls. She moved her hands into the space beneath my ribs, and I let out breath. "Another," she said. Her hands pushed, and stayed. "There you go." I felt panic hint. Most people resist abdominal massage, the tender core unguarded; it's too much. Many therapists don't like to work there either, vulnerable to the power of someone's stored trauma, but I was now so naked, and a hard stone lived there that I could not get at on my own. I wanted it loosed. She shaped the tissue and moved muscle, getting to a buried dungeon. She went on, in, and I told myself this wasn't too much, I could go in, too.

Tears had started, leaking a thin track to my ears. Flora stayed quiet, and the crying turned hard. I felt her hands inside my gut, sinew telling me some old story, and I had to attend. "Shh, shh, shhh," she said, not to silence the full-throated sobs, but to stay with me, the cooing of a real mother. My body began to heave, the sobs deliberate, one after the other, and I dissolved into the *shhhh,* the whisper, the backward falling that was not into empty rage and desertion, but with amber sun around us, late-day orange on the familiar skin of Flora's arms.

I kept my eyes open, regarded my unbroken nakedness to my toes. Flora hefted one arm under my shoulders, as I cried. She wrapped her other arm in front, gathered me to her, and then the dangerous miracle: I gave away the last things. Naked; naked breasts and hips, unguarded tummy, throat exposed, knees, bared thighs and bottom, naked, I let her hold me up, yielding to infant grief, and she kept me at her chest, her skin sticky where it melted to mine.

The word came as an animal — TRUST. *You trust her,* I thought. Peace. This woman looked after me.

After many minutes, we were reverent. She knew she'd reached a place no one had. We knew I'd let her. I didn't make jokes, as

I usually would, putting metal back into emotion. I wanted to savor the body's mysterious achievement. We marveled together.

She left to give me privacy. Astonished, I considered the depths. They would close back up, I knew, but in this moment I was ravished. I dressed, the sleeves of my shirt confusing, and opened the door, a small breeze passing in. Flora came back and held me, both of us standing. "Honey," she said. Her body felt small, now that I was up, her strengths absorbed back into her frame, but she was all there. You had only to look at her to see what shined forth. I had let myself be lifted, held, carried, had felt what it felt like. I couldn't believe it.

The next week, I came for the massage and — well, I should have predicted this — I did not know which way to go. I'd been so revealed that it felt dishonest to be less than that, but I also couldn't go around gapingly torn open. It was exhausting, had taken me liters of water to restore a capable self after that session, which I left in a trance that lasted into the following morning. Besides, tiny scraps of reserve and apprehension had begun to flutter against me again.

Flora talked on, and it grated. She had tax

trouble and renter's complaints. She was looking for a cheaper place to live but was worried about breaking her lease. She knew I needed an office.

"Why, you could rent my place," she said.

"I'll think about it," I said. I wanted to keep her attention on the massage. "I'll come and see it." But it was the wrong price, and it was all her viney plants, aging cats, splayed painting materials, family photos, kitchen disarray. She'd clean up and take her things, of course, but no. "I'd love to help you move," I said, "but I don't want to rent the apartment. Thank you for thinking of me though." I'd arranged each sentence several times. I got careful with offers, knew the nasty turn they could take right before they evaporated.

She left a message on the phone — her landlord wanted to meet me, said I could rent it. "I told him all about you," she said, singsong. I felt adamant and annoyed. Back off, I thought, don't manage me. Your affairs and mine are not intertwined. She had the flu, Sylvia said, and I stopped by with soup and flowers, staying put on the couch as she related symptoms for ten minutes. She asked me to refer more friends.

I did not want to take part in Flora's troubles. This distressed me. Wouldn't a friend help? Sylvia gave her rides when her car broke down. I struggled with what to offer, besides my custom and the money I paid. I cared, but I needed her to remain a grown-up, my grown-up, and she seemed to be careless with this charge. We weren't, after all, friends. We had our contract, the terms that had allowed me to be more naked than in any sex, aware of my body cradled. I had written the check for that.

When she moved, I came by the new place and, finding her not at home, left a bouquet of lavender on her windshield, no note. I'd biked and hadn't had room for pen and paper in my summer pockets. But, lavender the sort of language we used to speak together, she called to thank me. I listened to her voice mail, glad I'd avoided one of her sighing discussions.

We drifted, conversation grew parched. At a session, I tensed under her hands, drew back. She couldn't undo my stiffness. We weren't working together anymore. I was angry about this.

To my relief, Flora left town. Usually, though I tried to be supportive and amiable, I felt bereft when friends moved away. But I wanted Flora off me, my skin coated with her oils and clogged. I heard from Sylvia where she was going, without taking it in. Something to do with her dying father, a duty, but also care, a calling with her. Good: let that calling no longer be me.

A few years later, Flora moved back. Elated, Sylvia imagined the pleasures she'd share again with her friend, and how Flora's reappearance would better my life, too. I was wary. What would be expected of me, how had I failed and what would I be held accountable for? I carried the drama around.

I meant to call her but didn't do it. After several months I ran into her in the post office, the small-town denominator, an abrupt meeting, edged by old intimacy. We'd had something, we knew that. We'd cared, respected, and shared hard, beautiful hours. We'd loved. We stood in formal parallels by the large oak doors and caught up, but without visible feeling. I felt afraid and was trying to head off accusation, if it was going to show up. I'd let Flora be my mother, and then *mother* had marshaled its alarms and savagery, and I couldn't stay whole. Our agreement had evolved, loosened, and we were well into a relationship that promised to nourish — did nourish — but had normal limitations, human complications. Someone else might have rolled with it, paid no attention to the stripped contract, but the only thing I knew how to do, no matter what I told myself, was to get up and run.

BOUNDARIES

Ellen and I are formal with each other now, like people who have never met in person. She sends me short, uninflected e-mails, and I respond in a day or so with something short, too. She praises our children; I agree and thank her. We do not use exclamation points. Urgency has left us. Although our houses are across the tame Clark Fork River from each other, walking distance, and the kids are inseparable, we've secured perimeters to keep safe from contact. Our long, close friendship ended two years ago, and I'm not sure what we're starting.

If Abby had stayed, I'd have known Ellen mostly by report. They'd met in some previous city, had moved to Missoula at the same time. Abby introduced us at the All Women's Run. We stood around before the start. They talked and I listened, and Ellen listened to me and Abby. Each relationship its own container, the duos didn't blend. Ellen provided Abby with something I didn't, I thought. They used to backcountry camp, seek out remote waterfalls, adventures of self-reliance and physical strain. Abby and I liked to have long coffees in busy student cafés, make up reading lists of novels for each other. The serious runners gathered at the starting line and set off, and we followed at the walkers' increasing distance, three abreast on a windy day, which made conversation hard to share. We pushed jog strollers, while Ellen shouldered the weight of her solemn infant in a structured backpack. Abby had described this brilliant friend, her honors and scholarly pursuits, her pure physical endurance. Maybe Ellen had heard Abby talk about me, my intellect and achievements, but I doubted it. Consumed by my boy, I didn't show ambition and aptitude anymore. Those were no longer useful.

I asked Ellen about herself, a way of showing Abby respect, and her answers were brief, polite. She did not open. She didn't seem a match for Abby, whose warmth defined our first breezy moments a year earlier at the gym. I'd come for prenatal water aerobics, and entering the locker room I saw the woman's bare back, her shirt and bra already off. A copy of *The Nation,* unusual in Missoula, showed over the top of her tote bag and beckoned, but I chose a separate bench and turned my back, too, carving the false privacy. Several inches taller than me, the woman seemed to rule her stomach, its taut skin stretched to pale, except for the *linea nigra* that ran a darkened seam down the middle of her bare belly. I looked her body over, seeking the future. I remembered a day at the start of high school; in the claustrophobic proximity of the dorm bathroom, I saw breasts of older girls for the first time, unlike the breasts of my mother or grandmother — the rude freshness of the flesh, that warning. That was when I realized, nauseated and faintly aroused, that womanhood would come for me.

The *Nation* reader and I struggled with our bathing suits, clumsy fingers and swollen feet. We were grunting, effort overriding our discretions. How wretched we were, how many tasks had become humiliating. We looked up, and a smile burst across her face. We each asked, When are you due, before we said our names, then tumbled into that gentle, competitive monomania of pregnancy, collecting the specifics of OBs, digestion and sleep, supplement brands and yoga poses. We were preoccupied with comfort. She was four weeks away from delivery, and I still had months to go, endless and lagging. Nice to meet you, we said as we left the cocoon of the locker room for the pool, as we lowered into the weightless blessing of water.

A few days later we met for lunch, and sat on a sunny deck facing the river. I had put on the prettiest lipstick color, wanting a chance at a better first impression. We pushed our plastic chairs from the table to give our bodies room, moved our menus to the side. Tell me your story, we said, tell me all about you. Raised in New York, I told her, I felt at odds in Montana, where I'd lived for three years. The feeling wasn't going away. Briefly, my job history, as if that were salient; I only cared to talk about being pregnant. She, too, dashed off minor biography, then talked pregnancy, our headline subject, and I accrued details. I needed to cement my conviction about what I was doing, which was anyway moot. This was coming. Compelled beyond my reason, my education, my writing, I had volunteered to be pregnant, craved it. Abby seemed grounded and driven and reasonable. Yet she had also been compelled. What was happening to our bodies, to us? And what about

291

our marriages? Would they be okay? Abby's husband wanted to stay home with the baby. Christopher had gone back to school for a counseling degree, was working new, lengthy hours as a therapist, and already I saw him less. When Abby said she was planning to start divinity school, I thought she was kidding. No: *This* is what we're doing, we're having babies. At the dawn of a friendship, which seemed like it might be remarkable for her intelligence and my candor, her placid security and easygoing generosity, it was news I didn't want to hear.

"When are you leaving?"

"Don't worry, in a year," she said. "I still have to write my thesis."

I was the late arrival in her Missoula life. She already had lots of friends, whom I met the next week at her boisterous shower, except for Ellen, who was out of town.

I was surprised a few years later to see Ellen at a party. Christopher and I had hired a sitter for Daniel, and I'd spent most of the evening seated and inert, my newborn sleeping in one arm, as Christopher brought me a plate of food, a glass of juice and seltzer. When Jack woke, and breathed deeper into his muscles, which I could feel against my ribs, I split open the front of my shirt and nursed him. Abby had long since moved to Palo Alto, which I struggled to keep in mind was not, of course, a personal rejection. Every time I passed her old house, those first months, I cried, empty, heart-sore. It embarrassed me how acute my long-ing was for a miracle that would have changed her mind, made her stay. She hadn't met Jack, my new baby, which seemed all wrong because she'd been so much a part of Daniel's first year. In our rare and rarer calls Abby outlined theology courses, which I wanted to find interesting, but her busyness and excellent grades and philosophical investigation left me discour-aged in my mousy accomplishments, my awareness that all aspiration had been bludgeoned by domestic repetition, by the mass of baby-boy particulars that occupied my brain. It was better to speak of the babies, pose polite questions about hers as I waited for the moment to describe my sons.

Ellen stood in the kitchen, regarding the guests as they got drunker. She had no glass, her arms folded. We seemed to be the only two not drinking. I said hello, she said hello, and I remembered our first awkward-ness, but tonight we could summon our absent friend, and Ellen's face lightened, and her talk flowed, a mix of affection and sarcasm and acute perception. It felt like a way to have Abby back, to affirm the importance of that friendship. We united in a benign mourning.

"I was watching you with the baby," Ellen said. "You're very good with him. You're calm." I thanked her, bloomed, asked after her son. Later I said to Christopher, "Just to be really seen. Just to be *recognized.*"

Ellen and I compared the eerie intelligence of our children, how riveted they were by the inner workings of things. Daniel was four, Thomas six months younger. "It sounds like they'd be friends," I said. "You want to get them together?" I offered my house for the first playdate. We used them as the ruse, advancing toward each other, but not fast. I knew from Christopher that some people need to observe, take things in; they can't be rushed. "Safety sensitive," he used the term he'd learned in his training for "introvert." The personality that has always compelled me, why I married Christopher: *you* won't shudder and explode, you won't unseat me, you won't bite off pieces of me to feed yourself. I sought out people who promised safety. Ellen and I made a date for the next week, around her work schedule.

I watched for her car. She leaned deep

into the backseat, her feet on the sidewalk. She took a long time, as I stood at the window. Then she lifted a sleeping child out, all her strength and torque in managing her way up from the bent position without jostling him. She eased the car door shut with a slow hip, opened my gate. Thomas's head lolled off her shoulder, the straps of his polar fleece hat draped in the same direction. "I'm sorry," Ellen said. She spoke to me but looked at her son. "Just fell asleep on the way over." There was no question of waking him. We all knew that, not to interfere with the children's plans on our account. Some of us practiced it more diligently than others. "He'll probably wake up soon," she said.

She settled the drowsing boy on Daniel's bed, where my son inspected him before returning to his trucks and plastic animals on the freshly vacuumed carpet. Ellen declined coffee and tea and water. We shared updates of Abby, incredulous that anyone had started divinity school — started anything! — with a new baby. I was relieved we knew the same details, that Abby didn't favor one of us with better intimacies. Ellen nudged her son, but he slept on, severe seriousness plastered over his face. She looked over at him about once a minute.

Later, failing again, she said, "This is a little embarrassing."

"Don't worry at all," I said to be kind. I was perplexed by the tenacity of her discomfort. Hadn't motherhood taught all of us to give up formality, to relinquish the hope for plans carried through?

"I guess we should make another date. You could come to my house."

"Great, yes." I wanted to know her, this smart lawyer with the wry outlook, this woman who respected the heart's sobrieties. This woman who'd watched me with a newborn and told me I was doing it right. Ellen talked about the politics of motherhood, the confusions of leftover feminism, rather than the daily mess and the obvious obstacles. I loved that. She said, How about I call and we'll set something up, and I said, Sure, anytime.

Little by little, my patience rewarded, Ellen revealed herself. First the defining items, where she was raised, which law school, what her husband did, how she landed her job at the firm. I was used to deeper talk mixed with trivial musings sooner — the way women talk, assuming we will inevitably be intimate, so we may as well get there — but I'd be cautious. Ellen needed reassurance, even if I couldn't tell why. I wouldn't beg for her confidences, which she showed sparingly, which she guarded against some unknown threat. When she was almost relaxed she mentioned she'd been a night-club DJ through college and in her twenties; she'd get to bed at dawn. We laughed and laughed. What music did you play? Did you *dance*? She shook her head, the faraway of it all, our youthful personas assumed to broadcast what we were capable of, what we dared. I could picture a DJ — though not Ellen — elevated on the raised stage, her black T-shirt, the dark club, the frantic focus of discs and knobs, the shouted requests. A DJ, I told Christopher! Here's the Ellen you can't see, only I'm allowed to see her this way! The incongruous picture boasted too much frivolity for my subdued, introspective friend, until I realized the job provided the perch apart, her safe discretion. She could be visible, never known. Well, I would know her. "My new best friend," I told him. He nodded, used to my loyal passions, how they flared and dimmed, serially.

One hot night, several months into the slow unwrapping, I invited Ellen for dinner. Her husband, Laurence, was away, and she brought her boy. Our sons, if not true friends, accepted being together. Christopher and I sat under the canvas umbrella with Ellen, the table laid with food and plates, cool taking over the air, darkness deepening the backyard. Thomas and Daniel started to chase our cats, who ran up against the fence and darted away, the children after them, their limbs in all directions. "We're herding cats!" they chanted, screaming with laughter. We hadn't noticed the boys loosening, having fun, and it unnerved but pleased us, the sign that they were normal as well as exceptional. I'd made penne with garlic and cauliflower and a tart of nectarines and blueberries, cookbooks still open on the counter. Ellen didn't eat. She dished spoonfuls of food onto her son's plate, but the boy didn't eat either. "Can I get you something else?" I said. "Would he like macaroni and cheese?"

All that evening, looking at the still life on her plate, the roasted scallions and seasoned beets and arugula untouched, I went back and forth between insult and frustration. I'll have her over again, I resolved, entice her. I tried to make myself indispensable to my friends, a tactic I'd learned chasing down the gazes of my self-absorbed parents: need me. How necessary it was for me to offer and provide, to establish that I would attend to her. I felt unaccusable that way; I didn't like that such safety had to be the prominent compass, but it was me.

In the next months, I invited Ellen, and the conversation was rich, the observations pointed yet nuanced, the recognition of motherhood challenges mutual, and she never ate. I made my best dishes: sausage with black-eyed peas, grilled salmon marinated in grated ginger and soy sauce, cucumber salad. She ate none of it. I gave up. She was not comfortable with offerings, a fact I finally accepted. She was teaching me to look away from her, yet she'd chosen me, a woman intensely conscious, ready to pull apart each gesture, detail, mood, and ask what it meant. When she came over with Thomas, I'd leave her a glass of water on the counter. I had learned not to hold it out to her.

A couple of years later, she and I were at the farmers' market, the kids beside us. In my bag I had lettuce and garlic, fresh cheeses, local honey. She wasn't shopping, but entertained me with her commentary on the scene and people around us. We came to a stand with wide-leafed chard and exceptional cauliflower in white and purple. "I just hate cauliflower," she said. She sounded ready, a disclosure that had been needing to escape. Was she thinking of that first dinner at my house, the offending dish on the table? *Why didn't you say?* I thought, wishing to relive the evening. *I would have made something you liked.*

By age six, Daniel and Thomas were devoted and entwined, and Ellen and I were connected in the most dire way: for them. We praised them for finding each other, quietly praising ourselves. In our numerous daily phone calls we checked our opinions: Those big kids who commandeer the slides? They're *too* big! Those bulk bins at the health food store? There's corn meal on the floor, someone should clean up the raisins. We found elite security in agreement. And we both had our second sons. Jack was two, her son just a few months old. We applied to the private school with the solar panels and the prize-winning math team. The doors would open, of course they would, our brilliant children bound together for their academic careers, and we would carpool and sit next to each other at school plays and know each other for decades. As we filled out the applications, we phoned back and forth. What did you put for his interests? Do you see how many "volunteer" hours they require! When the rejection letter came, I phoned Ellen, not my husband.

I felt scared Thomas had been accepted. If she sent him out of our orbit, would I lose her, too? But he'd also been rejected, and our momentary joint wrath turned to fun we could have at the expense of ourselves — *How much we'd thought it mattered!* This was our merry joke, meant to distract us from our real dread, unaccountable disappointment.

The phone rang after we'd gone to sleep. Ellen was at the ER with Thomas, who'd broken his leg. She asked me to come and get her infant son, so she and Laurence could concentrate. I dressed, got there, found them through the admitting doors. Her face was tight and pale, her natural beauty invisible behind worry. Laurence didn't even make eye contact, pulled down deep. I looked for Thomas, but he'd been taken away, the family stranded in a gaping room. She offered the baby. I think he was about four months old then. "Can you bring him back in the morning?" she said. "He'll need to nurse." I carried him outside, uneasy with his smallness, and adjusted the lanky straps of Jack's car seat to fit him. I brought him home like a prize, a found kitten, waking Christopher as I settled him into the crib near our bed. I fell asleep listening to my best friend's infant make his noises, the sounds she must have documented every night, as if I had finally entered her sequestered heart.

In the morning I brought him to the hospital room, where Thomas's face was turned from the door, his expression dim and blank, not with pain, but with the spooky absence of pain. Ellen took the baby, asked after his night. We consulted over how many hours he'd slept, his mood on waking and on the ride over. I didn't say I wished I could have nursed him for her, saved her the trouble this particular morning. Or maybe I did say that. We would have laughed, our conspiracy of crude truths. We always pushed deeply into the inane and the grotesque of motherhood, into the dictates and phobias of our culture, gave each other permission to have really bad days and say so. Her face assumed more of its character as she found her baby's gaze. Finally, I had done something for her. She had trusted me, letting me drive away with her baby into the unpredictable night, and when the midnight came that I brought a son to the ER, she'd be there for me, too.

A few years later, I sprained my foot, biking in flip-flops. Pain stealthy while it traveled to the bone, I walked the bike out of the intersection to a gas station, where I asked for ice, ignoring how bad the foot felt, or not feeling it yet. As I applied the ice, propped outside against a white wall in the shade, the pain screamed forward. I couldn't get the bike home or get myself home. My family was out of town, so I called Ellen. Our friendship was reliable ballast in my daily life, Ellen the one I called when I felt my bitchiest and sharpest, when I felt depleted and overwhelmed, who groaned and laughed with me at how all our time and talent were enslaved to our children.

"I fell off my bike," I said, needing to be that little again.

"Do you want me to come get you?" Her voice was flat patience, consideration.

"No, I'll be okay." We hung up. I sensed that this involved politics between us we'd never used. I tried to think of another friend but then called Ellen back. "Please come and get me, I need you, please." Something in me always made it hard to ask for complete attention, afraid I'd be accused of selfishness or, worse, ignored. And something in her made it hard for me to ask her.

She left her kids with a sitter and drove to me. I climbed into the front, mostly by arm strength, while she lifted the bike into the

303

back of the SUV. Absent our precious and encompassing focus of the children, we were not talkative. She monitored the road. I was embarrassed to have pulled her away from other things and glad she didn't look at me, examine my naked need.

"Do you want to go to the doctor?" she said.

"No, that's okay."

"I'll drop your bike at your house," she said, "if you want to go."

"Okay."

She drove me to the clinic, where I made my slow way through the glass doors and across marble to the elevators, and I was glad, as I guarded the ghastly pain, that I had let myself ask her. Yes, this will take us further in, tighten us. As promised, she left the bike on my lawn.

As the boys grew and enrolled in separate schools and Thomas had dance class and Daniel started Aikido, I realized I'd never seen Ellen without the kids, save for that short drive. I had other friends for not-mothering time, women without children who met spontaneously for late drinks or a quick river float, who said yes to a last-minute movie. Spontaneity — always a little risky for me — was not part of this friend-

ship. We provided each other with an antidote to the long, long loving boredoms of
parenthood. We provided each other with
good company. I counted on Ellen's solem-
nity, her structured beams and mortar. She
liked my mischief and sense of play. Settled,
shoes off in her living room, we would watch
our sons, unknot their laces, sweep up their
abandoned LEGO pieces with our arms,
and converse in surreptitious undertones,
vocabulary chosen to elude them. Did we
talk of our hearts' desires, our ruinous
disappointments? No. We talked, albeit
smartly and with absolute candor, even
splendid vulgarity, about the thorny demands in raising our kids, our resentments
and frustrations, our terrifying moments of
uncertainty, the traps of masculinity we
hoped to teach our boys to avoid. We felt
stronger. Everything deserved comment,
their dreams, whether or not they liked
bacon, if they'd learned how to lie, which
mittens they preferred. How badly we
wanted to go to the bathroom without talking through the closed door, just once. So,
without them, we would have no need for
the hushed aside and sideways affection,
more assumed than demonstrated. We
would have had to talk directly to each other
and confront a troubling truth of our friend-

ship: something blocked further intimacy, real knowing. She barely mentioned her work, and I didn't ask, because confidentiality in a small town was hard enough. Anything she said about her marriage concerned only parenting decisions (on the other hand, I told her the details of my marriage; inspecting me and Christopher, seeking her reactions — our history, our tensions, our time in bed, our happiest privacies). When she mentioned law-firm politics, glancingly, I couldn't picture *my* Ellen involved. A busy stride down a hallway, depositions? I thought of it like this: let the world have the lesser Ellen in her temporary assignment. Her real work — devotion to her sons, her other masks dropped — she chose to share with me. But, lacking a complete picture, I wondered at who she was, the whole of her.

Once, Ellen cried. I sat curled with the phone on our basement steps, away from the family activity in the kitchen, and at first I didn't recognize the sound. A sputter, an extended sigh, and then it was clear what sound it was. We had long before agreed without acknowledgment that she was the grounded listener and I was the explosive confessor. For ethical quandaries I went to Ellen, where I found refuge in her serious, procedural thinking. Her order, her rules; they helped me keep myself together. I remember what she disclosed that day, what prompted her uncharacteristic tears (Ellen crying! Ellen unguarded!) and that she said, "Please don't talk about this to anyone," and that in her pain she became clear and supple and visible, which was lovely. I remember the satisfaction of having her recognize my empathy. She let me in.

It was the anniversary of my mother's accident. A few years earlier, she had suffered a car wreck, spent time in a coma, and nearly died. Our impossible relationship already in tatters, I had chosen not to go to her but to stay nested in the protections of my town, my home, my children's regard. I chose — as I had over years of Thanksgivings and boarding-school Christmases — my friends. Ellen, compassionate, sensitive listener, had accompanied me through the galling puzzle of that decision, witnessed the wrenching problem and irreconcilable pain, always with her steady, neutral gaze. I couldn't track exact dates with my mother, one of the effects of her lifetime of lying, so I hadn't been preparing for this date, but my body felt anniversary unease, reminding me, *You chose this isolation.* That spring day

I felt dangerously unloved. I needed to be included anywhere, at some table.

Christopher was away and I was alone with the boys, who were out of school on break. A lot of my friends were out of town. Ellen was around but overseeing a big conference. I knew she had public-speaking anxiety, that even in her established legal brilliance, scrutiny and exposure were hard for her. Being her friend, I wanted to ease things. I called and asked, could the boys and I come for dinner (that unspoken law between two families — the smaller crowd travels), could we spend the evening with her and Laurence and Thomas and the baby? I'd bring a couple of dishes, a salad, I said, a baguette. But I didn't say, "I'm thinking of my broken daughterhood." I needed a loneliness cure, a way to escape for a day, for a night, the reverberations of family damage; also I wanted Ellen to feel her friend's support, my desire to help move her through the big work weekend. Both were true; the first a little truer.

"Let me think about it and call you back," she said. I felt irritated.

"Of course," I said, polite. Call me back. She always had to call me back, on her schedule, her terms. I didn't want to wait, I wanted a *yes,* a *now,* a *come in.* But Ellen never said those things. I knew that.

She called. "I would love to have you and the boys over," she said, conscious precision. "But not today. I have a lot to handle."

Ellen was calm and clear, with textbook boundaries. I knew I was supposed to respect them, find comfort in the cool accuracy, which, when the friendship hummed along its chosen track, usually I did. But today I was distraught, vulnerable beyond reason, and at her definitive no, I felt defeated: she heard me ask for one particular thing, and she denied me. Why, when I needed a cure for the deprivation lapping at me, did I look to the restrained friend? That was my problem. Why did my good friend step away as I showed need? That, I felt, was hers. I was, at the time, endangered by depression, increasingly isolated in a terrible state, but I didn't know how to confess I was sinking. I wanted to cry, *Please come and get me.*

Christopher returned home, school resumed. Ellen did not call to make the dinner plan and, feeling exposed in my primal loneliness, I didn't call her. All at once we went silent, stopped making dates for the kids. It was so strange for us not to talk for even two days, let alone two, then three weeks. Hard and strange, and obvious. Was she mad? Had I pushed too far? I had, I knew that. I'm sorry, but you . . . Back and forth, I argued her part, then mine; her rebuttal, my petulant rage. Things muffled and unsaid, things I'd never called her on, were knocked loose and scattered in the open. Why do we exchange so many phone calls to make plans? I would not be the only one to accommodate our friendship anymore, wouldn't bargain for her convenience and safety. If she had made concessions for me, as she surely must have, I refused to appreciate them.

After months of this twilight I requested a date. We met at a coffee place downtown, the heavy wooden tables piled with people's schoolwork and laptops, the good cheer from the baristas' counter. I sat by the wall and watched for her, conscious in a tough, angry way that this betrayed her. She didn't like being on display. She came through the door, and when she neared I stood and hugged her. Physical affection had never been in our regular language, but today, after this bizarre separation, the reality of her body and mine signaled that we could overcome whatever bad flame burned in my head, where I was alone. This would be the real two of us. Real would be much better.

We sat with our prop cups of tea.

"The day I asked to come for dinner," I said. "I wonder if you knew how upset I was, before I asked; what was going on for me." Therapist-careful.

She let me talk a long while. Listening. She listened well.

I said, "When I ask for something specific, I mean, I don't, it's not easy for me, but when I do . . ."

Then she said, like a teacher, "I appreciate you telling me this. I respect your feelings." I waited. She was done, my heart sank. Ellen, clear-eyed, always ready for honest acknowledgment, wouldn't even agree we had a dilemma. She wouldn't participate.

"I miss you," I said. "And I love you." She straightened. "And, and I don't want our relationship tied exclusively to our children." I was flailing. I missed her strength, her steadying judgment. "I've been depressed, Ellen. I needed" — *What?* — "to talk to *you,* not with the kids, and so . . . and I've never been able to be alone with you."

"Well," she said, "my time."

"But I should count!" I regretted my force. "If our friendship matters, there should be time for it." I was pushing at her, exactly what I knew not to do. It had gone badly before. I imagined, with enduring dread, her sighing to Laurence about Susanna's narcissism. I always dreaded this when I spoke up for something I craved. But the friendship, I thought, should not be denied specialness. That's what made a friendship. That, and private repair.

She held her hands to herself, her bag on her lap; she sighed.

"We've known each other a long time," I said. "You, me, we know each other better and better. Right?" I wasn't even sure what I was asking anymore.

"I need to get back to you," she said. "Thank you for calling me, and for the tea." Undrunk. The formality stung.

We parted outside. I moved to hug her, trying to hear more from her, anything, and I had my face in her hair.

She stepped backward, held my gaze. "I think you're very brave," she said. Whatever, I thought. I knew I wasn't, not really. I hadn't said how plain angry I was; and I hadn't copped to the bind I'd put her in — Susanna's unanswerable need versus Ellen's locked boundaries. I was still hoping — this was pure me — that if I found the right words, expressed my true problem, I would somehow unleash the generous waters. I hadn't asked for what I really needed her to

give me, because you can't ask for everything; you can't ask your friend to fill up
the holes left gaping by two selfish parents.

In a few days she e-mailed. "It feels very
difficult to have a hard issue affecting our
relationship that we can't fully process. I'm
sad that this has been so painful and I hope
we can find a way to reconnect." I was tired
of her guarded script, this antiseptic order.

"She won't help fix this," I told Christopher, bruised as I read. This is not, as you
can see, what she said. She was looking, in
her way, for our repair, but in my way, pure
Susanna, I felt abandoned and couldn't rise
up out of it. Look, she offered to reconnect,
but I never responded to the e-mail. Feeling
unheard in my terms, I gave up on hers,
and inside me, where I possessed the friendship's certain riches, I shut her off.

I wish I had Ellen back, miss us. I wish I
had Abby back, unhappy at any bounty lost
in my life or taken away. I miss the rewards
of long-term work and company, our tiny
in-jokes and half-conscious intuitions. I
don't know how we recover, or if we should,
and that seems to me like my own inad-
equacy. Other people make up, forgive, keep
going. Why was I so rigid? Was I? We'd
reached a crisis, the friendship needed tend-

ing, both of us. I want some eloquent way to tell Ellen I knew this about myself — that I pushed at her and thus pushed her away. I knew I demanded a lot, challenged her safety; I knew I still wanted the friendship, or a fresh version, because our rewards of candor and afternoon levity were rich; that she must get something from me, too, and I wanted her to say that. We both like complicated relationships, wouldn't have trusted any other kind, yet I pressed at her anxieties, and she pressed at mine. We forged a compulsive magnet.

It takes concentration to avoid your close friend who lives just over the bridge, half a mile away, and the effort was at first its own busy trial, another of the aggravations, which now I was free to count up. I knew Fridays she'd come into Bernice's Bakery, because often I was there when she did, our routines coinciding. So, I noticed with a spiky, helpless sadness that she no longer did it. She'd made a decision to change her routine, because of us. Many Fridays I sat at a corner table, looked out at the negative space.

But I was also relieved, because the energy I'd devoted to careful Ellen and our careful friendship could now go elsewhere. I didn't have to be watchful anymore, hold my affections in check, allow for her to trade a million calls, or remember that she disliked cauliflower. I didn't have to speak in whispers, muffle my full voice, a habit she got me into in front of the boys. I was ready to shed aspects of that friendship; I was ready for more risk. If we begin again, will it be a reinvention? Perhaps in our few e-mails we're constructing a careful edifice, entombing a shattered friendship. We can't unknow the other's inevitable ways, but we've let a lot of time go by, clearing a space. We were one thing, and we're not that now; we may forge a third act, or we may not. I don't know.

Ellen sends a casual e-mail. For the first time in two years she admits something of herself. She has gotten an African gray parrot (she attaches a photo), "if you can believe it," she writes, which tugs at me, our lost intimacy, our knowing as a strong, daily habit. Ellen had always had an abhorrence of birds, and she knows I'll see, as only a longtime confidante could, that the shift she's made is significant. She chooses to show me she is changing.

Uncertain how to respond, I let a week go by. I drive her son home, saying I'd like a look at the parrot. I go up Ellen's front steps with the boy. I'm nervous, scared to present myself with no plan. When she opens the door, the sight of her, the first time we've stood before each other in two years, dissolves a great deal of the buttressed wall. I want to touch her, feel her hand. It's like seeing someone you'd been in love with, whom you'd talked yourself out of, or thought you had. A meaningful gladness comes over me, much stronger than the goodwill I'd prepared. I can feel, even under the lapses and the struggle and the tacit clashes we couldn't surmount, how much we gave and traded, understood, the ways our corresponding energies fueled the other's; how much room we made for each other as we each inhabited our unavoidable natures. Our rupture, which in pain I'd tried never to inspect, seems a tragedy, quiet in a busy world but one of my own great epics. I stand waiting, as if she will say, *Yes, Susanna, now. Come in.*

RITUAL

I see Adele in the public spaces of our town. We stand in the school corridor, waiting for our children to emerge from their classrooms. Almost daily we start a conversation with resumed warmth, but it's often rearranged by another parent whom Adele welcomes. She extends an arm, brings the parent close, wants to know how she is. Sometimes, with no chance to catch up, first- and second-graders a rush between and around us, we just embrace, but it's a generous pause in my day.

After twenty years in Missoula, nearly, my days contain these brief and crucial flirts, gestures of belonging. A row ahead at the movies, say, is a surgeon I consulted, with his girlfriend, the receptionist at Daniel's high school. His ex-wife gets her hair cut where I do. I wave outside Food Farm to the woman who owned a bookstore. Now she does massage. I pull over with a flat tire, and the person who stops to help used to run the food bank where I volunteered. The rustle of people in this small city is a flag of stitched and overlapping roles, coincident eras. My dentist used to be married to my neighbor; my pharmacist dropped off a prescription after I left it on her counter. We bring Jack to the walk-in clinic, and the doctor is a woman I once knew, who left for med school, and whose son, it turns out, is in calculus with Daniel. When I leave the house I prepare unconsciously for the pleasant social exhaustion of an intimate city. In the school hall, we wait for children who didn't exist when I first came to live here. We made people, joined city council; we've all adopted cats and dogs from our shelter. I have lived here long enough that important friends have moved away, that friends I liked and saw a lot have faded into acquaintances, that grudges remain although I've forgotten their source. Friends' teenagers take holiday jobs at the mall, or show up in the community musicals, unexpected singers. I drive past fields where the kids remind me they played Little League, and what I remember, guiltily, is the sun in my irritated eyes and the hungry hours on aluminum bleachers with a blanket. I greet three or four people within a downtown block. I know their names; I've forgotten names. And a few women, a rare few, are bound to me by key experience and disclosure, by admiration, by uncomplicated love. Adele is one of these. We are not best friends, although we have confided. We are dearly connected.

When I had the abortion, Missoula was still strange, eighteen months' residency hardly a viable tenure. I had no close friends here. I found out I was pregnant — an accident three months into marriage. For any other burden or transition Christopher would have been enough, but we were pushed apart by mutual devastation, had turned unfamiliar and silent. I needed warming, someone in front of me. The phone didn't serve, its connection only a trick. On a winter day I went to lunch with a woman I knew slightly (Patricia, I've told you about her), yearning for the right companion, but when I said, "I'm having an abortion," the light left her face and she told me not to do it, and we were each embarrassed. She tried to explain — hadn't meant to sound that way, wasn't judging, the years she'd been hoping to get pregnant. So I went to the preliminary appointments on my own, offered bare inner arm for the blood tests, read the forms by myself. Alone I attended to the mad, unceasing noise in my head as I recalculated weeks, days, this choice or that one. We made our decision, which is a story for another time. Christopher came with me for the abortion itself, but I told him he had to stay in the waiting room. I didn't want to look at him.

Always, Christopher made me glad and loved me, and I loved him, but each year I got into unconscious trouble around the anniversary, and hated him. How doltish and inept he seemed filling a doorway, how puny on the other side of the bed as he stood taking off his glasses, checking the alarm on his clock. I hated his pillow. I'd watch him and allow contempt to fill me, startled by my longing to do him inexplicable violence. Then I'd remember the date. His body, dumb and comfortable with maleness, would never have to give away what mine had. We'd endured the decision, done that together, and that part — the hard, hard education of being in a couple — I didn't regret. We learned respectful compromise, were prepared by it to face lesser conflicts, but in the long weeks of late winter leading up to each anniversary, I started my furious retreat and in my mind unmarried him. The burst of the actual date made me miserable, and I stormed around. As we got into bed, deliberately oblique, I'd say, "It was today, you know." Mutter. "The anniversary." I forced his confused look, his searching query, "Which anniversary?" so I could blow up, fling him away. I was isolated in this eddy of memory that wouldn't release me.

Ten years of that. I was talking one afternoon with my friend Donna, who had hired me as an abortion counselor soon after my own abortion. I'd needed to go to work in a clinic, work with women and for women, forget men. Somewhere in age between my mother's and my father's, Donna had watched me hesitate, attempt, stumble, stand. We had a teapot and cups on my table, a plate of bruschetta, shards of garlic shining with green olive oil. Abortion was a vivid and regular subject between us, and I adored her frank acknowledgment, straight language, our aggressive push away from shame. Beneath all our conversations ran her interest in my well-being. I was slowly learning to seek that, allow it.

"How are you, my dear?"

"It's almost the anniversary, not great. I get kind of crazy. Really angry."

"Crazy angry — that's always productive. Have you ever done anything, a ritual?"

I flinched. "No."

"Have you thought about a ceremony?"

"No."

My parents, their parents, the aunts and uncles, had disdained ceremony, secular and intellectual instead. I'd never attended a funeral for a grandparent. My sister and my half sister had both married, but I'd attended neither wedding, nor included anyone at mine, which had been more a civic task than a ceremony. I could run up against the family mistakes anywhere: ritual seemed an unworthy idea, ridiculous, common.

"I wouldn't know where to begin."

"You don't have to do it alone, you know," Donna said. She was leaving for a trip, but as we parted she told me, "Find someone."

I grew more awake than usual to the approaching date, intrigued in spite of myself by this idea. Inarguably, the right person was Adele. As if she couldn't help it — and the longer I knew her I saw she could not — Adele made people feel safe, acceptance her well-known forte. She conducted workshops in the schools on racism, trained the police department in sensitivity. The scope of experience moved her, the ugliness and mistake born of fear didn't faze her.

The first time I met her, eleven years earlier, Adele annoyed me because my house was not being painted. The painter

322

was dating her. Adele dropped by on a sunny day in her loose jeans and sat down on the front steps. The painter, Sara, climbed down the ladder, and from the kitchen I could hear the swishy murmur between them, the laughter's song, the silent pauses. Sara sat Adele down on the front steps, both hands around her face, and they made out. I was pregnant, which accounted for my many bad moods, for my impatience with people who were not completing tasks I'd hired them to do. This dewy girl, this trivial what's-her-name, was in my way. After an hour, she pulled herself up, and Sara walked her to the gate, her hand over her ass. I was glad to see her leave, maybe today Sara would paint the front door, but they stopped and kissed more showy kisses.

When I came outside later, Sara turned down the radio so she could tell me, anyone, about her delicious romantic find. I looked at the window trim. So what, Adele was an art student, so what, she came from blah blah and planned to study blah blah? "She's *ten years* younger than we are," I told Sara. Adele did not seem a serious person, hanging around just to make out. Who seems serious, when you're thirty and pregnant? You think you are the only one capable of a meaningful decision.

Later — this was after they'd broken up — Adele appeared at the clinic. Before sunrise she would escort women from their cars into the building. For hours she put her body between the patients and the protestors. Anyone who helped with abortion was heroic to me, and I regretted having called her unserious. When she saw me she'd smile her calm, starry smile.

When I was pregnant with my second child, Christopher and I went to the midwife's basement office. We'd returned to this comfortable realm for the reassuring instruction, the sympathetic company, and for the film of Brazilian women squatting to give birth. Seven or eight couples dotted the rug, each claiming a double place.

Adele entered with a man, who spoke only to say his name, Joe. Were they together, I wondered, or was he a donor? They sat across from us, Joe against the wall. Adele eased back into him, resting between his legs. Twins, she said sheepishly, radiantly. Her conviction was brave and gorgeous. Interested in each person, she proved a dedicated listener.

The women looked from one to the other, knowing what the men didn't know. We knew the heartbeat and interior graces, compensation for our own clumsiness; the beatitude as we renounced our bodies, our noble little parasites the higher calling. We knew, without saying, the watery rollover, tremor, seismic shudders, the steadiness of the baby's hiccups, the reliable stab from a kick to the kidney, and the intensity of orgasm primed with massive doses of estrogen. We ignored the men, let them prop us. Adele was the one who asked to hear their experience, and then they spoke.

I ran into Adele in the Good Food Store. Her births, news shared rapidly between the classmates, were legendary for their ease, and for being the only multiple among us. She was — they were — taking up an aisle, the twins bound into some sort of double baby carrier held to her by padded straps so that each baby obscured a hip. I was hardly coping with the demands of a baby and a child four years apart, and I felt aghast on her behalf — nursing times two, sleeplessness times two. I think I made a joke, and she did, too, our first private equality, and there was just so much *baby*. Adele, only in her early twenties, seemed unbreachably able, a sanguine girl-mother.

We started to get together, find mornings. We made chai in her kitchen, Adele with the wooden spoon in the pan as I added the milk. We settled on the floor, mugs beside us, her old Rottweiler asleep on the couch. Now and then she reached up to him to smooth his ears. Daniel, four years old, looked at books, chewed pretzel sticks, while the babies crawled into each other, her daughters and their huge smiles, climbing her, Jack a pumpkin in my lap. We talked about the small and numerous disagreements with the men. They had been our closest friends. We once sought their counsel, cared to advise them. She still wanted to, patient with Joe and herself, able to guide them back to any fraught subject after a day or two. Leaving her house, I always felt I might now possess a clearer heart.

That birthday I answered the door to find Adele with a small bouquet. She showed her relaxed smile, her offered love. It set off my panic — what will I owe and when? But Adele seemed to trust that her good faith would germinate and feed the world beyond friendship. Who lived so unselfishly, with altruism and pure concern? She did, which took me a number of years to determine, not because she was hard to trust, but because I didn't believe in such magnanimity. Adele required of me a leap of faith.

When their daughters were five, Adele and Joe married before the Mission Mountains on a blazing day in July, a bright sky, a high heat. I'd driven up from Missoula on my own. When I rounded the pass, emerged from the high-shouldered section of Route 93, the Missions stunned me, always did, and my car, pulled by the force that governed the valley, seemed bird-size.

Unfolded chairs made a wreath around the outdoor altar, and the vistas in every direction caught up together the sky, rock, valley bowl, the limitless grasses. Stately peace spread open before us, and beyond and behind. Kids ran about, alighting for a moment on mothers' laps, then off in their packs again.

The ceremony began. Rather than turn to their friend who presided, Adele and Joe faced us, and each spoke. They told us how we mattered and made them strong, gave them a home, taught them resilience. You care for us, they said, and we love you. I'd never heard anything like it, this inclusive ceremony. Adele defied definitions, added to them, broadened them, and illuminated what only the kindest friend could, which was a way to accept oneself.

So I asked Adele to help me with the abortion memory, feeling a bit of a fraud, guilty at taking up her time. I didn't believe in my own use of the word *ritual.*

Warmly and at once she said, "I'd love to do that for you."

I didn't know what specifics to request, how to proceed. But I knew I could show Adele my ineptitude, and she would hear my unkempt longing. She would find the gravity, see to the reverence. She came to my studio during her lunch hour.

"What are the important elements of this for you?" she asked.

"Um, water? The woods? Somewhere that's . . ." I felt ridiculous. "Sacred?" *Sacred*?

"Do you have a place in mind? I know some places." I nodded. "There's a stand of cedars, it's not too far." That was good. She said, "And what about an offering?" Completely blank, I started to cry, confronted by the skepticisms of a broken-apart family and overwhelmed by the borrowed strength of a tender woman who called me her friend.

She drove, and we went way up Rock Creek, past many spots Christopher and I used to fish when we'd first explored Montana, freshly arrived together. I'd decided that was the place. We'd known nothing then of this heartbreak and conflict that would weave into our lives, hadn't even a glimmer.

328

We thought, *We're in love,* but we'd been cutouts, not yet even the firm molds that would be filled. I didn't go fishing with him anymore. I was talking about him to Adele, exasperated and complaining — he chews, he clears his throat, he snores. "I hate feeling this," I said. "That nothing he can do is right, how distant he seems from the man I loved."

"Maybe there's another way to see him," she suggested after thinking about it. "To ask him what it's like."

"I don't want to hear him. I want to stay angry."

"Maybe," she said, "staying angry doesn't really help you."

She parked by an ancient wooden fence, gray and bleached pale by sun, and we got out. Yellow butterflies clung to the ground in lacework around our feet, and the enchantment began. From the backseat I retrieved the small clay figure I'd made, the "offering." I'd had to go to a pottery studio to buy the clay, a weighty brick with a plastic coating to keep it moist. I hoped Christopher wouldn't see me bring it in from the car, I didn't want to explain it. Outdoors beside the house one afternoon, I'd let my hands shape whatever came, and a feminine form emerged, which embarrassed me as trite, some sort of rounded, reclining woman. It had dried in the sun, and on the seat it left chalky brown dust. We headed across the creek over an old bridge and into the snows hidden from the spring sunlight in the deeper part of the canyon. I stopped talking. Soon we were up to our thighs, pushing into drifts, and getting wet. I didn't want to work hard, still resisting the mission, its seriousness, but with Adele next to me, I did work. She let me walk on, pick the spot, and we came to rest at the bank a ways up, a place where the water was loud, the stream running hard with spring runoff. Red, brown, and green rocks, mixed with gray, were visible on the bottom.

We looked down at the water. I didn't know if I should start, how to be. "What do you need to say?" Adele asked. "You can say whatever it is." I knelt on the tough ground. My abortion had happened ten years before, no close to its harrowing chapter. To Christopher I'd pretended the episode was over, the sour memory the only remains, but I still felt the muscular truth, the places in my body that had held, had fought, had released. I always felt them.

"I'm sorry," I said for the first time. I was self-conscious. Adele moved away. "I let you

330

go." The sound of my voice was wrapped in water as I placed the clay into the current. There was room to say more. "I'm sorry, Christopher. I'm sorry, Susanna. Goodbye, baby. I set all this down, and I'm saying good-bye." I rested on my knees in the melting snow and watched the heedless creek reshape the contours of the figure. Silent, Adele sat on a low rock. I returned to her and settled, and she put both arms around me. Against her, I cried, draining the angers, the sorrows. Not even Christopher knew them. They existed in the words, the water, the murmured recognition, between women.

I did not go back up Rock Creek for the anniversary the following spring, or the next. The March date came and went, softer. It's been a few years. Christopher goes to fish there, as he always has, but I've never told him where I took Adele. I don't need him to know. He knows I changed something and that that changed something for us. In the school hallway at the sight of Adele, I am steadied every time. I picture the winter's gaunt riparian brush, the clearing snows and the place on the bank where the water hurries past, where this calm and

unprejudiced friend blessed my first ceremony.

REAL ESTATE

We shared a circle that senior spring, really at the last minute. Loosened by all I'd accomplished and antsy to go and show off in the open world, my attention for the last of college was scattered, the people see-through. I wasn't taking on new friends *here*. Amidst our huddles of playgoing and bargoing, Connie was the firm column in the theater crowd, her words the sharpest and most ardently argued, infallible entertainment. My playwright boyfriend was the classicist, his roommate the jester, Neil the handsome actor, Tina the pure angel on stage; but Connie, the dramaturge, would say the wonderful, ghastly thing, stop the whole room, and get it right, and then slam down her dissenters. I didn't want to consider her powers, because I was supposed to be the smart, insolent woman. But she did not mimic fearlessness. She bristled, commanded, and we knew that Connie — her *work* — was special in a way that transcended envy. She and Jim were already together, but I never thought of her in a couple. My boyfriend resented her lauded recognition and her prodigious skills, her drive. "She's amazing," he'd say to me, not happy. "What a mind." He encouraged me not to think well of her.

I look at that twenty-one-year-old me, susceptible to his thin impersonation of love, his bitter, thin authority, and I hate how little I cared to heed my instincts — about him, about Connie — how readily I ignored a remarkable woman. It was easier to be scared of her, to step out of her way and nurse my own meek jealousies.

A few months after college, Connie's name appeared on the opening credits of a TV series. We'd heard rumors too watery to take seriously, but look! Oh, hey, we *know* her! We watched the popular show, my boyfriend riveted, his scorn the soundtrack. I joined him. Who did she think she was! Who deserved that level of success already? Connie — paid God knows what — betrayed the rest of us. We couldn't bear our striving to look childish.

I broke up with that man eventually, lost a thousand-dollar deposit on a wedding dress left unclaimed at the bridal store. Events filled my years, and I was pushed on to fresh pursuits of jobs, friends, apartments, men, travel. I married after moving to Montana, and I had a baby. Before a trip to New York with our infant son, we put out the word for a place to stay. Another friend knew that Jim and Connie, who were not coming back from LA anytime soon, had a brownstone, and in a rush of impersonal messages left between me and Jim, we were granted permission to use it, a New York rescue. They had a boy, too, red-haired like our son. We could use his crib, his bath toys. Feel free.

"I have these old friends, from college, they're letting us stay," I told Christopher, but in Brooklyn their furnishings, framed posters, book collection, spoke of nothing more personal to me than catalog content. I couldn't say to Christopher, "Yeah, Connie's always loved Italian pottery." I didn't know her, hadn't even seen her since an indifferent, mass good-bye at graduation nine years before. She worked ferociously, profusely, had some unnerving drive, and I'd heard that Jim took care of their son and everything else. What to make of it, the aggressive reversal: the woman doing this and the man that? The woman seizing wide latitude. Something felt faintly dangerous, an unnamed treachery, uncomprehended, but — Thank you for the house! We slept in their bed, ground our coffee in their grinder and washed towels in their machine, where Jim had taped up a kind note of instruction. We kept their keys in our pockets and ran up and down their red Brooklyn stoop as if, for ten days, we were them. What if *we* made Hollywood money? What if these magic towels and rugs belonged to us? At the end, we bought a bottle of excellent wine (one we'd never have purchased with our real dollars) and put it on their dining table. I left the bright, literate note you write to people you don't plan on knowing. By the time we boarded the plane, we'd dismissed our unuseful fantasies.

On a ravishing day when the wind was high and all the air cleaned, I drove up and up into the Pacific Palisades. I'd come to LA with baby Daniel to visit my friend Steffie, who said she loved babies, and really did, welcomed mine. She'd borrowed a high chair for our visit and squeezed it into her small kitchen. Such friends had principal status in my straitened life. Most of my old friends, men especially, did not disguise their boredom, and they expected me and us to talk about them. I didn't have the energy. Steffie, raised in the Midwest with brothers and sisters, who doted on new nieces and nephews, was actually interested in what my son would eat, or if he sunburned easily. She was unbothered by where I changed him, and she spoke to him. We had often laughed at our disparate upbringings — my urban sarcasms and entitlements, her lakeside summers, family weddings — but now I felt, in stupendous, unsayable terms, grateful for her plain faith in bonds, for her example of loyalty. I felt I was becoming someone she recognized, that she liked me better than ever this way. At the same time I faced the rough problem of diluted identity.

That morning Steffie needed to work at home, and I was touring around Venice with my agitated baby, his collapsed stroller in the trunk of the rental car. Our disrupted routines — nap *now* instead of then, read now, nurse now — left me anxious and exposed in a colossal city, where my friend glided, stony muscles revealed by workout clothes or backless dresses, her penned eyeliner in place all day, a velvet thread. Once, I'd lived in LA, some other me, had had the low Hollywood assignment of D-Girl. I had sped on and off the freeway arteries, eaten Asian salads at outdoor tables, my fruited iced tea always refilled. This was after the playwright boyfriend, and then the banker boyfriend, when I was trying on independence with a mania fueled by my first significant salary. Steffie and I had lived together in Santa Monica, a stucco bungalow. We threw a party, and people came, which seemed to us, the morning after, like the real miracle. They came for us. We were noticeable. What did I matter now, beyond the range of my baby's adamant reach? The identity of mother had stolen up behind me, made me renounce plans, ideologies, wardrobes, allowed me no time to shape new ones.

I know! I thought, and called Connie's house. Old friends could show me something of my origins. Unflappable Jim said, *Come on over,* as if I'd be petulant not to. I drove and parked, disbelieving at the address, the trail of numbers part of California's big arrogance. The rosebushes in front of the house were perfect, the hard breeze brightening them. The white fence at knee height was movie-set perfect, almost suspect. Connie as the woman with flowers in fat bloom? I couldn't even picture her outdoors, our briefly mutual life limited back then by classrooms and temporary quarters, rehearsal spaces dark with stage black. Here was her husband, who tended the baby and baked and was wonderfully calm, who commented with no malice on the idiocies of Hollywood and sudden wealth, and on the funny sorority he shared with mothers at the playgroups. He enjoyed the shock of his splendid house. Their son was at a playdate, and Jim was giving his own solitary hours to us, to someone else's baby. He took me from room to room, and he joked about the length of the tour, the numerous closets with their recessed bulbs, the soft wool carpeting upstairs. The baby was heavy and hot in my arms, his skin stuck to mine by sweat. Jim brought us into the stylish kitchen and poured us apple juice, ice cubes from a dispenser. It was a house to make you sick with envy, if it belonged to your best friend, who'd achieved that much more than you had, while you both pretended neither of you noticed her rewards. But Connie and Jim were not my best friends, not even close friends. I just knew them. They were information.

Connie, said Jim, was supposed to get back but was still at a script meeting, or something with producers, and I said, Ah, right, but felt wan. He drove us to the beach, where we followed my son in the sand. I didn't see Connie that day, but I saw her goods and spoils, the whimsical chandelier and tall wineglasses, the oversize couches and terra-cotta floors, her windows gaping over the open valley toward the sea. The evidence of Connie's achievement roared, but the woman, engaged by work and absent, didn't smell or move like anything. I couldn't remember her voice, the gestures of her shoulders or hands. A few months later she dropped a note. She'd liked a piece I'd written; and the star on her TV show, she said, so *difficult*. In a day otherwise dull with routine, I felt flattered. Ten years went by after that.

"You're really something!" Connie wrote after I published a book. "When's your reading? I'll come if I can." I'd lost track of her, unaware of her many plays, collected essays, her Tony nomination, esteemed prizes and Pulitzer consideration, and felt embarrassed. I should have kept up, battled my provincial absence from New York. But she didn't seem to care. When I saw her in the city she hugged me with might, surprisingly fraternal. She was more expressive than I remembered her being, what, twenty years ago? Had I forgotten a better friendship, memory's focus too keen on that disappointing boyfriend? She urged me to come over, see her house (a different brownstone), meet her kids, and *write more.* She took a piercing interest in what I thought.

I readied for closeness, my way with women, what we did. We'd go in now, wouldn't we, divulge our hearts' hurts, our marital pleasures and discords, we'd talk about what we'd hidden in college, held back? But we did not, a bafflement to me. We did not get soft. When she called, or I called her, we'd be in our respective studies, mine above the carriage house, hers atop her brownstone. Our husbands cared for our families and left us alone to work. We talked of writing, the nagging challenges and small breakthroughs. With appetite, Connie recounted the insults and idiosyncrasies she witnessed, described the notorious playground of the entertainment world, unfair with male antics. Her voice tightened as she argued her rights, her resolutions, and her firm intention not to be fucked over. She pushed back against every oppression, and I agreed and agreed, even though she didn't wait for me. Connie and I made the money, supported our families. Fuck, yeah, I thought, as Connie turned out play after play, book after book, as she sought my input and championed my efforts. We did not hide talent or dim our confidence but delighted in them, used them. We didn't dwell on the word *woman;* we were beyond that.

My next time in the city I stayed with her, a bed made up in the sunny, brick-walled office where she worked. It was wonderful in there. Comfortable and good taste, enough room to sprawl pages and magazines. A cluster of petite Orangina bottles stood in the little fridge so you didn't have to run all the way downstairs. She brushed off thanks. I'd come for the release of her novel, peer solidarity as distinct from friendly support. The first afternoon, me ragged from flights but pumped up by the city, we stood in her kitchen, Jim's thriving garden visible through glass walls. Jane came — a producer or screenwriter? From London? — and the room filled, charged by three women in righteous, amiable conflict. Jim had set out banana bread, the warm loaf unpanned and divided in thick slices. He came in briefly and put out cheese, went back to his own work. We leaned on her counter, into the evening, and drank steeped black tea — Connie was particular and interesting about its preparation — and then wine, then vodka. Our mutual urging seemed to spark the darkening room and sharpen our passions, which grew more intense as Connie — Jane called her C, I could, too — dove into education, art criticism, Broadway economics, the Catholic fucking *Church.* We shouted, we trumpeted. We barely mentioned our children.

In my copy of her novel, Connie wrote, "To Susanna Sonnenberg you have the key to my heart! Many many thanks for your constant wisdom and clear-eyed love. It is my friends who make me feel at home in the world. I am truly grateful that you are among them." The mix of formality — my whole name, we were not sisters — and sudden effusion, a spring fleetingly revealed. I was taken aback and gratified that she assessed my "wisdom," "clear-eyed love," qualities I hoped others saw, but about which I was always unsure. *My friends make me feel at home in the world.* Yes. That one I got, the scaffolding of friends. We'd never discussed it, too intimate. Not everything, Susanna, has to be discussed, dissected, investigated. Just being is a possibility, being and going along and making an example. I was touched by this unfamiliar warmth from her, the glimpse of her heart, to which, she'd said, I held a key.

343

■ ■ ■ ■

My father was dying suddenly. The afternoon my stepmother called, Christopher was camping and unreachable. Harsh and strange, my stepmother made it clear the boys and I couldn't stay with her. I phoned C. Could we sleep there, could my boys be absorbed into the summer activities of her family while I did whatever this was? It was a lot to ask. "Yes, of course yes," she said, "don't even worry about it." But I worried a little. I was not one of those people who could rally naturally in spontaneous crisis, and I didn't want to be witnessed discombobulated by a woman so directed and industrious. Nor was I easy with asking, nervous as usual about uneven power, tallied debts. I felt already all that I owed her. A couple of months earlier, she'd invited me to join a group of writers at her house in the country. Two houses, actually, the small one across the road from the other, her own pond, her own fish. She had come to my door as I unpacked.

"Do you like your room?"

"I love it, C. Thank you for everything."

"Oh, good. Well, then." She left the doorway, on to the next guest.

Each evening the writers assembled, dropped down into roomy chairs and plush couches. The playwrights, as they all were, passed around the day's pages, held readings. We made loud suggestions, peppered each other with convulsive jokes and broad, witty insults. When I read, they listened. Connie had cleared a space for my work, as if I were an oracle. Her respect was an unpronounceable gift to me, a tremendous encouragement. Then we made dinner, the men, the women, the kitchen a tight hive of bodies, some of us at the oven door, some with wine bottle and corkscrew, or mixing together greens and chèvre and diced red pepper. Magnificent noise came from blue stories, elaborate epithets and curses, rabid opinion, and from laughter in bursts so loud and shared, sometimes none of us could speak over it. Connie ruled us, her fervent topics instruction for the evening: theater! health care! poverty! honor! The generosity of our benefactor was too great to describe, although we tried, eight of us, night after night, in our toasts. She branded me with her lion-like faith. I was thriving in her kindness.

Now I was standing in her kitchen, again, beautiful Brooklyn, ample brownstone. She'd waited up, and she hailed me as I opened her gate with the key she'd given me. "The boys are asleep," she reported. "Everyone's fine." A glass of wine? She poured, we almost drank, my phone rang. I stepped apart from this friend and her version of me, unsure who this call would ask me to become. My sister said our father had died, not this moment but the moment before, in the hospital room I'd left forty-five minutes earlier.

I closed the phone. A black tunnel came for me, narrow focus, blank hands.

Connie stood, not drinking, a high pitch to her attention.

"He's dead," I said and tried to exhale, a vain grab at normal. "My father died." I lost contact with her, my vision pinned on the butcher-block countertop, the orange tiles of a house-cleaned floor, the fresh dishtowel in a folded square to the side of the sink. Each detail stung in how meaningless it was, how absent animation. I couldn't look up; I hardly knew her. Nothing in our history had primed us to bear a moment such as this.

"I'm sorry," she said, in a slow, soft voice I'd never heard her use. She reached both hands and picked up her glass, handed me mine. "Hey." Slow, soft. "To your father." I echoed her, raised the numb glass, tipped its first sip in, must have swallowed.

She will always be in this, my altering moment. She wasn't a best friend, but Connie
is fixed, salient in my history of friendship.
Perhaps that left us both awkward, the
unplanned intimacy so florid we knew we'd
have to mark it, calculate the entwining. She
asked if I was okay, courteously. "Yeah,
okay," I said, a lie. Each sentence, each
sandwich, each tap turned on, in the next
months would be that same lie, the pronounced betrayal of previous certainty. I
would forget ambitions, come apart. Anger
was already starting: I looked at her and
thought, *your* father is not dead. No one is
dead, except my father and part of me.
Neither of us imagined, two decades ago at
someone's birthday party in an Indian
restaurant in Somerville, that I'd transform
before you in your Brooklyn kitchen, that
you would be the unforgettable friend. We
never agreed to be sealed this way.

I knew I'd put her on the spot, presented
a scene that demanded response. I wanted
to apologize. "Come on," she said, taking
the glass from my hand, setting it somewhere. She turned off the warm lights of
the kitchen and we went upstairs together.
On her landing, the floor below mine, she
wished me well for sleep. Into the following
year, I called on many friends, closer and

fonder, better known, who understood my family. I called on their varied ways of giving me a home in the world, but in that new orphaned hour, sheltered in her house, Connie gave me a last, firm look before going to bed and made me feel instructed and very strong.

The Four Seasons

Marlene suggested the bar in the Four Seasons. I would have said yes to any plan. In the two days since my father had died, I'd wandered, trailed, traipsed my city, had put my children on a plane home to their father, who'd returned from camping. I'd stood alone at crosswalks, sat down in unexpected parks, unable to change this; gathered with friends who loved me; I'd drunk a lot of white wine for the chill in my mouth and the softness of mind and muscle that followed the alcohol. I couldn't handle the hiss of the subways and the muddle of close, heated bodies, so I'd been riding the bus, staring from the window, consuming details that meant little of streets I once knew deeply. They told me nothing of myself. My city was changed. I didn't know where to go.

Marlene wrote, "Oh Susy," a cry. She'd known me as Susy. In her note, she encouraged me to call, and I did, having to concentrate on the sequence of numbers as I copied it from laptop screen onto a notebook page. Paper, the contents of my bag, standing up — every action, every object required exhausting focus. I made the call in a gray stretch of hot shadow against a building on the Upper West Side. It was one of the short streets between Broadway and Central Park, where the neighborhood wedges itself into an awkward triangle, conceding briefly the true topography of the island. I'd never thought before of the island as terrain. If I faced west I could watch the double avenue, sense the Hudson's expanse, and, turning east, I saw the spark of green from the park's trees. When Marlene answered I said, "It's Susy," and I was, and we fell straightaway into comfortable, miserable speech. I strained to hear above the churn of air vents around me, exhaust pipes, the high-pitched, rhythmic pierce of work trucks in reverse. When Marlene spoke my name, I felt thirteen and liked it, my age when my father started seeing her. She said, "Can we meet, I really want to see you." I said, "Just tell me where, when." I had nothing I was meant to do.

When I was in eighth grade my father's MS

started to worsen, and he stopped driving. He could still cook, deliberate gestures, his hands shaping the ground lamb, his fingers able to pluck at the little hill of chopped parsley, the coarse grains in the salt dip, but he could not rely on reflex, fast changes, and he had to give up the car. One weekend, Marlene drove my father and herself up to my school in Connecticut, her black terrier on his lap the whole way. My mother, as it happened, had introduced him to Marlene. Her best friend, Bev, brought Marlene to a party my mother gave, and they conspired to throw this young reporter at him. They watched from across the room. When he asked the reporter out and took her out several more times after that, my mother was furious, excluded. The intentions of the adults were mysterious, and I could not get a grip on who wanted what. My mother seemed excited one minute, dismissive the next, loved to tell people what good friends she and my father were, such a progressive divorce, but she wasn't pleased when he stopped flirting with her.

I got into the back of the car, behind my father, glad to avoid his gaze, which could stun me. Marlene slowly drove the road that wound through the campus, and she asked what's that, what happens there, so I could point out what mattered to me, using the arcane terms of segregated life. She and I hadn't done much together. Once, she'd taken me to a movie, R-rated but not shocking; and she'd given me *The White Album,* pressed in white vinyl, when I still didn't get the Beatles. The undeniable cool of this present informed my view of her.

In the backseat I was dreaming, gone. The night before — how many hours, I counted backward — a boy had kissed me. It was my first French kiss — the phrase itself delicious — and I replayed it: tiptoe on the steps of my dorm, aware of curfew minutes away, and the broadness of his upper body, the dry taste of boy, the colliding textures on his face of smooth lips, scratchy cheek. His hands were too heavy on my shoulders. I reviewed the tiny moment of last air, right before his leaning in became his mouth on mine, which had sent an addictive charge into my body. In the car, the charge again coursed, a devastating, honeyed sensation. I was lost to an erotic spell as Marlene and my father debated dinner, her sweet voice teasing him.

I was bursting to announce, to just let this out, but my father would mock me, ruin it. He took too great an interest in my crushes, managing to be both prurient and belittling, and I had to keep this from him. It must have shown, though, my body alight — does it show, can't you see my lips are different? Am I discovered? I scanned the campus for the boy, who was nowhere to be found.

They stayed in a motor court, as my father insisted on calling it, and Marlene unlocked the door and threw it open, guiding me inside. I walked the dog from the parking spot, amused by her trot and tug. I sat on one of the beds. My father despised attention as he worked his slow legs, so we'd left him to get out of the car alone, and I talked to Marlene, dropped a hand over the side of the bed to find the dog's ears and nose. It was casual, without moment. Starving for good women, I loved her.

"You know what?"

"What, Susy?"

"I had my first French kiss last night." The boy himself was less and less relevant.

"What happened?" Marlene said, a spark to her. She wanted to hear me tell. Before my father made it inside the room, I confided the strangeness and excitement.

"But don't tell him," I said.

"I would never tell him."

That weekend, I had an easy time with my father, Marlene coaxing his good moods. I was still afraid of him, no one could wipe that out, but it was a novel fear, loose rather than vigilant, relaxed by the new instinct that being his adult daughter would be better than being his child. We'd been estranged, as I, age twelve, had renounced his swift lacerations and undermining indifference. I took two years off from him, protecting myself. I credit Marlene with a crucial thaw between us. They weren't together very long and when they ended, over what I never knew, I was bitter. "Why didn't you marry her, I didn't want her to go," I said. He said she wanted someone healthy instead of ill, but he always spoke of their romance with deep affection. She had introduced him to something in himself. To me she was a necessary, wonderful mercy.

I'd never been inside the Four Seasons, had just a notion of its status, the midtown anchor of opulence. New York, that day, those days, was breaking apart into two pieces, the familiar and the disconcertingly unknown. The very familiar Lenox Hill Hospital, home in childhood to my mother's back surgeries and overdose revivals, and then last week reknown with the dowdy repetitions, the day after day leading to my father's death. In contrast, the aggressive sheen of corporate retail confused me, a false overlay that obscured my historical markers.

For the first time in days, with the hotel ahead, I felt composed. I could rise to the occasion, after being submerged. My eyes were lined with a steady hand, my lip touched with pale color. Just enough to be pulled together. Today, which bore no relation to the day before, I knew the contents of my bag and where my wallet was. I knew which pocket held my cell phone. These seemed like fundamental miracles, after the earthquaking of my heart. I moved amidst the cars, the bicycles and food carts, the wandering and the hurry, people with their lively bodies. I had to be careful with myself.

I was swept off Fifty-seventh Street into the theatrical magnificence of the lobby, where I was meant to be overwhelmed by architectural decision, trains of fabric, and acres of high ceiling, and I was. A dose of Asiatic lilies drugged the air. The unoccupied couches and empty carpets in stately greens and browns. A rise led to the elevated restaurant that looked out over the lobby, and a solicitous man in well-cut black showed me to a table by the window. His cuff snapped as he indicated my seat. The window was its own dramatic residence, primped with sheer muslin and velvet, layers of enclosure. Beyond the glass, the sunlit street had become a prop, an adornment. Filtered through white tulle, sun fell on the tablecloth, a warmed spot, and I sat on a tightly upholstered armchair, scattering my loose self, as my sunglasses, phone, wallet, pen, notebook, all found a separate place on the table. I could live in this coached oblivion. I asked for Sancerre, the wine that had become my friend this week simply for its pretty name, which I didn't need to think about when I ordered.

In thirty years, I'd seen Marlene once. The year before my book came out, but when I'd finished it and felt an unflappable confidence, Christopher and I went for drinks at my father's, where Marlene and her husband were expected. I was terribly nervous to see her. The girl-me loved her forever, as she was. After she and my father split up, she'd married and moved to the country. She had sons, grown men now. My father still — well, not today or yesterday, not anymore — talked to her frequently, sent e-mails and token books, thought of her and told her so, still flirting. But she wasn't in the regular circle. My stepmother did not like to admit the women who had mattered.

On their way to a party, Marlene and her

husband could only stop for a drink, half an hour, an hour, they were saying in the hall as they took off their coats and greeted my stepmother. I waited for Marlene to see me, as shy as a new student, and we put out our arms, pressed shoulders, ladylike and gracious but not more. We gathered our chairs in the bedroom, my father our focus, the way he liked it. We made light conversation, a convivial mood, holiday reports. How grown I felt as I handed Marlene her wineglass, then a glass to her husband. Of course, I *was* grown, past forty, but I wanted her to see all that had happened, all I'd become, to review the years she'd missed. I talked with her husband, partly afraid that my eyes on her would betray old worship and make me foolish, but now and then I looked, willing the appearance of my familiar reckonings, and she was still there, girlish and a little flustered, too, and it charmed me.

Marlene walked toward the table, and I stood. We looked into each other, took the measure, sat down. "Have you eaten?" she said. I'd read the menu. A sandwich cost $27. I objected on principle. "Oh, Susy, please have the sandwich, please." Okay. I let her take me to lunch. I needed an immediate mother. My stepmother the day before had exiled me from the apartment for good, no explanation beyond, "This is too awkward." I can't remember where I slept, helped by some receiving friend. My stepmother, whom I'd loved for thirty years and had believed loved me, had thrown callous ill feeling at me through this whole thing, and disorientation ruled my latest interactions. But it was too much, not for now. I'd think about it later.

There was catching up, my children's lives and Marlene's, our work, but mostly, we talked of my father, a confidential and vivid closeness. I imagined how we looked, not friends, but a mother, her daughter. Marlene forged ahead with the beloved and the obnoxious, memories of my father rising and blending together, just as mine were, ungraspable details I wanted to catch before they evaporated. As if they'd evaporate.

"Do you know what he called my husband? After I got married?" she said. "A golden retriever."

"Oh, God."

"My husband didn't like that," she was laughing. We had more wine. We tattled on my father with intense affection, profound knowledge.

"You know he adored you."

358

"Well, yes," I said. "But we had a hard time the last couple of years." This was hurting terribly. My stepmother had chosen the day after he died to tell me I'd wounded him. That he'd been disappointed, waiting for me. Nothing could help me digest her choice, her need to dispatch her rage.

"He never stopped talking about you."

"He didn't?"

"Susy. He was so proud of you."

She said it simply. In the week my father died, it was the only time anyone said this. Marlene, again and at the right moment, wound his humanity with mine, made us father and daughter, daughter and father.

As We Both Know

When I agreed to move to the big blank of
Montana with Christopher, I asked him to
come with me as I said my good-byes. I
wanted to introduce him, have people see
he was *it*. We drove around the East Coast,
my inventory of friends in Boston, Provi-
dence, New Haven, family members in New
York. In Sag Harbor, April and Marina
pulled us into the kitchen, sat us at the
broad table and asked to hear everything.
"Tell us!" We loved to tell that story, only a
few months old.

As I talked, April listened with acute attention. "So *beautiful*!" she exclaimed at the
slight asides, the passing detail: I had to wait
for Christopher to unlock the car door . . .
He'd just come back from a run, when . . .
She revered each step in the dawning of
love, the joining. She gazed at Marina,
whose ranging, coppery curls and red
lipstick made her the focal point of any

room. We all stared, the delicacy and sleepy, erotic energy, those wrists. Love shaped April, decided her. April and Marina exalted sex as sacred and did it saying *cunt* and *pussy,* spilling mock secrets, letting raunch erupt. "Stop it! Oh, don't!" Christopher blushed, already uncomfortable at playing the fourth to our three. It's *good,* I wanted to tell him, when women say the real everything, allow each other, wield dirty talk as part of living; but I was startled, too. Marina lowered her eyelids, and April touched those curls. I leaned forward and loved them.

I was in my early twenties when I first knew them, long before I'd met Christopher, and I liked their act of "April and Marina." How lovely it was to observe, to applaud, and how blushingly, beautifully, they invited the witness. One of those couples, perfectly coupled. They knew they were an example, took that seriously. I was living in Sag Harbor, the strange job with the movie producer, and they'd bring me to the beach, Marina's towel in the middle, conversation as her head turned to me, then April, then me. We ate sandwiches of watercress and cheese and sat up to peel fruit. April wore long-sleeved linen to shield her freckled skin. After a few months, plenty of beach, and couscous for dinner or miso soup laced with seaweed, months of affectionate argument, advice, me charging over to their house for a dose of them or to borrow a book, I understood that Marina was simpler, a bright burn. April had shadow mixed in, a whole spectrum.

April worked at my father's magazine, another brilliant redhead in his small kingdom, but she was unusual for being sexually unassailable. He enjoyed her mind and willing vulgarity, and he published her poems with enthusiasm, proud to start her career. Then he began to mock her earnestness, both to her face and out of earshot, and her emotional purity, and her deeply felt intention. He had no room for those. He started to ignore her life, which puzzled me, and must have done worse to her, the promise of belief withdrawn. His scorn grew fiercer, his derision pointed, which made her more my sister. Where did she go wrong, I wondered. Did she wonder?

She didn't stop loving him. He baited her, insults delivered in his lilting, flirtatious purr, and she'd erupt with laughter, batting him back down. With fierce generosity, she teased him, able to celebrate his whole way, his every way. She accepted imperfect selves, or at least my father's, something I couldn't. Only a saint, an acolyte, could do that, I thought, someone bathed in holy distinction. April embodied grace while I was still transfixed by the grace of Marina's performance, and my own.

April knew grief, her underwriter. She knew torments, leaden histories. I heard many, many details, entrusted to me in her sure voice, serene as an intangible harp, but I didn't store them. They were too much. Anyway, she seemed to be storing them. I benefited from the thoughtful woman she'd become, the startling poet, as she dosed me with canny assessments, eyed my new friends and lovers, held steady against my father. In Sag Harbor I'd arrive in the wet afternoons and tuck up on the deep cushions of the couch, as she sat on the floor, leaning back, her head propped by the side of my leg. Marina was elsewhere on the phone, her pretty voice in a separate room. April talked about Merrill, Lowell, and Adrienne Rich, their humanity, about Elizabeth Bishop in Brazil, about conversions, suicides, about meaning and God and the face of cruelty, about longing. She talked about ecstasy. She thought importantly but within reach, disciplined mornings at her desk, surrounded by the inscriptions and quotations she'd transcribe onto torn slips and back with colored paper. These were tacked around the room at eye level, the inside of herself turned into beautiful landmarks. I looked down at the handwriting on her white pages, at her piles of maps. She'd made each torment into something calm, each calm step a useful one. Everything served.

Christopher and I had been in Montana six months when someone told me April and Marina had broken up. But April's last letter came a few weeks ago! I worried what would become of her. She was the boyish one, her haircut boxed against her head, her shirts buttoned, jeans formless, and her plain gait; but she was the one so easy to bruise, her rapt face about to crumble at any second. The peaceful kitchen was dismantled, the books peeled from every shelf in the house and crated, arrangements made. I was angry. A beautiful building had come down in my neighborhood, my path altered.

She moved into the city after falling in love with her married therapist, an adventure she related in frequent letters to Montana, which were hard for me to read. I'd put years of effort into undoing my English teacher's harm, into assessing power's damages. Exploding with fresh happiness, she wrote me the minute details — the first, blunt mutual admissions, the first time she met the husband and the little boy, held the infant, the business of hauling stuff to a new apartment, having room made for her in a family. She was driven to mother the children, fulfilled. Grounded now with Christopher, I practiced stern emotional safety, our religion. We discussed April's mistake. It seemed so clear that she'd put herself at risk, self-defeating. I wanted to offer her my support, the way she'd given hers to me, but I didn't approve of her choice. There was no other way to put it. I didn't approve.

In April's new living room on the Upper West Side, she and I were on the rug with my red-haired boy. How wrong, April engulfed by the tumultuous city. She always liked the floor, truth there. Daniel was walking, and I felt eternally weary with the responsibility of him, having to know where his next foot would come down. I sought guidance: Can you show me how to be a mother? Can *you*? Can *you*? Can you watch me *being* a mother and tell me I am fit and right and good? I needed my old friend, in her infinite capacity for struggle, to give me that, but she was repeating the story of falling in love, relishing the thrill. Here was their bedroom, their bureau and shared drawers, here the black-and-white family scenes framed already in the hallway. "Go on," I said. "Then what?" I pretended to share her joy, to approve the evidence that my dear friend had been violated by a therapist with awful ethics. My habit, my calling, in those days, was to match the other person jot for jot, be the mirror so she wouldn't look away, but how indecent to fake April to her face, take advantage. April simply gave herself to you. She trusted that if she loved you, you were worthy of her enormous gift.

The shrink arrived, had a good handshake, gave happy April a kiss, but I loathed her, appalled by her sloppy, professional breach. I could barely talk. Exploiter, I thought. Abuser. And now, at the end of the visit, time to leave them to their wrong kisses, I'd have to gather the baby's bits and debris, stuff sticky objects in the diaper bag, push elevator buttons, walk out through lobby doors and into the wind chasing up Broadway. I wanted refuge. April didn't have it for me. She sheltered others.

I returned to Montana and couldn't write to her. All I could think was haughty injunction: *This is a bad idea. You'll be sorry.* I didn't want to be that friend, because that wasn't a friend. But then *what?* I wanted her to triumph over moral violation — as she'd always done — and she hadn't. Our exchange of letters stopped, and I gradually noticed. It had been a month; then six months, et cetera. Christopher and I talked about our own terrible histories, protecting each other as if that were the single decree in the marriage oath. We named the abuses of trust we'd grown up with. We reviewed the exploitations of unfed hunger and sweet availability. I didn't want April to be that girl, used in that way. I could only think "Don't," and I didn't say it. When you stop saying to your friend the curse or hope you really think, then who are you? Who are you together? In a few ragged steps, I abandoned her.

I would count the years since I'd had that friendship. I knew no other woman who exclaimed with astonishment and reverence, let the ecstasy be named and up front, who was so feverishly open to the range of human mistake, always interested to explore it further. No one else had given me clues to real grace and sexual honesty, or had honored terror. I'd ask my father for news of

April, because I missed her uneasily. I hoped he'd say she asked after me, and I waited. After a while, my physical memory of her dimmed, and I found when he talked of her that I was listening to a story of his friend, not mine. She became someone I'd met. *April's over,* I'd think, and I'd mourn. Had she forgotten me, too, the way I looked and sounded and thought? Then the familiar judgment would present itself, this time not about her choice, but about myself, how I'd ruined something precious — well! she'd forced me to! — and I'd shove her from my mind, ignore failure. How long had I been gone from New York? How long had my father been teasing me to move back? She was part of all that, far away, the childish me I had renounced.

I flirted again, the impulse long shut off.

I flirted with a man, someone I met through work. Being a mother was my principal purpose, a Susanna for those two people: they needed her, *this* Susanna. My marriage was straining, chafing, but Christopher and I were not worried about it, knew it would endure. We were good at talking. Now the kids were in school, the day's hours open and mine. The flirtation grew bolder, hungrier. The hunger scared me, a stowed appetite looming up. The man lived in New York, we'd met once, the tantalizing lunch and the unspoken; hands frozen on the white tablecloth. E-mails held us together, held us in check and at the same time allowed strategic lapses.

One day I stood in my kitchen, my body accustomed to the drugged arousal that had replaced conscious thought. Some deep plan was buzzing inside me — get to the computer, get more; what next heat would he bestow? I was shutting the fridge, and its chrome handle woke my hand, woke me, and then, I felt one *pow* blow of all I'd forfeit if the attraction wreaked its powers. I'd never known such hot fear.

Aghast, I faced exposure — not just wife, not just mother to my sons, but the all; not just the devout notion of ethical safety, I was also *this,* this fucking mess, aching for true, dense, bold expression. I was unpredictable.

It was breathtaking, too much awareness to hold alone. *April,* I thought, craved. Uppity and know-it-all, I'd judged her. I hadn't let her luminous light cast itself on my waiting upheavals. Eight years earlier I hadn't anticipated the heart's implacable wants and the dangerous strain of longing. Nor could I have understood the futility in the attempts to reconcile what would never be reconciled. I had thought April just gave in, let herself be used, and I'd punished her in the way I'd been taught: I dismissed her.

After dropping the boys at school I went to the bakery and took a sunny table, a plate with a blueberry muffin, a cup of coffee. I opened a notebook and wrote "Dear April." I understand better now, I wrote, not everything, not properly, but a little bit, have edged closer to ambivalence. You were struggling, I wrote, to live fully. Forgive me.

I wasn't looking for absolution over my crush, its reckless peril, but for a way to tell her, "I get it." I wrote several pages but didn't send them. I was scared she'd ignore my letter; so I held on to my sure loss rather than risk a new pain. I'd sacrificed eight years of friendship out of ignorance: You don't deserve April, I was thinking. It was, of course, a different debt that worried me, other people I was terrified might vanish.

Anyone I'd ever known received an invitation to my New York bookstore reading. My father, in his palatial wheelchair and easily tired, couldn't come. I'd tell him about it, my stepmother would tell him. I was waiting for him to mention my book, acknowledge its contents. April, her name right there on my laptop screen, wrote back with congratulation and her news. After eleven years, she'd left the shrink. Her teaching career was good, her writing rich, she was the essential stepmother to two teenagers. "When you're here, come have brunch in my studio."

I brought bagels from H&H, and she received them as if they were rare and deeply special. She'd always been good at reverence, and I was drinking this in. It used to mean little to me. We'd all teased her, my father, even Marina. Back then, I had to get going, argue, match my father, be on, see things, go to bed with people, no reflection. I watched her hands around the white bag and saw how the simple act was made complex and sacred.

She set the bagels on a square of cutting block next to a tomato and a red-waxed piece of cheese. There was the knife. I sliced the tomato as she split the bagels and toasted them, fussed at the kettle. We shared the kitchen space. I looked around, slowed myself. Unless you've lived in New York, you've never imagined daily life in a room of only a few footsteps, but I recognized the real-estate coup, the splendor of high windows presiding over a wide street and the triumph of sealing out the noises from below with an air conditioner. Her walls were papered here and there in her hand, the careful transcribing of words that belonged to reactionaries, dear friends, Neruda, Cavafy, Sanskrit translations. Yoga had replaced romance and everything, besides poetry and her stepchildren. I listened with a mixture of respect and creeping boredom, which I transformed into learning because her scrupulous mind interested me: April would think differently about yoga than anyone else did. Her body was much changed, formed anew by the discipline, muscular yet more yielding, and visible. Startled each time I looked at her, I kept commenting on her body. She joked that she had dresses now. She opened her closet and showed me one.

We spread plates on the patch of floor and sat on pillows, lifting the food, setting it back down, lifting the napkins. It was a quiet room, where we could be noisy with filling in and catching up. People had died, things that mattered had been written, since we'd last sat together. People had been born. My father had remained important to her, and we compared affectionate and aggravating stories of him. I confessed about the man and the one kiss, which I'd told no one. April asked for the specifics and the unconsidered. She talked about the new woman she loved, who didn't love her yet, and about her much-broken heart; grief; I talked about my sons, my stumbling marriage, my father's sharp silence; grief. I told her of the letter I hadn't sent her, and she pushed for the heart of the matter, calm no matter the revelations. I admitted my shame at abandoning her, my watchful protective judgment. "I was wrong," I said. I came clean, and we were restored to each other. The friendship had only been in hibernation. I'd let years of such generous acceptance and investigation slip past, what we could have shared: *You will never do that again.* She asked me to read the opening of my book to her, closed her eyes, then at the first sentence she burst in to note the verb tense, picked up each word and looked at it, which flattered me. She made me feel I had created a perfect thing from dread pain. I felt appreciated in my own precisions.

After brunch, I gathered things to carry to the sink but she stopped me.

"Leave them," she said. "I like them there for a while. When you've gone, they'll make me happy that you were here, that we ate together." She walked me the three paces to the door. I loved her grounded feet, the unabashed royalty of her affection. She

373

watched with me for the elevator, the hallway spiced with the flavors of ancient dinners, and oh! those topics we'd forgotten! next time! "Good-bye, honey," she said, pleased and laughing. "I'll see you tonight," and then her voice changed to lullaby, her last goodbye a reassurance. I knew that I'd given her as much as I'd received.

In the full bookstore later, I looked up from the page and found April in the dense crowd, her steady look right on me, filled with love. I held this as I performed, then as I answered questions. There were strangers and forgotten colleagues and friends who had traveled from other states, and there were people outside on the cold street. Both aunts, all my cousins; childhood friends, high school acquaintances, lovers from college, and after; my agent, editor, publisher, publicist; my husband, my stepmother. Also in the room was the pervasive whisper of my mother, who might appear, but if she had, what would it have mattered? How could she have breached the fortress of friendship?

I am lucky that April forgave me. Our correspondence became central to my thinking, a place I unscrolled and wandered strange territory. I delighted in her letters, which were raw, a torrent of poetry, immediate crudeness, smart passions. I wrote to her about every little thing — a school play, sore muscles from pruning in the garden — and huge things, the unsalvable sting as Daniel, growing older, found me less interesting; my creative attempts and hopes. But mostly and voluptuously we spoke about desire and writing, the vulnerabilities and awakenings, the necessity of loving and fucking intensely, of writing. We recognized each other, paid tribute, allowed forbidden sentences. Hello, Comrade, she wrote; Dear Adventurer, she wrote. We mused on the ecstatic dangers. April loved to study the complications of ambivalence.

When I finally slept with someone else (I was away from Missoula, writing), the next morning I called April. I was fretting and afraid, also bursting from sex. "I know this is trouble," I said, "but I had to."

"I know," she said. I rushed the details, and she gasped happily, stopped me for clarifications I was too scared to note — not about the event but about my heart and feeling.

"No, April, but this is terrible, a true disaster." My voice was shaking, off-kilter. "I'm bad."

"That's one way to look at it," she said,

allowing the truth in that. "But, honey, you sound *alive* and joyous!" We pondered the competing pulses of life — the safe home, the happy cunt, the cherished children, the greedy artist. In a letter afterward, she wrote that she loved to see "the beautiful, drenched place that you are in, in bed and at the desk, which as we know are inseparable." As we know.

As we know.

Over the next week it was April who encouraged my fiercest honesty, who witnessed my perplexed, unstoppable claim of appetite and identity. She prepared with me my courage, so that when I had the painful and unprecedented conversation with Christopher, I was awake, but not afraid. He and I made our new, extraordinary way, our marriage reimagined and reshaped, richer veins mined. April fortified me. I inhabited the messy self, and she loved me for "the way you live every scrap of it."

It is morning, night's tired exhale that has reached its thin light. It was all ICU, my father's breaths and the seeming hours of pauses, my collapse in the cab, the phone call in Connie's kitchen. I've brought my children to the airport, sending them home to Montana after the sudden New York week, allowed to pass with them through security and see them down the jetway. I have never done this before. Please stay in the gate area until the plane has taken off, I'm told, so I do that, set my bag on a plastic seat, and stand against the glass, facing the tarmac and my sons, who cannot see me. The woman next to me stares out, a tissue held at her chin, eyes riveted to the plane. She's crying.

"You have a kid on it?" I say.

"I shouldn't cry," she says, holding up the Kleenex. "It's the tenth time. He goes to his dad."

"It's always the same, hard every time?" I ask. "It's my boys' first time."

"Oh, they're fine, they like it," she says. "It's no problem for them."

With silent natural need we put our arms around each other and watch as the plane pulls back and leaves workers to scatter and meander on the ground. There is more grief in her than just this, and there is more grief and catastrophe in me, but we don't mention those, we stay with our airport script. The jet reaches the runway and speeds up, and we watch it lift its impossible weight, our three boys, and pierce the haze of yellow dirt and heat. "Good luck," she tells me, shouldering her bag.

■ ■ ■ ■

My sister and I have been together for the last five days, a rare occasion. She has three young children, lives up the Hudson, and we try to see each other when I get to the city; but it's always been with kids, and our father. This is not my first sister, with whom I shared childhood, whose grueling rage defined her single brief visit to the hospital room. This is Hattie, my father's third daughter, born when I was eight. In the last decade she and I have grown close, a tender advancing that means everything to me, more than I can say. More than I can write. I can't call her "half."

Hattie and I took a break one day from the ICU and wandered up Lexington to H&M, propelled by a mutual simple hunger for clean clothes. We were so tired, but I danced in the store to the aggressive pop song, made her smile. We bought the same loose tank tops and wandered back. "One sec," she said. She went to a low wall near the hospital entrance and sat, pulling her tobacco pouch from her bag. I sat next to her. Even as we longed for each other, for sistering and good connection, we always practiced a certain formality, as if both aware that our relationship — sane, crucial — was our responsibility alone. We had no shared references of childhood experience, no shared mother. We had to *make* this. But, with blood's deep mystery, we knew each other, too. In the cafeteria, she'd watched me open a sandwich, cover the tuna with potato chips, and close it again. She murmured, "Texture girl." No one had ever noticed the habit or knew that this was exactly what it meant, this was me. She rolled her cigarette. Everything was allowed this week. She drew a drag in and held the cigarette to me, and I took it from her hand. One taste, a pleasant dizziness, and I gave it back. We'd never sat as two grown women alone together. At my father's bedside, this awful week, we'd shared with each other a strange holiday, sustaining.

I walk out of the airport, have to find my way back to the city. I've never been in that fatherless city. On the train I nearly choke, breath and sobs mixed, unleashed now that my children are gone. A man who stands near me, uncomfortable, asks if I'm okay, I nod sobbing yes, he looks elsewhere. In Penn Station, the density around me in all its sticky business presses close, hurries hard. I pick my way among people, eyeing and hating them, in awe of their goals and morning starts.

I'm supposed to meet Hattie and our stepmother at my father's apartment. It's only 8 a.m., and I have beaten through so many recent hours. I'll go to Seventy-second Street, two express stops, I can manage. Thronged and hot, hot gusts from the vacant tunnels, the pulse of bodies on the platform, I send April a text and she answers, "Just awake. Come." I have to be with her. Not with Hattie right now, the matching daughter struck down, nor with my stepmother, who has been, all week, barricaded in her furies. Not with my children, sweetening good-byes and loss for them. With bravest April, patron of grief, unafraid. One day this week she'd taken Daniel and Jack for the ten hours I spent at the hospital. She'd calmed and fed them, taken them to the Natural History Museum, paid them kind attention, made certain they trusted that their mother would be herself when she returned. They love her now. I wedge myself and suitcase into the subway car, nearly asleep with all I don't want to feel, and nearly laughing with the insolent surge of too much feeling. Inside my head, I talk myself in and out, up and down, make nonsense lists that lead me to nothing.

At Seventy-second I haul my bag up the stairs, released into the sunny middle of Broadway, and turn in April's direction, the way opposite the apartment my father no longer inhabits. I hurry, peeling away the block until I'm at her building. Upstairs, she's left her door cracked, and I push in. She looks out from the bathroom, toothbrush in her mouth, a hand up. We stare, I don't speak. We let the about-to steady us. I stand in the middle of the room, April's sunlit surfaces and faded colors and the notecards on the walls with her powerful scrawl. I should be sweaty, but my body feels nothing.

Finished in the bathroom, she comes close. We kneel on the carpet, facing, two halves of something fitting, or trying to. We sit and stretch our legs, an empty diamond between us.

I say, "He died last night."

It's the only time it will be the first time I say this. Tomorrow I will have to say, "My father died the night before last," which won't mean what I'll need it to mean. We drop into each other to cry and clutch at this. Shoulders pressed into shoulders, I feel her wet face with my cheek. She has lost her old friend, her champion and great editor. She has lost more than my children have, who didn't know my father well, more than my husband has, who always stood outside our relationship. And something other than what I have lost. Am losing. Together, we don't stop this. It's a particular kind of comfort. The comfort of not being comforted. I do not worry that my wrecked heart will be mishandled. I do not have to fix it up quickly.

April reaches to her desk for a handker-chief square, which she holds to me. "It's only because of your father that I even have a handkerchief," she says. She smiles, cry-ing. "He taught me to be an English gentle-man." We laugh and I blow my nose, and at the same time we weep.

"Tell me," she says. She knows that the events of death, which I have stored for nine hours, must be gathered. She knows narra-tive will be important. I talk through every moment in the slow wash of clarity. "And then," I'm saying. "And then," and she's nodding. When I'm done speaking to her open, constant face, she gets up, leaves me resting my back against cushions.

She says, "Have you eaten?"

I consider this. "I should."

She says, "Hold this," and puts a peach in my hand. The rounded fruit flesh gives against my fingers. A morning peach. It is *this* morning. She blends yogurt and blueberries, slices of another peach, and hands me a glass filled with a pale purple. I tell my throat to open: take this in, stave off the empty, screaming high.

In her bathroom, my guts open up, cramps and loose shit that don't stop. I don't care. I wonder what I care about. I know I have to leave. I wash my hands and say good-bye. There is no other human possibility except April, who can grieve and laugh, too, who can keen and eat. She holds me up and holds herself, and she can space apart the exquisite in this anguish. I wonder if she knows how crucial she is. She does, which is her gift. She doesn't disavow the force we make, the ways we climb into places not yet defined or moored, and expand there. Not many people can do this together. As we both know.

I am not capable anymore today and don't remember red or green, the rules I'm meant to follow. "Walk me there?"

"Of course, honey."

She delivers me in front of my father's building, passing me to some other mourner, with whom I'll ride the elevator, and I ready myself for the next of this unday. That part will demand skills and graces I don't think I own, underwritten by her hold, her tears, the food she put into me.

In the next days I come to her often. She has pressed a set of keys into my hand. "Whenever you want to be here, just come." She brings tea to me, and I let her, which is hard. "I know, honey," she says. "We're both mothers, that's what we do, that's where we're safer. But can you? Accept this right now?" I accept. Memories churn and flood my mouth with more of my father, and more, unstoppable, and April listens, or she cries, adds her pieces of him, which in hunger I collect. Over the following months, she will call me right back, she will stay on the phone, she will conjure him for me in ways familiar and in ways I never knew. She'll witness my wail and collapse, my venom, astonishment, my slow changes, and she'll say, "You're beautiful." In her studio, the first day, the next day, the next, April takes my bag from my shoulder, sets it aside, guides me to the carpet, talks to me in her serene voice. She makes us fried eggs at the stove, orange yolks spectacular in the whites, delivered from the black skillet onto the plates that rest beside the window, and she brings the plates to the floor. We eat.

THANK YOU

This book was written with crucial support from Nancy Washburn and Tim Washburn, Marta Pierpoint and Ross Tillman, and Karin Stallard; and from Theresa Rebeck and the Lark Theatre Company, One Writer's Place, the Virginia Center for the Creative Arts, and the Corporation of Yaddo. It is my privilege and great fortune to be guided by Nan Graham, my generous editor. I thank her for her faith and unflagging attentions. Thank you to Eric Simonoff, my agent, devoted ally and friend, whose words of encouragement always steady me. I am grateful beyond measure to Andrew Peterson for his tremendous love and generosity. And thank you, Ezekiel and Otis. My life with you is rich, sweet, and so happy.

ABOUT THE AUTHOR

Susanna Sonnenberg is the author of *Her Last Death*. She lives in Montana with her family.